Events That Changed the World in the Twentieth Century

Events That Changed the World in the Twentieth Century

edited by
Frank W. Thackeray
&
John E. Findling

THE GREENWOOD PRESS
"EVENTS THAT CHANGED THE WORLD" SERIES

GREENWOOD PRESS
Westport, Connecticut • London

Library of Congress Cataloging-in-Publication Data

Events that changed the world in the twentieth century / edited by
  Frank W. Thackeray and John E. Findling.
      p.   cm.—(The Greenwood Press "Events that changed the
  world" series, ISSN 1078–7860)
    Includes bibliographical references (p.   ) and index.
    ISBN 0–313–29075–X (alk. paper)
    1. History, Modern—20th century.   2. Revolutions—History—20th
  century.   3. Military history, Modern—20th century.   I. Thackeray,
  Frank W.   II. Findling, John E.
  D445.E82   1995
  909.82—dc20   94–38488

British Library Cataloguing in Publication Data is available.

Library of Congress Catalog Card Number: 94–38488
ISBN: 0–313–29075–X
ISSN: 1078–7860

First published in 1995

Greenwood Press, 88 Post Road West, Westport, CT 06881
An imprint of Greenwood Publishing Group, Inc.

Printed in the United States of America

The paper used in this book complies with the
Permanent Paper Standard issued by the National
Information Standards Organization (Z39.48–1984).

10 9 8 7 6 5 4 3 2

Contents

Illustrations

Preface

This volume, which describes and evaluates the global impact of ten of the twentieth century's most important events, is the first in a multivolume series intended to acquaint readers with the seminal events of modern times. Future volumes will cover the most important world events of earlier centuries. There will also be a series of volumes specifically addressing the American experience.

Our collective classroom experience provided the inspiration for this project. Having encountered literally thousands of entry-level college students whose knowledge of the world in which they live is sadly deficient, we determined to write a series of books that would concentrate on the most important events affecting those students (and others as well) in the hope that they would better understand their world and how it came to be. Furthermore, we hope these books will stimulate the reader to delve further into the events covered in each volume and to take a greater interest in history in general.

The current volume is designed to serve two purposes. First, the editors have provided an introduction that presents factual material about each event in a clear, concise, chronological order. Second, each introduction is followed by a longer interpretive essay by a recognized authority exploring the ramifications of the event under consideration. Each essay concludes with an annotated bibliography of the most important works about the event. The essays are followed by four appendices that give additional information useful to the reader. Appendix A is a glossary of names, events, organizations, treaties, and terms mentioned but not fully explained in the introductions and the essays. Appendix B is a timeline of twentieth-century events. Appendix C traces the population growth of selected countries during the twentieth century, and Appendix D lists states that have achieved independence since 1945.

The events covered in this volume were selected on the basis of our combined teaching and research activities. Colleagues and contributors made suggestions as well, and for this we thank them. Of course, another pair of editors might have arrived at a somewhat different list than we did; but we believe that we have assembled a group of events that truly changed the twentieth-century world.

As with all published works, numerous people behind the scenes deserve much of the credit for the final product. Barbara Rader, our editor at Greenwood Publishing Group, has consistently lent her support and encouragement to the project. Our student research assistant, Bob Marshall, worked diligently to fulfill our every request. Special thanks go to Brigette Colligan, who cheerfully, speedily, and efficiently typed and retyped what appeared to be reams of material. As always, Kirk Klaphaak applied his computer-oriented magic to the manuscript with salutary results. We also wish to thank Indiana University Southeast for supplying funds to hire our student research assistant and for providing one of the coeditors with additional time away from classroom responsibilities to complete the manuscript. Many thanks to Roger and Amy Baylor for opening their hearts and their establishment to us, thereby giving us a congenial, enlightened atmosphere for wide-ranging discussions on every conceivable subject, including our manuscript, at the very time when our campus sometimes seemed less than enthusiastic about fulfilling that role. Various students and colleagues, but especially Kimberly Pelle, Kathy Theilen, Rachael L. James, Tom Prebys, Brent Freiberger, Andrew Trout, and John H. Newman, have consistently encouraged us to persevere. For their warm words of support, we are thankful. Most important, we wish to thank the authors of the book's essays. All were cooperative and punctual, and all presented us with insightful, articulate analysis. Without them, there would be no book.

Finally, we wish to express our appreciation to our spouses, Kathy Thackeray and Carol Findling, and to our children, Alex and Max Thackeray and Jamey Findling, who nurtured our dreams, supported our work, tolerated our idiosyncrasies, and overlooked our idiocies as we grappled with our manuscript. For that we are grateful.

Frank W. Thackeray
John E. Findling

Death and destruction on the Western Front. The fighting on both fronts during World War I took an unprecedented toll in lives and property. (Photographic Archives, University of Louisville)

1

World War I, 1914–1918

INTRODUCTION

In 1914 Europe stumbled into a catastrophic war that lasted for more than four years and claimed the lives of millions of soldiers and civilians. The causes of World War I are complex and multifaceted. They have stirred debate among historians and laymen alike ever since the war ground to a halt in 1918. It seems clear, however, that the outbreak of war was an unintended consequence of an extremely tense international order in which the Great Powers of Europe eyed each other with varying degrees of hatred, envy, fear, and suspicion.

The event that detonated this powder keg was the assassination of Archduke Franz Ferdinand, the heir to the throne of Austria-Hungary, at Sarajevo on June 28, 1914. This act of political terror infuriated Austria, which concluded that Serbia, a small Balkan country, was behind the assassination. When Austria threatened Serbia, the Serb government appealed for protection to its ally, Russia. Meanwhile, Austria received strong encouragement for its confrontational stance from its ally, Germany. As the crisis deepened, Russia consulted with its ally, France; and France, in turn, entered into discussions with its friend, Great Britain. When Austria sent an ultimatum to Serbia and the antiquated Russian army began to mobilize, the dominoes fell. By early August 1914, World War I had begun.

In light of the terrible destruction that followed, it is interesting to note that not only the European governments but also their populations went to war with great enthusiasm. Huge crowds filled the streets of Europe's capital cities, wildly cheering the declarations of war. Not only was this first general war since Napoleon's campaigns of 100 years earlier greeted with enthusiasm, there was also a universal conviction that the war would be a short one and that "the boys would be home by Christmas."

As the war progressed, more and more countries became involved. At the start, however, the major combatants were, on one side, Germany and Austria-Hungary, which, together with their allies, would be known as the Central Powers; and, on the other side, Great Britain, France, and Russia, which, together with their allies, would be known as the Allied Powers or Allies.

From the start, the Central Powers found themselves fighting a two-front war; that is, they were forced to fight simultaneously in both the west and the east. Aware of the grave dangers inherent in a two-front war, the German general staff had drawn up the Schlieffen Plan, which called for Germany, in the event of war, to mass the bulk of its army in the west in order to deliver a quick and devastating knockout blow to the French. After defeating the French, the German army could turn its attention to the east and destroy the Russian army at its leisure.

Employing the Schlieffen Plan, the Germans came very close to capturing Paris in the first month of the war. They were barely stopped at the First Battle of the Marne, when the French took advantage of gaps in the German lines caused by the transfer of some German units from the Western Front to the Eastern Front, where the Russians had unexpectedly mounted an offensive. Ironically, these German troops were not crucial to the outcome in the east. Although the Russians, under Generals Alexander Samsonov and Pavel Rennenkampf, had moved westward into the German territory of East Prussia, their attack was so confused and poorly coordinated that a smaller German force defeated both Russian armies at the twin battles of Tannenberg and the Masurian Lakes. These huge German victories in the east focused the spotlight on Generals Erich Ludendorff and Paul von Hindenburg, two of the most effective military commanders in a war notable for undistinguished if not abominable military leadership.

The failure of the German offensive in the west and of the Russian offensive in the east shattered all illusions about the war being a short one. Instead, both sides settled in for a protracted struggle featuring trench warfare. Trench warfare called for each side to concentrate great numbers of men in a series of parallel fortified ditches, or trenches, and to attack in massed formations in the hope of breaching the enemy's lines. Those on the defensive would exploit their dug-in positions to repel the offensive. The nature of trench warfare, with its massed assaults into the teeth of entrenched defensive positions, resulted in truly appalling casualty figures. World War I quickly became a war of attrition in which each side readily sacrificed incredible numbers of its own men in order to exhaust the enemy, "bleed them white," and thus achieve victory.

During 1915 the war on the Western Front witnessed wave after wave of British, French, and German soldiers attacking across barren "no man's land" into the face of entrenched machine-gun nests. Although the casualty figures skyrocketed, the front barely moved. Much of the military action in that year took place on the Eastern Front. Having failed to destroy France in 1914, the Central Powers in 1915 sought to drive Russia from the war. In a series of coordinated attacks, the Central Powers regained Galicia, expelled Russia from Poland and Lithuania, and invaded Russia proper. However, victory proved elusive. Although the Russian army was poorly led, poorly equipped, poorly fed, and beaten on the battlefield, it nevertheless relied on its seemingly unlimited supply of men and the vast expanses of the Russian countryside to remain in the field as a viable foe.

During the first months of hostilities in the east, it became obvious that Austria-Hungary was not up to the military task at hand. Austria-Hungary's offensives, even against tiny Serbia, failed, and often Germany had to come to its rescue when the Russians pummeled its army. Consequently, by 1916 Austria-Hungary had virtually surrendered its freedom of action to Germany, and it was relegated to this inferior position until the end of the war.

In 1915 the western allies (France and Great Britain) invaded Turkey, which had entered the war on the side of the Central Powers in October 1914. This attack, known as the Gallipoli campaign and fought chiefly by soldiers from the British Empire, ended in defeat for the Allies. Nevertheless, the Allies now determined to destroy the Ottoman Empire. By virtue of a secret treaty concluded in 1915, Russia was granted the right to fulfill its long-standing desire to annex Constantinople and thereby gain control over the straits leading from the Black Sea to the Aegean Sea and the Mediterranean. Subsequently, the British, led by Colonel

T. E. Lawrence, successfully incited the Turkish Empire's Arab populations. In 1917 the British issued the Balfour Declaration, pledging themselves to support the establishment of a Jewish homeland in Palestine.

As the British were becoming bogged down at Gallipoli, Italy, having
been promised territorial gains at the expense of Austria-Hungary, entered the war on the side of the Allies in May 1915. Also during the early
stages of the war, the Allies, especially Great Britain, moved against Germany's African colonies. Japan, Britain's Pacific ally, grabbed Germany's
colonies in Asia and the South Pacific.

In 1916, while the armies of the Central Powers slowly chewed up the
fading Russian army, the military spotlight shifted to the west once
again. In particular, two battles on the Western Front that year came to
symbolize the futility and mindless bloodletting that were hallmarks of
World War I. In February the Germans launched a massive attack against
French positions in and around the fortress town of Verdun. The objective was to bleed the French and hasten their surrender. However, the
French determined to hang on, and under the tenacious leadership of
General Henri-Philippe Pétain, whose pledge "they shall not pass" lifted
French morale, France withstood the German attack, but at a terrible
price. By the end of the battle, the Germans and the French had each
lost 350,000 men. Later that same year, the British launched a massive
attack against German positions along the Somme River. After several
weeks of intense combat, the Allies had gained a mere fifteen square
miles at the cost of 410,000 British dead and 190,000 French dead. The
Germans lost 500,000 men.

The staggering number of casualties can be attributed not only to incredibly stupid strategic planning and leadership, but also to the perfec-
tion of already existing weapons of mass destruction and the
introduction of new ones. During World War I, the machine gun and
heavy artillery were employed with devastating effect. Weapons used
for the first time included aircraft, tanks, poison gas, and submarines.
Their effect was no less devastating.

In particular, the submarine and its effects transcended the battlefield.
At the onset of the war, both sets of belligerents declared a blockade in
the belief that they could starve their opponent into submission. While
the Allies relied chiefly on Britain's fleet to maintain their blockade, the
Central Powers placed their hopes in Germany's submarines. The
German submarines were quite effective, but the type of campaign they
waged was flawed because, unlike surface vessels, they could not stop
and board their intended target. Rather, they could only sink their targets
in an indiscriminate fashion, demonstrated quite dramatically in May

1915 with the sinking of the passenger ship *Lusitania* with the loss of 1,200 lives, including 118 Americans. The United States, a neutral country that had protested the blockade actions of both belligerents, erupted in anger at the sinking of the *Lusitania.* The United States threatened war against Germany, a prospect that caused German leaders to modify their submarine campaign. However, at the start of 1917 Germany once again decided to wage unrestricted submarine warfare. This decision played an important part in the American determination to enter the war on the side of the Allies in April 1917.

The only major conventional clash at sea occurred in spring 1916 when the German fleet ventured from its harbors and fought the British fleet at the Battle of Jutland. The clash was essentially an accidental one, and although the German fleet probably gained a slight victory (German guns proved better than English ones, and the Germans sank twice the tonnage that the British did), it retreated to port and never again sallied forth to challenge the British.

While millions of men slaughtered each other at the front, important changes occurred at home. World War I introduced the twentieth century to the concept of "total war." Subjected to the requirements of a war effort of unprecedented scope and size, each belligerent government eventually adopted policies that interfered profoundly with normal civilian activity in order to marshal all available human and material resources. Perhaps the best example of this development is found in the policy of national conscription that placed all able-bodied young and middle-aged men at the state's disposal.

The now regimented populations were also the target of incessant campaigns of state-sponsored but often distorted propaganda designed to boost civilian morale and generate support for the war. Meanwhile, the war effort drained the financial resources of the state and eventually bankrupted almost every belligerent. Standards of living also declined, and each state struggled to find substitutes for items that were no longer available, including labor, as women performed heretofore exclusively male tasks.

Germany, under the organizational genius Walter Rathenau, practiced total war most effectively. Rathenau successfully organized Germany's productive capacity and directed German scientists in the production of many ersatz, or artificial, items that served to mitigate the effects of the Allied blockade. Such steps enabled a resource-strapped Germany to fight effectively for more than four years. Those countries least successful in waging total war (Russia and Austria-Hungary) found their chances for success, even survival, rapidly diminishing.

In fact, the failure to shoulder the crushing burdens of modern warfare led to the collapse of Russia in 1917. In March of that year, revolution broke out in the capital, St. Petersburg, which had been renamed Petrograd at the beginning of the war. Nicholas II, the Russian tsar, or emperor, quickly abdicated; but the chaos intensified. While the situation at home continued to deteriorate, the Russian army mounted a summer offensive under General Alexis Brusilov. As had been the case in 1916, when Brusilov launched a similar campaign, he was defeated.

With Brusilov's defeat, the Russian army began to disintegrate. At home a power struggle was under way to see who would fill the vacuum created by the collapse of the tsarist state. In November 1917, the Bolsheviks, a small, radical group espousing Marxism and led by V. I. Lenin, seized power. Believing in the inevitability of a global, working-class revolution, the Bolsheviks sought to withdraw Russia from the war. Negotiations ensued during which the Germans drove a very hard bargain. These negotiations resulted in the March 3, 1918, Treaty of Brest-Litovsk, which validated the German victory in the east. The Germans could now devote their full attention to the Western Front. There, however, circumstances had changed dramatically.

Russia's departure from the war roughly coincided with the U.S. entry into the war. In early 1917, an increasingly desperate Germany, now fully under the control of Generals Ludendorff and Hindenburg, decided to resume unrestricted submarine warfare in an effort to starve Great Britain into submission once and for all. This decision infuriated the United States, which declared war on Germany on April 6, 1917. Several months later, in January 1918, U.S. president Woodrow Wilson issued the Fourteen Points, which for the first time clearly set out Allied war aims.

Both the American entry into the war and the Fourteen Points, following closely upon the triumph of Bolshevism in Russia, gave the Allies a huge boost in morale. Moreover, the prospect of unlimited American men, money, and material seemed to ensure that the Allies would eventually win the stalemated conflict. However, the United States would take about a year to move to a war footing, and the bloodletting on the Western Front continued unabated throughout 1917.

The French, under a new commander, General Robert Nivelle, determined to continue the failed tactic of the massed assault. This time, however, French troops mutinied, refusing to go on the offensive. Unbeknownst to the Germans, the French army was on the verge of collapse. That catastrophe was avoided when Pétain, the hero of Verdun, replaced Nivelle and restored discipline. In order to save his army, Pétain abandoned the doctrine of attack and took up a defensive posture awaiting the arrival of the Americans. The British, however, continued to press forward. Fighting in "Flanders' Fields" at Passchendaele and Ypres, the British army absorbed staggering casualties at the hands of dug-in German forces. In October the Southern Front flared when the Austrians routed the Italian army at Caporetto. Approximately 300,000 Italians surrendered, while more than 400,000 deserted.

The failures of 1917 might have been enough to break the Allies had it not been for the entry of the United States into the war and the coming to power of Georges Clemenceau in France and David Lloyd George in Britain. These hard-nosed leaders, who sometimes rode roughshod over both their political opponents and prevailing legal standards, were determined to achieve victory.

Their determination proved helpful as the war reached its climax in 1918. Freed of major military responsibilities in the east, the Germans now transferred the bulk of their forces to the Western Front as they prepared for an all-out onslaught against the British and the French before the Americans could arrive to tip the scales in favor of the Allies. Launching their massive attack in March 1918, the Germans came perilously close to success until they were defeated in July at the gates of Paris in the Second Battle of the Marne. The failure of the German offensive foreshadowed the end of the war. With American troops pouring into France at the rate of 250,000 a month, the German armies lost all chance of victory.

In September 1918 the German generals informed a shocked Kaiser William II that Germany was defeated and dumped further responsibility for the conduct of the war in his lap. In Austria-Hungary, the empire itself was disintegrating as each of its component national parts started to go its own way. On November 11, 1918, an armistice took effect. After more than four years of the bloodiest fighting the world had ever seen, the guns stopped firing.

In January 1919, peace negotiations opened at Paris. The Paris Peace Conference, as the negotiations were called, tried to deal with the many consequences of the war. However, Soviet Russia, already a pariah among nations, was not invited to the conference, and defeated Germany was effectively barred from participating in the discussions. As for the victorious Allies, they tended to squabble among themselves and could never agree on whether to impose a truly Draconian peace or a generous peace. The main product of this flawed effort to bring peace to Europe was the Treaty of Versailles, signed on June 28, 1919, five years to the day after the assassination of Franz Ferdinand at Sarajevo.

INTERPRETIVE ESSAY
Marilyn Shevin-Coetzee and
Frans Coetzee

In 1914, as temperatures soared during one of the hottest summers on record in Europe, tempers flared as well. Lacking conveniences such as air conditioning that late-twentieth-century readers take for granted, and bound by heavy conventional fashions, the peoples of Europe were challenged by both the weather and events. The heat was an irritation, possibly a catalyst rather than a direct cause of World War I, the origins of which can be traced to deep-seated economic, military, diplomatic, and political developments. Ironically, the very technology that brought the Continent closer together, such as the telegraph and the telephone, helped to tear it asunder. Eventually, a combination of long-term causes and short-term accidents combined to precipitate the first total war.

The most serious of these crises was triggered—literally—by the assassination in Sarajevo of the heir to the Austro-Hungarian throne, Archduke Franz Ferdinand, and his wife, Sophie, on June 28, 1914. The assassin was Gavrilo Princip, a teenaged Serbian nationalist. On July 23, 1914, Austria-Hungary issued an ultimatum to Serbia; Serbia's response, while conciliatory, failed to prevent Austria-Hungary from declaring war on Serbia five days later. Russia responded by mobilizing its military, prompting Germany to do the same and eventually to declare war on Russia on August 1, and on France two days later. On August 4, after German troops violated the Belgian frontier, Britain honored its treaty obligation to protect Belgian neutrality and entered the conflict on the side of France and Russia. As the Continent plunged into war that evening, British foreign secretary Sir Edward Grey observed: "The lamps are going out all over Europe. We shall not see them lit again in our lifetime."

Grey's somber assessment was at odds with the prevailing orthodoxy, which depicted the process of mobilization as one greeted everywhere with enthusiasm and nationalistic fervor. War as Christmas, as a holiday to be celebrated, not a calamity to be mourned, a spiritual release from the mundane banalities of everyday life, a transformation of the degeneracy inherent in modern culture by means of the elevating impact of a higher, common moral purpose—these were among the sentiments with which Europeans anticipated the conflict. In part, these suppositions were sustained by the mistaken presumption, shared by participants in all countries, that the war would be something of a sporting match, brief and glorious, concluded by Christmas. Propaganda posters in Germany of young, beautiful maidens handing flowers or beverages to soldiers departing by train to the front, and of men, young and older, rushing to volunteer before they missed out on the fun, further emphasized the refreshing sense of unity and camaraderie that bore a welcome contrast to the domestic discord of the prewar years. A British poster appropriately entitled "Are you in this picture?" depicted Britons from all social classes waiting in a long line to enlist in the army. The *Burgfrieden* (Fortress under Siege) or the *Union sacrée* (Sacred Union) expressed the sentiment that under external pressure the nation would come together and rally around the flag.

Yet this picture was incomplete and in some ways misleading. If some Europeans looked to the war optimistically, still others viewed it through less rosy spectacles. The grounds for a more guarded response to the outbreak of hostilities would become apparent as the combatants' lack of preparation was revealed repeatedly. In underestimating the conflict's duration, the opposing nations failed to take requisite measures to ensure the uninterrupted flow of food for both soldiers and civilians and the stockpiling of raw materials for weapons and munitions. The British presumption that they could continue to conduct "business as usual" typified the initial response.

European expectations of a brief conflict were conditioned by the short and decisive Prussian campaigns against Austria and later France in 1866 and 1870–1871, which suggested that one Great Power could defeat another with relative ease. In retrospect, military planners should have taken their cue from the American Civil War, which dragged on for four years with staggering casualties. Of course, the first few weeks of campaigning in August 1914 conformed to expectations as the various armies jockeyed for position. An observer from the Napoleonic Wars would have recognized much. Cavalry still cantered at the head of columns, soldiers trudged on foot, horse-drawn carts laboriously pulled supplies. But once the German advance into France was stymied at the Battle of the Marne (September 1914), war on the Western Front settled into a prolonged and bloody stalemate.

That stalemate reflected the fact that technological advances favored the defensive. Barbed wire, which had confined cattle on America's Great Plains, proved even more effective in impeding the advance of men. Machine guns employed to deadly effect by imperialists in Africa and

Asia were now turned with equal success against the soldiers of the European powers themselves. And the devastating bombardments of heavy artillery forced troops to burrow ever deeper merely to survive. By early 1915 parallel lines of German and Allied trenches stretched virtually from the Belgian coast to the Swiss frontier. The constant shellfire tore up the once pristine countryside, and the pitted terrain between the trenches, a morass of mud, corpses, shell craters, and tangled wire, appropriately became known as no man's land.

The contradiction between the initial dreams of a brief, glorious, and inexpensive victory and the seemingly ineffectual efforts of soldiers to win more than a few yards of bloodsoaked ground at tremendous cost fostered disillusion, apathy, cynicism, and disgust. Like the myriad faces of war, the literature produced in response to the conflict was both varied and prodigious, ranging from outright nationalistic propaganda to realistic portrayals of battle to pacifistic appeals. Clergymen, physicians, and workers at the front became journalists, recording their personal experiences for posterity. In France, Dr. Georges Duhamel, a respected physician who voluntarily served for four years as a medical officer (his novels being translated into English as *The New Book of Martyrs* and *Civilization*), and Henri Barbusse, whose *Under Fire* detailed the miseries of war, were among the controversial and thought-provoking authors active during the war.

The main wave of famous war novels, however, began to appear a decade or so after the Armistice, by which time many authors felt that they had achieved the distance necessary to write about so painful an experience. Those publications (such as Robert Graves' *Goodbye to All That* and Erich Maria Remarque's *All Quiet on the Western Front*) testified to the profound sense of irony by which soldiers sought to comprehend their ghastly experiences, to the loyalty they felt to the comrades for whom they fought (rather than for the grandiose war aims trumpeted by the governments), and to the feeling of isolation they sensed when they returned on leave to civilians who had no comprehension of the realities of the front.

And yet these very civilians were essential to the war effort. Given the unprecedented scale of the war and the military leadership's inability to secure a decisive knockout blow, it gradually became apparent that victory would be secured through a slow process of attrition. This situation ensured that civilian production, whether of weapons, munitions, or foodstuffs, would be critical to the outcome. Accordingly, considerations of civilian morale on this second or "home front" took on additional importance, and governments devoted themselves to cultivating enthu-

siasm for the war. Perhaps never before had the visual arts been con-
scripted to such a degree to stimulate enlistment, to promote female
employment, and to vilify the enemy as lacking in human decency and
respect. Indeed, the pen proved as mighty as the sword, and art no
longer existed for its own sake. Along with literature and film, it had
become politicized, manipulated by supporters and opponents of the
conflict alike to deliver a specific message.

The benefits of propaganda were already known to nineteenth-century
figures such as France's Louis Napoleon (Napoleon III), whose successful
presidential campaign was aided by an impressive array of placards,
buttons, and other such paraphernalia. As Europe's electorate expanded
and politics took on greater significance, the use of propaganda increased. Posters not only carried easily remembered slogans or catch-
phrases, but their visual graphics also served to reinforce a particular
message. One need only recall what might well be the most famous of
all American war posters—that of Uncle Sam as a recruiter for the war.
Dressed in patriotic red, white, and blue, this fatherly figure beckoned
males of enlistment age to answer the call to arms and thereby protect
their country and its values, threatened by Germany and its allies. European governments commissioned posters that glorified the act of re-
cruitment as well: on the one hand, young men were pictured in
uniform, showered with the adulation of beautiful young women and
adoring crowds; on the other, prospective soldiers were reminded, even
if indirectly, of the horrors of war that could befall their innocent mothers, wives, and children should they fail to heed the call to arms. Images
of the bestial Hun or the animalistic Cossack were invoked as barbarous
threats to one's own humane and civilized existence.

In view of food shortages and other hardships caused by inevitable
disruptions in supply and demand, and to ensure the continued cooperation of civilians and soldiers alike, Europe's governments increasingly
disseminated propaganda that often contained only a small modicum of
truth, but whose impact proved devastating for their opponents. Above
all, Germany's invasion of neutral, defenseless Belgium and its ruthless
destruction of cathedrals, libraries, and other historical buildings served
the Allied propaganda machine extraordinarily well. Claims of German
barbarism against property and women not only enabled Germany's enemies to justify their participation in the war, but also served to reinforce
the idea of a holy Christian war waged against the German barbarians.

While governments churned out propaganda posters and literature
directed at their nemeses, peace advocates and disillusioned soldier-
writers also used literature and the visual arts to express their version

of the war, although state-imposed censorship often tempered their impact. These works all revealed uneasiness with the pursuit of war and its brutal character. Some were written during the war, but much of the war literature was published as a postscript to the authors' experiences and memories, whether of the conflict itself or of life on the home front.

Artists, too, created a visual testimony to the war with their paintings. Cubism remained the style of choice of many artists at the front. Dissonant, irreverent, and dissociated from the past, cubist paintings portrayed the helter-skelter nature of modern warfare, one that departed from traditional conventions and whose impact was more destructive than its predecessors. But on the home front in France, for example, artists preferred a more traditional approach to their works. This classicist revival, which began in earnest after 1917, was due in part to Italy's entry into the war in 1915 on the Allied side. Italy's association with classical civilization, humanism, and Christianity served as a counterpoise to Germany's barbarism; thus, the Allies could justify their war against Germany as one waged to preserve Western Civilization. And since France was part of the Latin tradition, French artists in particular responded to the call with portraits of Roman ruins, protective antique goddesses hovering above wounded soldiers, and well-known figures such as Dante urging combatants to continue their struggle against the barbaric enemy. In an effort to reinforce the bonds between classical Rome and twentieth-century France and to uplift the French national spirit, artistic figures like that of Marianne took on classical qualities. Indeed, posters, portraits, picture cards, and paintings evoked special symbolism, some carrying overwhelmingly nationalistic messages, others evoking pacifistic images.

But propaganda, whether persuasive or not, was by itself insufficient to mobilize societies effectively for the conduct of total war. Each combatant nation's leadership faced the same dilemma: how to fill the ranks with hundreds of thousands of recruits while simultaneously maintaining (or even accelerating) industrial production in the face of the inevitable disruption that the transfer of so many men would entail. This dilemma was the driving force behind the significant extension of state intervention throughout Europe. One common response was for the state to "militarize" the labor process and civilian war production, imposing military-style discipline and penalties for disruptions in the factories. Likewise, private enterprise might be subordinated to governmental regulation, as in the case of the British railroads under the Defense of the Realm Act, or that of French munitions workers, who were forbidden to strike. Governments soon found, however, that the unregulated departure of manpower to the front, while applauded by generals seeking replacements for the escalating casualties, proved counterproductive by denuding key industries of skilled workers. For without the requisite shells, no number of soldiers alone would suffice. With the passage in 1916 of the Auxiliary Service Act, German workers were transferred from less crucial civilian jobs to military industries. Agriculture, too, was susceptible to the same difficulties, especially given the degree to which it still relied on manual labor.

The longer the stalemate at the front persisted, the more acute these problems became. As a result, some skilled workers were actually withdrawn from front-line service or prohibited from joining as members of reserved occupations. But the principal solution lay in reconstituting the work force itself. By simplifying job tasks, semi-skilled workers could substitute for skilled men departed to the front; even more dramatically, by tapping pools of potential female labor, employers could maintain production. In the process, of course, women gained access to occupations from which they had often been excluded, and they also became accustomed to earning regular wages. In France, women accounted for one-quarter of the personnel in war factories, numbering some 1.6 million workers. Russian women assumed greater prominence in the transport and utility industries; German women engaged in engineering, metallurgy, and chemical production in numbers six times greater than on the eve of the war; British women were a mainstay of munitions production. Some scholars have suggested that by permitting greater access to paid employment and, to some extent, to occupational choice, the war proved a liberating experience for women. In this way, women gained an added measure of satisfaction from their contribution to the war effort, while men were forced to concede, however grudgingly, that many tasks once segregated by gender could now be performed with equal facility by female workers. One could also point to the concession of female suffrage in Britain and Germany as evidence of the newfound roles for women.

Did gender lines blur so rapidly and completely? One reason for doubting that they did is, first, that the rapid upsurge in female employment in war-related industries proved a transitory phenomenon; women workers were displaced as economies readjusted to a peacetime footing and soldiers returned to the jobs they had left. Second, female suffrage remained a contentious issue, denied in France and implemented in Britain on terms more restrictive than for male voters. Third, during the war itself, whether employed in the industrial or agricultural sector or engaged in domestic service, women still bore principal responsibility in the traditional female sphere, the home front, and for enduring the rigors of domestic life, such as the seemingly interminable lines for food, often in short supply.

The shortage of critical foodstuffs, exacerbated by the absence of plans to govern distribution and prevent price inflation, led eventually in Germany (beginning in January 1915), France (selectively in 1917), and England (in 1918) to rationing. Although intended to provide a basic minimum caloric intake for citizens, in reality the system often did not alleviate the food shortages. Many, including working-class children and pensioners on fixed incomes, still found food difficult to obtain, especially in view of the prevailing practice of allocating the best food to male workers. England and France appear to have suffered the least, while privation was more severe in Russia, Austria-Hungary, and blockaded Germany. In Austria, for example, while in 1916 some 40 percent of all strikes were prompted by food shortages, by 1917 the figure had climbed to 70 percent. Beginning in the spring of 1915, Russian women agitated against shortages and inflated prices.

In these circumstances, frugality and thrift, not to mention ingenuity, were preached as the best way to endure the hardships of the home front. It is no surprise, therefore, that the conflict witnessed the cultivation of numerous small so-called "war gardens" and the publication of many cookbooks designed to instruct working-class wives on the principles of nutrition and the more practical matter of stretching inadequate and even unappetizing ingredients into each day's breakfast, lunch, and modest supper. State intervention to limit the wartime pressure on standards of living also included the introduction of rent controls, but such action was not universal. In France, for example, the price of housing escalated to new heights and led to serious overcrowding.

Given the repetitious slaughter on the battlefields, the accelerating pressures of labor in the factories, and the accumulating tensions of civilian life, it is perhaps surprising that authority was maintained for so long. But the sense of common sacrifice implied by the *Burgfrieden* and the *Union sacrée* could persist for only so long in such an environment. The most obvious breakdown of authority occurred in Russia in 1917, followed by Germany and Austria-Hungary the following year. The various combatant nations' efforts to mobilize their societies for total war implied that the rewards of the conflict would be commensurate with the great effort expended. For nations that could not secure victory, however, the prospect of defeat implied the likelihood of revolution. While one cannot ignore the deep-seated social and political antagonisms that fragmented all three nations before 1914, it was the experience of the war itself that brought about a collapse of authority.

However, it would be a mistake to regard revolution as the sole war-time challenge to authority. Dissent emerged in a variety of ways—on the factory floor, in the food lines, and in the trenches. The later years of the war saw an upsurge in strike activity throughout Europe that continued to escalate as the war dragged on (it is worth recalling that even early in 1918 there were few signs that the war's conclusion was imminent). The expansion of trade unions suggested that a stronger working-class presence in economic and political life would be a per-manent feature of the European landscape and a potential challenge to the status quo. Nearly a century before, in England, a Chartist radical had defied anyone "to agitate on a full stomach," and by 1917 there were growing numbers of restive citizens to confirm his dictum on the relationship between hunger and protest.

Dissent emerged not just among civilians but also among the men in uniform. In 1917 substantial sections of the French army were wracked by mutiny, ending only with an understanding that the French military leadership would avoid needless or ill-conceived offensives. The German navy in Kiel mutinied in 1918 when official orders for a suicide mission to atone for the fleet's inactivity infuriated crews tired of their officers' incompetence and their own idleness. In Russia the situation was more complex, and after a first revolution in March 1917 that resulted in the abdication of Tsar Nicholas II and the formation of a Provisional Gov-ernment, the Russian army continued to fight, seeking victory to validate the previous three years of extensive sacrifice. A quantitative superiority, however, was no substitute for the qualitative edge enjoyed by the Ger-mans; and in the wake of further defeats, the Bolshevik platform of peace, land, and bread grew more attractive. A second revolution in November 1917 led to a Bolshevik takeover and eventually to a pro-longed civil war.

Even Britain was not immune to upheaval. In the spring of 1917, a massive series of strikes disrupted the vital engineering and shipbuilding region of the Clyde in western Scotland, and similar outbreaks in Wales and Lancashire took their toll as well. Most spectacularly, Dublin echoed to the sound of gunfire in April 1916 when Irish nationalists in the so-called Easter Rising proclaimed an independent Irish Republic, only to be forcibly repressed by British troops and hanging judges.

Socialist principles also persisted during the conflict. Initially, of course, such ideological considerations were largely, though not completely, submerged in the widespread support for the war from socialist parties. Germany's Social Democratic Party (SPD) approved war credits, many members of Britain's Labour Party rejected pacifistic appeals to abstain from the war, and French socialists supported the sacred union. But as the war progressed, socialist parties suffered a decline in membership, for the movement was divided, not just in its attitude toward capitalism, but also over whether to continue the conflict in the face of mounting casualties or to sue for peace. In France socialist membership dropped by two-thirds to some 30,000 by the war's end, while in Germany SPD membership plummeted by three-quarters to 243,000 in 1917.

However, the critical role of organized labor in wartime production strengthened the hand of trade unions. In France union membership rose from 355,000 in 1913 to 600,000 by 1918, while in Britain the comparable gain was from 4 million in 1914 to 8 million by 1920. Germany was the exception here, partly from the departure of union members to the front, and partly from the severe restrictions placed on unions by the government, especially the so-called silent dictatorship of Generals Paul von Hindenburg and Erich Ludendorff in the war's later stages. Absolute numbers, however, do not convey the degree to which the terms of debate over the role of labor had shifted. In some measure, the wartime extension of state influence could be regarded as an experiment in "war socialism," and thereby a partial vindication of labor ideology (in Britain, for example, the Labour Party, encouraged by its wartime experience, adopted a more explicitly socialist constitution in 1918). By the war's end, Germany and Russia had socialist governments, and five years later Britain experienced its first Labour administration.

In November 1918 the guns fell silent (though Russia would be wracked by civil war), but despite the widespread desire for a "return to normalcy," in U.S. president Warren Harding's famous phrase, restoring domestic stability proved problematic. No aspect of the war received greater attention (or condemnation) than efforts to fashion a lasting peace settlement. Part of the problem lay in the fact that Germany's military collapse occurred rapidly in 1918, by which time the battles had still largely been waged on other countries' terrain. In fact, despite its victory over Russia, the German war machine was as exhausted as those of France or Britain, and unable to resist the weight of American numbers as fresh doughboys poured into Europe (the United States having entered the conflict against Germany in April 1917).

The peacemakers—or rather the victorious powers, for Germany was not represented but only summoned to sign a treaty—met at Versailles to establish a framework for postwar Europe. In doing so, they were guided by their interpretation of the war's origins. In practice, this meant recognizing the rights of subject nationalities to self-determination and stripping defeated Germany of its colonial empire as well as severely restricting the size and equipment of its military. Accordingly, the peace-makers redrew the map of Europe, erasing the collapsed Austro-Hungarian and Ottoman empires, and creating a series of new states in eastern Europe, which, it was also thought, could provide a buffer to protect democratic Europe from Bolshevik contamination from the east. In retrospect, many of these states proved too small to withstand either German or Soviet expansion in the 1930s. Furthermore, many were badly splintered by ethnic rivalries.

Yet the limitations of the Versailles settlement were not confined to geographic issues. The enormous financial and human cost of the conflict, and the prospect of tangible rewards for persistent sacrifice, encouraged discussion of reparations to be paid to the victors by the defeated nations. Germany, widely regarded as the aggressor, was assigned full and sole responsibility for the war's outbreak and, therefore, for the damages incurred in its conduct (the famous Article 231, or War Guilt Clause, of the Versailles Treaty). Such a posture only assisted extremists within Germany who contended that the Allies, so careful to recognize the rights of nations in other cases, were determined to trample on those of Germany. Making Germany bear the burden of the war was unrealistic (especially given the fluctuating estimates of both the total cost and Germany's capacity to pay) and unwise, burdening that nation's first democratic government, the Weimar Republic, with an economic and emotional albatross.

In the end, Sir Edward Grey's prophecy proved correct, for World War I was a watershed in history. In some respects it accelerated existing trends (such as the growth of state intervention), and in others (such as the position of women) it failed to produce a decisive shift. But in many other respects, European life was very different after the war. Most countries' economies had been dealt harsh blows from which they did not fully recover, as was evidenced in the prolonged fiscal crisis beginning in 1929. Liquidated investments, accumulated debts, and disrupted trade all bore witness to the conflict's impact. Liberalism, which had seemed so confident of progress during the nineteenth century, appeared out of touch with postwar realities. Promoting the rational mediation of disputes had not forestalled war, and the claims of the sovereign, respectable individual withered in the face of state authority and the slaughter. After 1918 ideologies extolling the group and collective action, such as fascism and communism, and urging physical violence as a liberating experience, proved more attractive than the old liberal ideals. Indeed, it is difficult to imagine the success of either the Russian Revolution or the Nazi seizure of power without the groundwork laid by the war itself. Moreover, U.S. military involvement in the conflict, and its crucial financial role in postwar economic life ensured that, despite strong isolationist sentiment, the United States was now tied to European affairs. Therefore, the principal trends of twentieth-century European history are all tied to the experience of the first total war.

SELECTED BIBLIOGRAPHY

Audoin-Rouzeau, Stephan. *Men at War 1914–1918.* Providence, RI: Berg Press, 1992. An investigation of the ordinary soldier's experience as reflected in trench journalism.

Becker, Jean-Jacques. *The Great War and the French People.* Leamington Spa, England: Berg Press, 1985. The best account of civilian life in France during the conflict.

Bourne, John. *Britain and the Great War 1914–1918.* London: Edward Arnold, 1989. A helpful synthesis of recent scholarship on both the home front and military campaigns.

Braybon, Gail. *Women Workers in the First World War.* London: Croom Helm, 1981. Still a standard account of its subject.

Ekstein, Modris. *Rites of Spring: The Great War and the Birth of the Modern Age.* Boston: Houghton Mifflin, 1989. An imaginative and wide-ranging cultural study.

Feldman, Gerald D. *Army, Industry and Labor in Germany 1914–1918.* Princeton: Princeton University Press, 1966; reprinted 1992 by Berg Press. The pioneering study of civil-military relations.

Ferro, Marc. *The Great War 1914–1918.* London: Routledge, 1973. A good starting point.

Fischer, Fritz. *Germany's Aims in the First World War.* New York: Norton, 1967. Originally published in German in 1961; a fundamental but controversial study of the expansionist aims of German elites.

Fussell, Paul. *The Great War and Modern Memory.* New York: Oxford University Press, 1975. Sensitive exploration of the aesthetic side of the war, based on British sources.

Hardach, Gerd. *The First World War, 1914–1918.* Berkeley: University of California Press, 1977. The best brief introduction to the economic aspects of the conflict.

Joll, James. *The Origins of the First World War.* London: Longmans, 1981; 2nd ed., 1991. A wonderfully lucid and balanced introduction to a complex and controversial topic.

Kocka, Jürgen. *Facing Total War: German Society 1914–1918.* Leamington Spa, England: Berg Press, 1984. The only substantial study in English of German class relations during the war.

Marwick, Arthur. *The Deluge.* London: Macmillan, 1965; 2nd ed., 1991. A pio-

lative powers. While Russian moderates were satisfied with this con-
on, Russian radicals rejected the Duma and demanded renewal of
lutionary activity. Although the tsar circumscribed its powers after
, the Duma remained in existence and in March 1917 was trans-
ed into the Provisional Government.

e Provisional Government's great rival for power in revolutionary
ia was the Petrograd[2] Soviet (Council) of Workers' and Soldiers'
uties, which inspired imitators throughout the country. Formed in
ch 1917, the Soviet featured representatives from Russia's most rad-
political parties, including the Social Revolutionaries, the Menshe-
, and the Bolsheviks. The Soviet also included a fair number of
genous leaders from military units and the factories who did not
ally belong to any radical faction.

e Soviet favored an undefined form of socialism for Russia and de-
ded more radical action than the Provisional Government was will-
to undertake. By virtue of its revolutionary stance, the Soviet more
ly reflected the desires of the common people than did the Provi-
al Government. However, in its early days the Soviet lacked unity
urpose and clear leadership. In fact, its component parts often
ned with each other. Furthermore, the Soviet had no experience at
erning. Consequently, the Soviet shied away from seizing power
the Provisional Government, preferring to act as a parallel but com-
ng force. In sum, the Soviet enjoyed considerable popular support
had no clear vision of the future, while the Provisional Government
a marginally better idea of what it wished to accomplish but lacked
ular support.

uring the spring and early summer of 1917, the Provisional Govern-
t of Prime Minister Prince George Lvov failed to establish control
the deteriorating situation. The Russian economy continued to col-
e, the war dragged on, and the poverty-stricken Russian peasants,
constituted the overwhelming bulk of the population, pressed their
ands for land. Slowly the composition of the Provisional Govern-
t moved leftward until Alexander Kerensky, the only socialist mem-
of the original Provisional Government, was named prime minister
uly 20.

hile elements of the moderate, nonrevolutionary left gained power
he Provisional Government, the Bolsheviks, the most revolutionary
he socialist parties, increased their strength in the Soviet. This devel-
ent was directly attributable to the return to Russia from exile of the

e Russian capital St. Petersburg had been renamed Petrograd at the start of the war.

neering book arguing that the war produced profound social change in
Britain.

Offer, Avner. *The First World War: An Agrarian Interpretation.* Oxford: Clarendon
Press, 1989. Unconventional and uneven, but often brilliant.

Robbins, Keith. *The First World War.* Oxford: Clarendon Press, 1984. Thematic
rather than narrative approach.

Stevenson, David. *The First World War and International Politics.* Oxford: Clarendon Press, 1988. A persuasive study of the various countries' war aims
and the obstacles to a satisfactory peace settlement.

Stone, Norman. *The Eastern Front 1914–1917.* London: Hodder and Stoughton,
1975. A standard account.

Turner, John. *British Politics and the Great War.* New Haven: Yale University Press,
1992. The best detailed study of coalition governments and the collapse
of Britain's last Liberal administration.

Wohl, Robert. *The Generation of 1914.* Cambridge, MA: Harvard University Press,
1979. Elegant comparative analysis of the hopes and eventual disillusion
of the younger, university-educated generation.

ians, who had been forcibly brought into the Russian Empire, now demanded their independence.

Facing such a bleak prospect, Lenin and his followers concluded that their first priority must be to strengthen their grasp on the levers of power while simultaneously keeping faith with the Marxist ideology that had sustained them for so long. To that end they began their rule with a flurry of decrees, including the Decree on Land, which sanctioned peasant seizure of estates belonging to the well-to-do, and the Decree on Peace, which called upon all belligerents to enter into negotiations designed to achieve a just peace. In December they followed up on the peace decree when they concluded an armistice and opened peace negotiations with the Central Powers.

In addition to issuing popular decrees, the Bolsheviks tightened their grip on power when in December they established the Cheka, or secret police, and ordered it to ferret out and destroy all real and potential opposition to Bolshevik rule. Then, in January 1918, the Bolsheviks forcibly dissolved the democratically elected Constituent Assembly that had been expected to create a new set of governmental institutions for Russia. The Bolsheviks, who had done poorly in the fall 1917 elections, winning only 170 of 707 seats, regarded the Constituent Assembly as a threat to their power, and shut it down after allowing it to meet for only one day.

Meanwhile, the peace negotiations proved difficult. Meeting with German representatives at the small Polish town of Brest-Litovsk, the Bolsheviks discovered that their adversaries intended to extract major concessions from the fledgling regime. Bolshevik efforts to evade the German demands failed, and on March 3, 1918, the new Soviet state was forced to sign the humiliating Treaty of Brest-Litovsk. By the terms of the treaty, Soviet Russia gave up control over Poland, Finland, Estonia, Latvia, Lithuania, and Ukraine. It lost 60 million people, or more than one-quarter of its total population. It also surrendered more than one-quarter of its arable land, railways, and factories, and three-quarters of its iron and coal production. Only Germany's ultimate defeat in World War I enabled the weak Soviet state to recover some of its losses at Brest-Litovsk.

Many Bolshevik leaders balked at signing the Draconian peace, but Lenin carried the day when he argued that peace was absolutely essential for the retention of Soviet power in Russia, even if it meant that the war had to be concluded at virtually any price. Lenin maintained that peace would give the Bolsheviks a "breathing space" in which to build socialism in Russia. However, his optimism proved unfounded, as civil war broke out only weeks after the treaty was signed.

As with most civil wars, the Russian one was a bloody and brutal conflict. Emotions ran high, and both sides committed numerous indescribable atrocities. The Bolsheviks relied on their newly created Red Army, the product of Leon Trotsky's prodigious organizational skills. Their opponents were the Whites, an unlikely mixture of liberals, moderate socialists, radical but anti-Bolshevik socialists, army officers, monarchists, and conservatives. Ultimately, mindless reactionaries and fanatical Russian nationalists gained the upper hand and directed most White operations.

During the course of the civil war, the Bolsheviks instituted a policy known as War Communism. War Communism was designed to achieve two goals simultaneously: the marshalling of all available resources in order to prosecute the civil war, and the rapid transformation of Russia into a model Marxist state. To that end, the Bolsheviks under War Communism nationalized both land and industry, outlawed private trade, implemented a system of rationing and government distribution, and introduced the forced requisitioning of food and labor.

Although War Communism seriously disrupted Russia's already chaotic economy and earned for the Bolsheviks the enmity of millions, it probably helped the Reds to win their war against the Whites. Even more decisive for the Red victory, however, was the ineptitude of the White forces. Despite receiving help in the form of intervention and a blockade from several countries, including France, Great Britain, Japan, and the United States, the Whites failed to dislodge the Reds.

Basic to the White failure was their inability to coordinate their forces. Rather than a single, unified unit, the White army really consisted of several different armies, each under independent command, each following its own course of action, and each pursuing its own goals. Furthermore, the ultranationalistic Whites alienated the various minorities located on the periphery of the old Russian Empire, that is, the very places where the White forces had congregated to launch their attacks on the Bolsheviks. Finally, the Whites failed to win the hearts and minds of the vast peasant population. In fact, their behavior during the conflict as well as their stated desire to return to a prerevolutionary form of land tenure frightened and angered the peasants, without whose support the Whites' chances of success were slim.

The Russian Civil War dragged on for almost three years and, together with the famine it caused, resulted in the death of several million Russians. When the Bolsheviks finally emerged victorious in early 1921, their Russian state was a complete shambles. Nevertheless, the Bolsheviks had triumphed. The revolution was over, Lenin and the Bolsheviks had won, and the future of Russia was theirs to command.

INTERPRETIVE ESSAY
Bruce F. Adams

In 1917 Vladimir Lenin, leader of the Bolshevik Party, which would soon seize control of Russia, was living in Zurich, Switzerland. For most of the past sixteen years he had lived in self-imposed exile from tsarist Russia, watching intently events in the country whose government he had worked all his adult life to destroy. Once, when revolution had broken out in 1905, he had returned to St. Petersburg, hoping to help topple the tsar, but he had had to flee again when Nicholas II's forces crushed that revolution. Yet for more than twenty years he had sustained his faith that a socialist revolution would soon occur in Russia. Now in January 1917, he was heard to say, "We of the older generation"—Lenin was forty-six—"may not see the decisive battles of this coming revolution."

He was wrong, of course. Nicholas II was forced to abdicate less than two months later. One of the critical questions of twentieth-century history, endlessly debated by historians and taken up with renewed vigor since the collapse of the Soviet Union, is why this revolution occurred. Did the forces of worker discontent and revolutionary organization, which the Bolsheviks watched and tried to mold, make it inevitable, as Marxist-Leninist theory held? Or was the revolution an accident, a product of the economic collapse and suffering caused by World War I in Russia? Was the nature of the Bolshevik government also foreordained, or was it too the product of local and temporary circumstances?

To understand the impact the revolution had, both within and outside Russia, we must understand the contradictory answers to these questions. The people who made this history acted as they did in large part because they believed one version or the other. And history is after all not so much the story of the past as a continuing argument about how to tell that story.

We must also understand the long-term trends of Russian history. The revolution going on in Russia in the 1990s resembles the 1917 revolution in many ways. In both, the empire ruled by the Russians disintegrated and large numbers of refugees fled from war-torn lands. But in one important way these two revolutions are very different. After the 1917 revolution, the Bolsheviks began to construct wholly new forms of government and society that were threatening to their neighbors. In the Gorbachev and Yeltsin years, however, the Russians have tried to develop a more democratic government and a more open market economy, both of which are welcomed and supported by Russia's developed and powerful neighbors.

Despite his momentary doubt in 1917, Lenin would later insist that the revolution was the inevitable product of historical forces. And for the next seventy years, until the recent era of *glasnost* (openness), Soviet historians almost unanimously supported this view. In the West, however, most historians adopted a different interpretation. As they understood Russia's history up to 1917, Russia was evolving in the direction of Western constitutional monarchies and democracies, and not only was the revolution not inevitable, it violently contravened the general direction of Russian development. Revisionist historians have been challenging and modifying this so-called liberal view since the 1960s. But since the breakup of the Soviet Union and the recent democratic developments in Russia, liberal historians have retorted that the revolution and the following seventy years of communist domination were but an interruption in this general trend.

The Russian Revolution was, as practically all revolutions are, not so much an event as a process, a long period of instability that proceeded through several stages. It began in February 1917 in the midst of the third bleak winter of war. Almost 8 million Russians had died by that time, more than in the rest of the combatant nations combined. Enemy armies occupied much of western Russia, territory including more than a quarter of its industry and about a fourth of the prewar population. In unoccupied Russia much of the rest of the population suffered from unemployment, inflation, hunger, and cold. Most Russians had lost confidence in their army, in the tsar's government, and, most important, in Nicholas II himself. This was particularly true in St. Petersburg, Russia's capital. When yet another strike broke out there in late February, it quickly turned into an enormous antiwar demonstration, with tens of thousands of marchers calling for the tsar's ouster. This time the police were unable to suppress the demonstrators, and the army was unwilling to do so. The demonstration had become a revolution.

Russia's other leaders, including elected representatives to the Duma (a legislature established during the Revolution of 1905), generals in command of the armies, captains of industry, and leaders of other public institutions agreed that the only way to restore order was to ask Nicholas II to abdicate. When they insisted, he did so reluctantly, and they formed a new interim government called the Provisional Government. They did not mean to seize power and keep it. Rather, they intended to hold elections for a Constituent Assembly, which would write a constitution and oversee the election of a permanent government. The leaders of the Provisional Government believed above all else in the rule of law. And although it would lead to their destruction, they also believed that Russia must continue fighting alongside democratic France and England against the kaiser's Germany.

Reaction in Russia and in the Western democracies to this first revolution was immensely enthusiastic. The rapid growth of industrialization, urbanization, and higher education in Russia had by 1917 created a powerful middle class with liberal aspirations and a large working class that shared at least its distrust of the tsar. The former group dominated the tsarist-era public institutions, such as the Duma, and provided the foundation for the first Provisional Government. The interests and aspirations of the latter group were represented by the Soviet (Council) of Workers' and Soldiers' Deputies, which was established in St. Petersburg on the same day as the Provisional Government and which gave its conditional support to the new government. Both groups welcomed Nicholas II's fall and the opportunity to restructure their country.

European and American leaders shared their enthusiasm. The U.S. government recognized the Provisional Government within a week of its formation. (It would take it sixteen years to recognize the Bolsheviks.) In his first speech after the event, President Woodrow Wilson welcomed Russia to the "partnership of democratic nations" and spoke of "the wonderful and heartening things that have been happening within the last few weeks in Russia." Like Russia's European allies, Americans were pleased to see democracy developing in Russia. Having recently decided to commit the U.S. military to the war, they were probably even more pleased that the revolution might strengthen Russia's resolve and ability to fight Germany.

But the honeymoon for the Provisional Government was short. Continuing the war drained industry, finances, and manpower, thereby diminishing the people's loyalty and goodwill. All the problems that had led to Nicholas' ouster only got worse, and left-wing opposition to the war and the Provisional Government that now waged it grew rapidly. In just six months, three Provisional Governments fell as each failed to deal with shortages and the suffering they caused. Each new coalition government included more socialist ministers, and each was more torn by conflict than its predecessor. Ministers who proposed a solution to one of the problems found their way blocked by others who found it too radical—or too retrograde. The only real solution to Russia's problems probably was to make a separate peace with the Germans, but that was unacceptable to the government.

In June 1917, at the request of its allies, the Provisional Government launched a major offensive against Austria and Germany. The Allies hoped that a simultaneous offensive on both fronts would break the stalemate that World War I had become and push Germany to surrender. The Russians hoped also that a successful offensive would restore order to their army, whose morale had been sapped by earlier defeats and high losses, and thereby shore up support for the government. The European allies were not disappointed. Drawing more German troops east allowed them a measure of success in the west. But the Russians were more than disappointed. Early victories in the new offensive were quickly followed by defeats; the German counterattack turned into a rout. Whole units often refused orders to attack after this, and the desertion rate soared. The Russian army did not recover.

From July to October the Provisional Government continued to decay, tearing itself apart with internal squabbles while an ever-stronger Soviet organization and the growing Bolshevik Party picked at it from outside. By October, of all the major political parties from the center to the far left, only the Bolsheviks had remained outside the Provisional Government and consistently called for its ouster and an end to the war. While every other group was tarred by the common brush of failure, the Bolsheviks alone stood against the war and remained unblamed for its disaster. When they revolted on October 25, they overthrew a government that was barely standing.

The new Soviet government, which was essentially identical to the leadership of the Bolshevik Party, was not greeted with the same enthusiasm that the first Provisional Government had been. Most Russians were probably uncertain what the Bolsheviks intended to do. It would have been strange if they were not, as the Bolsheviks themselves did not know what they intended. On some major issues they did not hesitate. The night they took power Lenin announced to the Congress of Soviets that henceforth all land belonged to the peasants and the factories belonged to the workers. Exactly what that meant or how it would work was not immediately clear, but it placated large segments of the angry population. On the issue of the war the Bolsheviks equivocated. The Allies were fearful that the Bolsheviks would follow through on their repeated promises to leave the war. But the Bolsheviks feared German conquest, and a majority thought that they could mount a "revolutionary war" to defend the socialist revolution and inspire German troops to turn on their officers. A minority, led by Lenin, feared that they would not survive the Russian people's anger if they did not pull out. They played in the middle ground on this issue from October 1917 to March 1918, much of that time following a policy they called "neither peace nor war."

What seems to have saved the Bolsheviks at this point was their determination and the relative weakness of their enemies. Only one other party, the Socialist Revolutionaries (SR), enjoyed widespread popularity. Most of them were too close to the Bolsheviks doctrinally to oppose them with force, and the Bolsheviks had stolen much of the SR thunder with the Decree on Land. No other group, including the army, had the following or even sufficient confidence in itself to mount resistance. The Bolsheviks, on the other hand, were dedicated revolutionaries and true believers in the historical inevitability and justice of their cause. They were prepared to destroy their opponents with force and violence.

The election to and the meeting of the Constituent Assembly illuminates this point. The Provisional Government had waited until September to set a November date for the election to the assembly. It had been in constant crisis since March and wanted to postpone so important and potentially divisive a meeting until the war was over. Finally, however, the Provisional Government could no longer avoid it. When the Bolsheviks came to power, they debated whether they should allow the election to take place, fearing they would not win; but they did not want to appear undemocratic and dictatorial. In fact, when the election took place the Bolsheviks won only 24 percent of the national vote, while the Socialist Revolutionary factions polled 57 percent. The assembly met for one day in January 1918 and elected an SR chairman. When the delegates attempted to reassemble the second day, they found their way barred by Bolshevik guards and were disbanded. There was much grumbling and some editorializing against the Bolsheviks' high-handedness, but no armed resistance.

The work of the Cheka illustrates the point more clearly. Shortly after the October revolution, Lenin authorized Felix Dzerzhinsky to establish the Extraordinary Commission to Combat Counterrevolution, Sabotage, and Speculation. Its ostensible purpose was to restore civic and economic order by arresting speculators, saboteurs, and other criminals. Very quickly, however, it became a political police. Unrestrained by the rules of procedure that had controlled the tsarist police, the Cheka quickly arrested many thousands of people. Often ignoring its own rules, it dispensed quick "revolutionary justice," imprisoning, interrogating, trying (or not), and executing prisoners without turning them over to the courts. In 1918 the Cheka executed more prisoners than the tsarist regime had put to death in the previous 300 years. It did so again in 1919.

Opposition to the Bolsheviks was slow to organize. After the Bolsheviks disbanded the Constituent Assembly in January and pulled out of the war with Germany in March, however, opponents started to gather. Military opposition began in several areas, led by former officers of the tsarist army and politicians from a wide range of parties. By mid-1918, while large parts of Russia were still occupied by the Germans (the war was not over until November), civil war had begun. It would rage for more than two years. Although it was much shorter than the world war, and for the most part fought with weapons far less destructive, it was bitterly contested and vicious. Five million more Russians died in this war. All of the problems begun by the world war—industrial dislocation, unemployment, and inflation—intensified. In 1921 Russian industry produced less than one-fifth of what it had produced in 1914. Because both sides fed themselves by ravaging peasant villages and took reprisals against villagers who had "helped" their enemies, very little was planted in spring 1921, and the harvest that fall was too small to feed the country. Another million Russians died in the subsequent famine of 1921–1922.

Another form of opposition to the Bolsheviks ineffectually organized in 1918–1919. The Allies were afraid that the Bolshevik withdrawal from the war would allow Germany to concentrate its forces in the west. They were also concerned about social unrest in their own countries. If they allowed communism to be established in Russia, it could encourage labor and social democratic organizations in the West to revolt. The Bolsheviks believed that world revolution was about to begin and, beyond that, that their revolution could not survive unless it did. In March 1919 they had established the Communist International, or Comintern, whose raison d'être was to "export" revolution. Calling their intervention an effort to reopen a second front against Germany, near the end of the war the Allies landed small British, French, and American forces at Archangel and Murmansk, Vladivostok, and the Crimea. The Japanese, who were not part of the alliance but who took advantage of the Russian Empire's collapse to do the same, occupied parts of Russia's eastern maritime provinces and eastern Siberia. These foreign troops had few serious engagements with Bolshevik forces and rendered only insignificant assistance to the White forces in the civil war. They did little to affect the outcome of the civil war and less to affect the course of the world war. The fact that the intervention continued beyond the end of the world war showed, however, that Western leaders were worried about the threat of international communist revolution.

As well they should have been. No sooner had the war ended than communist revolutions broke out in several parts of Europe. Like the Russian Revolution, these all stemmed from local movements and problems, but undoubtedly the Bolshevik revolution inspired their leaders. Communists took power briefly in Bavaria and in Hungary. Demonstrations, riots, and terrorist activity occurred in many other countries. In free elections shortly after the war, communist, social democratic, and labor parties made large gains. In several European nations, legislation establishing parts of the modern welfare state was soon passed. This was more a consequence of the world war than of the Russian Revolution, but the Bolsheviks' apparent success increased the need to placate radical political forces.

In some countries, including the United States, postwar radicalism and fear of communism brought on a backlash, called the Red Scare. In the United States many radicals in unions and other labor and political movements were foreign born, often recent émigrés who had not yet become citizens. The decades around the turn of the century had seen a huge wave of immigrants come to America, many from eastern Europe and Russia. When several large strikes and a few anarchist bombings occurred in 1919, many Americans saw in them a communist revolution brewing and pressured the government to act. In August 1919 Attorney General A. Mitchell Palmer established in the Department of Justice a General Intelligence Division headed by J. Edgar Hoover. In November 1919 and January 1920 they raided suspected radical organizations all over the country, including one called the Union of Russian Workers, and arrested almost 7,000 people. Although the police and federal agents violated the civil rights of many of these people in their investigations and interrogations, very few turned out to have committed offenses for which they might be deported. The Red Scare petered out quickly in mid-1920.

One of the major consequences of the revolutions cannot be separated from the war and the peace settlement. By the end of 1918, the tsarist empire had been torn apart. In the Treaty of Brest-Litovsk, which the Bolsheviks signed with the Germans in March 1918, Russia lost western and southern territory, including more than a fourth of its population. Germany's subsequent surrender nullified this treaty, but the treaties signed in Paris in 1919 ratified most of the territorial losses. Finland, Estonia, Latvia, and Lithuania became independent states. Taking territory principally from Russia, Poland also became independent. Romania received former Bessarabia. As has happened again in the 1990s, many other areas populated by non-Russian peoples took advantage of the disorder to claim their independence also. This was particularly true on the periphery of the country in areas that had been joined to Russia relatively recently. Georgians, Armenians, Uzbeks, and others experienced a few years of independence before reconquest and reabsorption into the Soviet Union.

The most important consequences of the revolutions, in Russia and outside it, were changes in the nature of Russian government and society. The Bolsheviks did not know in 1917 what sort of government was suitable for "building socialism," and they argued bitterly about it until Joseph Stalin ended all discussion. Initially, in part because their first several years in power were passed in continual crisis and insecurity, the Bolshevik leadership agreed that they would need to be a "dictatorship of the proletariat." The Bolsheviks shared power with no other party. As a matter of fact, they suppressed rival parties, often violently. Within their own party, however, for the first ten years they tolerated wide-ranging discussion and dissent. In theory this dictatorship was meant to be temporary and would "wither away" as socialism made government almost unnecessary. But by 1928, four years after Lenin died, Joseph Stalin had maneuvered his way to preeminence, silenced his critics, taken control of the levers of power, and established a personal dictatorship. In 1929 he began to collectivize agriculture and to industrialize rapidly. Employing great violence and brutality, Stalin achieved his twin goals; however, more than 20 million Soviet citizens died in the process.

Russia's neighbors feared this dictatorship, which abetted revolution abroad and which mobilized its people and its industrial forces in part by proclaiming (and often believing) that war with the capitalist states was inevitable. Because of this mutual fear and distrust, Russia remained a pariah, an outcast among the European nations. Even before Lenin's death this outcast status drew Russia closer to Germany, the other European pariah of the 1920s, which was blamed for causing World War I. These fears and relationships helped create the European alliance system that led into World War II and helped shape the period of postwar tensions that we call the Cold War.

The origins of this dictatorship form the other major historiographical issue of the Russian revolutions. One camp claims that Stalinism, as the whole system came to be called, was the product of Stalin's personal character. Proponents like to claim that had Lenin lived longer such a brutal dictatorship would not have developed, a proposition that cannot, of course, be tested. Since the collapse of the Communist Party of the Soviet Union and of the Soviet Union itself in 1991, many communists have preferred to blame Stalin personally for the great tragedies of his era, thereby preserving the belief that the revolution could have evolved very differently. These sentiments first surfaced (albeit quietly) after Stalin's death in 1953.

Historians on the other side of this argument find Stalinism to be a logical development of the earlier dictatorship. Writers in the West have been as divided on this issue as on the question of the causes of the revolution. Most research, however, seems to suggest that the nature of the Bolsheviks (most of whom were professional revolutionaries), their experience in the very bitter civil war, and their dedication to the idea of building socialism led logically, if not inevitably, to a Stalinist sort of dictatorship. The ruthlessness with which enemies were eradicated from 1917 to 1921 and the frustrations experienced in building socialism by 1928 came together in Stalin's violent dictatorship.

Russian society was also changed radically by the revolutions. Not only did the Bolsheviks not know in 1917 what sort of government they needed to create, they were not at all certain what socialism looked like. What did it mean that the workers owned the factories and the peasants owned the land? Was it private ownership or collective ownership? Did it allow for some farms and factories to flourish and others to fail? What would become of former owners and specialists, members of the upper class against whom the proletariat had presumably revolted? Were the products of labor to be redistributed? What role did the state play in all this?

In the civil war years, the Bolsheviks nationalized all large-scale industry, banks, and the means of communication—what they called the "commanding heights" of the national economy. They took from everyone else whatever they needed to feed the Red Army and fight the war, particularly food from the peasants. Altogether this policy was called War Communism. Like practically everything else in these first years, it was considered a temporary expedient.

The real problems surfaced again when the Bolsheviks controlled the country and had the freedom to decide what they really wanted to do. They could not agree. Until the so-called Stalin revolution at the end of the 1920s, they dithered and argued bitterly over policy. The New Economic Policy (NEP) that was begun in 1921 allowed for a mixed economy. The "commanding heights" remained in the hands of the government, but farming, small-scale industry, retail sales, and services were left to the private sector. And the private sector flourished as the state sector did not, reproducing the very inequalities that socialism was meant to end. Radical Bolsheviks, veterans of the civil war, and poor workers and peasants resented the successful NEPmen (those who profited from the New Economic Policy) and wondered why they had suffered through the revolution and war. When Stalin acted to build his version of socialism, he crushed all independent economic activity (and essentially all intellectual activity) and brought everything within the state sector. The state did not wither away, but came to dominate people's lives by means of an enormous and pervasive bureaucracy.

The Russian Revolution deeply affected life in Russia, much of the rest of Europe, and eventually the entire world. What it ultimately produced bore little resemblance to the dreams of most of the people who made it, but that is true of all revolutions. Until 1949, when the Chinese communists won their civil war, the Soviet Union stood as the world's only socialist society. Its reputation was tarnished and its international following diminished after the horrors of the Stalin years came to light, some in the 1930s and many more after 1953. But until at least 1989, it continued to provide hope and an example for some communist parties around the world who wished to make their own revolutions.

SELECTED BIBLIOGRAPHY

Acton, Edward. *Rethinking the Russian Revolution.* London: Edward Arnold, 1990. This survey of literature on the revolution concentrates on histories written since the 1960s.

Daniels, Robert V. *Red October: The Bolshevik Revolution of 1917.* New York: Charles Scribner's Sons, 1967. Concentrating on events in the capital, Daniels concludes that the Bolsheviks struck when the Provisional Government was on the point of collapse and came to power largely by default.

Deutscher, Isaac. *The Prophet Armed: Trotsky, 1879–1921.* New York: Vintage Books, 1965. This is the first volume of the classic three-volume biography of Trotsky.

Fischer, Louis. *The Life of Lenin.* New York: Harper Colophon Books, 1964. Probably still the most readable, thorough biography of Lenin.

Keep, John L.H. *The Russian Revolution: A Study in Mass Mobilization.* New York: W. W. Norton, 1976. An important history of the revolution concentrating on events outside Petrograd.

Leggett, George. *The Cheka: Lenin's Political Police.* Oxford: Oxford University Press, 1981. Appendices include biographical sketches of Cheka leaders and statistics on arrests and executions.

Lincoln, W. Bruce. *Passage Through Armageddon: The Russians in War and Revolution, 1914–1918.* New York: Simon and Schuster, 1986. A well-written scholarly account of Russia's collapse in World War I, the complexities of the 1917 revolutions, and the establishment of Bolshevik power.

————. *Red Victory: A History of the Russian Civil War.* New York: Touchstone, 1989. A thorough account of the politics, personalities, and battles of the civil war.

Pipes, Richard. *The Russian Revolution.* New York: Vintage Books, 1991. A huge (944-page) narrative and analysis of the revolution by a leading conservative thinker.

Rabinowitch, Alexander. *The Bolsheviks Come to Power: The Revolution of 1917 in Petrograd.* New York: W. W. Norton, 1978. This work focuses on the Bolsheviks in Petrograd and finds spontaneous activity by soldiers and workers to be a major cause of the revolution.

Reed, John. *Ten Days that Shook the World.* New York: New American Library, 1967. A colorful, not always accurate look by an American sympathetic to the Bolsheviks.

Rosenberg, William. *Liberals in the Russian Revolution: The Constitutional Democratic Party, 1917–1921.* Princeton: Princeton University Press, 1974. A history of liberalism and of the leading liberal party in the revolutionary years.

Shulgin, V. V. *Days of the Russian Revolution: Memoirs from the Right, 1905–1907.* Translated and edited by Bruce F. Adams. Gulf Breeze, FL: Academic International Press, 1990. The only memoir in English by a major conservative figure of the revolutionary period.

Stites, Richard. *Feminism, Nihilism, and Bolshevism, 1860–1930.* Princeton: Princeton University Press, 1990. The best history of radical women before and during the revolutionary period.

Trotsky, Leon. *The History of the Russian Revolution.* New York: Monad Press, 1980. An insider's look at events by one of the Bolshevik leaders.

Tucker, Robert C. *Stalin as Revolutionary, 1879–1929: A Study of History and Personality.* New York: W. W. Norton, 1973. A biography of Joseph Stalin, a minor figure in the 1917 revolution who became the leader of the Party and the nation by 1928.

Von Hagen, Mark. *Soldiers in the Proletarian Dictatorship: The Red Army and the Soviet Socialist State, 1917–1930.* Ithaca: Cornell University Press, 1990. The formation of the Red Army, the civil war, and the years following to 1930.

Von Laue, Theodore H. *Why Lenin? Why Stalin? A Reappraisal of the Russian Revolution, 1900–1930.* Philadelphia: J. B. Lippincott, 1964. An attempt to explain the sources of the revolution and the Soviet dictatorship.

Wildman, Allan K. *The End of the Russian Imperial Army: The Old Army and the Soldiers' Revolt (March–April 1917).* Princeton: Princeton University Press, 1980. The collapse of the tsarist army in World War I and how it helped lead to the revolution.

Adolf Hitler and Benito Mussolini take the salute. Fascism promised to bring a new world order, but only renewed global conflict. (Reproduced from the Collections of the Library of Congress)

3

The Rise of Fascism, 1919–1945

INTRODUCTION

Fascism is defined as a system of government characterized by a rigid one-party dictatorship, forcible suppression of the opposition, the retention of private ownership of the means of production under centralized governmental control, belligerent nationalism and racism, and glorification of war. Although fascism's intellectual antecedents are rooted in the nineteenth century, it is universally regarded as one of the most important twentieth-century movements. Fascist regimes under Benito Mussolini in Italy and Adolf Hitler in Germany not only spawned numerous imitators, but also introduced unique political, economic, and social forms. Eventually, fascist aggression plunged the world into the cataclysmic World War II.

Benito Mussolini (1883–1945), the son of a poor blacksmith, led Italian fascism. A socialist like his father, Mussolini abandoned a teaching career, joined the Socialist Party, and became editor of its official newspaper, *Avanti* (Forward). When Mussolini shockingly rejected the socialist commitment to neutrality and urged Italian entry into World War I on the side of the Entente, the socialists expelled him from their party.

Mussolini founded the Fascio di Combattimento, or Fascists, in Milan in March 1919. With no clear goal in mind other than self-advancement, Mussolini led his fascists on an ultranationalistic course. He also condemned the capitalist socioeconomic system. With time, the nationalistic stance hardened; but strident attacks on socialism, especially Marxism, replaced the criticism of capitalism. Mussolini, who depended upon contributions from Italian businessmen, converted his party into a staunch champion of property rights and the existing social order. Thanks to his attacks on socialism and his nationalistic demagoguery, Mussolini also gathered support among the middle class. Nevertheless, the Fascists remained on the political periphery. In the 1921 parliamentary elections, they managed to win just 35 of the more than 500 seats contested.

To give his party the muscle it lacked at the ballot box, Mussolini created the *squadristi,* black-shirted paramilitary street gangs that brawled incessantly with Fascism's opponents. In October 1922 the *squadristi* responded to Mussolini's command to "march on Rome" and seize power. Although the legitimate government possessed the resources to crush the Fascist threat, it lacked the necessary leadership and willpower. Consequently, Mussolini's bold gamble succeeded, and the Fascist leader was named prime minister.

Although Mussolini headed only a coalition government, it was quite apparent that he was in charge. In a matter of months he easily converted Italy's parliamentary democracy into a fascist dictatorship. However, since he never fully controlled several independent institutions, including the monarchy, the military, and the Roman Catholic Church, he had to proceed cautiously when dealing with them.

In practice, Italian fascism was often inefficient if not chaotic. Overlapping and competing layers of bureaucracy created numerous opportunities for corruption. The chain of command was unclear, and so were the regime's ultimate goals.

By the end of 1926, Mussolini had many essential elements of his dictatorship in place. A stringent censorship muzzled the press, and the Fascist Party wrested control over local government from elective bodies. The Fascists also dominated the educational establishment. With the exception of the Fascist Party, all political organizations were abolished. Labor, considered the bastion of socialism, attracted special attention. Fascist labor unions replaced independent ones, and labor lost the right to strike.

Mussolini continued his cozy relationship with Italian big business, which delightedly applauded his rough treatment of the unions. He subsequently developed the concept of corporativism, which divided all Italian economic life into a number of units, or corporations. The corporations allegedly represented all the concerned parties, including business and labor, but in fact they were dominated by Fascists, who nevertheless were careful not to antagonize factory owners. Attempts to coordinate the national economy in order to achieve autarky, or self-sufficiency, failed in the face of inefficiency, corruption, and Italy's dependence upon imported raw materials.

The Fascists also fashioned government-like institutions that gradually superseded the state apparatus. To enforce their rule, the Fascists created a secret police, the OVRA, and arrested a number of opponents, who were incarcerated in political prisons. However, it was not until 1938, after Mussolini had moved close to Hitler, that the Italian fascists began to discriminate against and harass Jews and other racial minorities.

Mussolini initiated the "leader" principle, which subsequent fascist chieftains eagerly copied. Mussolini, supported by his sprawling propaganda apparatus, claimed for himself the title Duce, or leader, and increasingly portrayed himself as infallible. One of the regime's most important slogans was "Mussolini is always right."

This same propaganda apparatus denigrated liberalism and democracy, and glorified brute strength and mindless violence. "Action," often with no particular purpose, became a way of life. Mussolini tried to dress his people in a dizzying array of uniforms, and the government proclaimed numerous causes for battle, including a battle for grain and one for population, the so-called battle for births. Italian nationalism was virtually sanctified, while a cult of male virility took on such proportions that Mussolini himself was shown engaging in the most ludicrous physical activity, including leaping through burning hoops.

In foreign affairs, the fascist credo of "action" assumed a bombastic and often expansionistic form. Mussolini began his foreign policy adventures with a bang—literally—when in 1923 he bombarded the Greek island of Corfu. For a number of years afterward he occupied himself with domestic matters, including the 1929 Lateran Accords, which regularized relations with the Roman Catholic Church. However, by the mid-1930s Italian fascism was on the move. In 1934 Mussolini rallied behind Austria's arch-conservative government to prevent that state from succumbing to the Nazis. The following year, Italy attacked Abyssinia (Ethiopia) in northeast Africa in a bid to revive Italy's colonial empire. In rapid succession, Mussolini reversed his course and teamed up with Adolf Hitler, intervened in the Spanish Civil War on the side of General Francisco Franco and the Spanish Falangists or fascists, acquiesced to Hitler's 1938 annexation of Austria, and finally joined the Germans in World War II, a decision that ultimately led to the destruction of both Mussolini and Italian fascism.

Mussolini's counterpart in Germany was Adolf Hitler (1889–1945). German fascism, called National Socialism or Nazism, was considerably more virulent than Mussolini's Italian version. Hitler was the son of a minor Austrian customs official. As a young man, the lazy and untalented Hitler failed to gain entry to art school, and drifted first to Vienna and then to Munich, where he joined the German army at the outbreak of World War I. Hitler enjoyed his military experience and was decorated for bravery.

At the close of World War I, Hitler returned to Munich, where he immersed himself in radical politics. In 1919 he joined the National Socialist German Workers' (Nazi) Party, and two years later he emerged as its leader. The Nazis, a fringe party at best, adopted an ultranationalistic program that denounced both the Treaty of Versailles and the Weimar Republic, the democratic state formed in the wake of Germany's defeat in the war. The Nazis originally flirted with socialism, but later came to condemn it. Hitler added a unique racial element to German fascism, proclaiming the superiority of the Aryan, or German, race and calling for the subjugation of "inferior" races, especially the Jews, whom he blamed for all of Germany's problems.

In 1923 Hitler led a failed coup d'état, the so-called Beer Hall Putsch, and was sentenced to jail, where he wrote his autobiography, *Mein Kampf*. Released from jail in late 1924, Hitler resumed his leadership of the Nazi Party, which continued to be politically inconsequential. In the 1928 elections the Nazis garnered only 2.6 percent of the popular vote and elected only 12 deputies in the 491-seat German Reichstag, or parliament.

Nazi fortunes improved dramatically when the Great Depression struck Germany in late 1929. When the economy collapsed, the German voters, who were never entirely satisfied with the democratic republic, turned to the political extremes. In the 1930 elections the Nazis increased their popular vote by more than 700 percent and elected 107 deputies, which made them the second largest party in the Reichstag.

The economic collapse provoked a political crisis, and another round of elections in 1932 served to confirm the Nazis' popularity. Consequently, it was not at all remarkable that Hitler, as leader of the largest political party in Germany, was named chancellor in January 1933. Like Mussolini, Hitler originally headed up a coalition government, and like Mussolini he soon dispensed with his partners in favor of dictatorial rule.

Immediately after the Reichstag building burned to the ground in a suspicious February fire, Hitler issued a decree suspending civil rights in Germany and began to arrest his opponents. A week later, new but less than totally free elections resulted in a Nazi landslide, with Hitler's party capturing almost 44 percent of the vote and electing 288 deputies. At the end of March 1933, a now docile Reichstag passed the Enabling Act, which gave Hitler's government the right to enact laws at will. Democracy in Germany was dead; the fascists now ruled.

Before the year was out, the Nazis had opened their first concentration camp at Dachau and were busy filling it with political prisoners. All political parties other than the Nazis were outlawed as the fascists imposed a one-party state. Independent trade unions were dissolved as well, replaced by the Labor Front, a Nazi organization officially dedicated to the well-being of the German working class but in fact charged with keeping German labor quiet. The first of numerous book-burning spectacles during which Nazi thugs torched millions of volumes deemed to be subversive, decadent, authored by Jews or communists, or in some way unfit for the master race, also occurred in 1933. The racial side of German fascism made itself felt in April 1933 when the Nazis organized a nationwide boycott of Jewish shops.

German fascism continued to consolidate its grip on power in 1934. The Law on the Reconstruction of the Reich destroyed the independence of the German *lander*, or provinces, and a system of Nazi-controlled People's Courts replaced the existing German judicial structure. Hitler also secured his personal position. On June 30 he carried out a bloody purge of the Nazi Party. This purge, known as the Night of the Long Knives, eliminated Hitler's real and potential rivals, such as Ernst Röhm, head of the party's SA (Sturm Abteilungen), a paramilitary organization consisting of Nazi hoodlums.

A few weeks later, German president Paul von Hindenburg, the antiquated World War I general, died. Hitler seized the occasion to unite the offices of chancellor and president in himself, thereby institutionalizing the concept of the infallible leader, or Führer. As with the Duce in Italy, the German Führer could do no wrong.

Hitler also followed the Italian example when he promoted the absorption of the state by the party. However, in the German case the Nazis went much further. The Nazi Party gradually expanded its authority to perform functions normally carried out by the state, while the state's traditional governing institutions either disappeared or became superfluous. The Nazis energetically encouraged *Gleichschaltung*, or coordination, which aimed to invade every nook and cranny of German life in order

to Nazify all human activity. With *Gleichschaltung,* the Nazis planned first
to atomize German society and then to rebuild it according to Nazi spec-
ifications.

That *Gleichschaltung* was never fully realized is at least partially attributable to the rampant inefficiency and corruption of German fascism.
Nazi party bosses frequently behaved like feudal barons, jealously
guarding their fiefdoms, ceaselessly squabbling over minor details, and
slavishly competing for the Führer's favor. Nevertheless, German fascism
clearly affected society more profoundly than its Italian counterpart. Hitler developed more effective means of control, especially the brutal and
omnipresent secret police, or Gestapo, under the command of Heinrich
Himmler. Joseph Goebbels, Hitler's chief propagandist, orchestrated a
constant stream of nationalistic propaganda that further buttressed the
repressive Nazi regime. Romanticizing the past, glorifying Hitler and the
present, and promising a triumphant future, Goebbels' propaganda machine enveloped Germany in a cloud of hallucinatory smoke.

Hitler was more successful than Mussolini in bringing independent
institutions under his control. After first allying himself with big business, Hitler came to dominate it. By the late 1930s, German businessmen
and their factories were virtually subject to the Führer's command.
German industrialists quietly accepted their reduced status since they
retained ownership of their property and enjoyed the profits that their
businesses generated. In the case of the German army, a proud bastion
of traditional conservatism and the Prussian aristocracy, Hitler managed
by 1938 to discredit its leadership and to fill its command ranks with
loyal Nazis.

German fascism clearly reflected Hitler's obsessive racial hatred. It
turned its full force against society's "outsiders," especially the Jews. In
1935 the Nazis imposed the Nuremberg Laws, which deprived Jews of
their German citizenship, forbade Jews to marry non-Jews, and set quotas for Jews in the professions. In November 1938 Hitler unleashed his
Nazi hordes in an orgy of violence directed against the tiny (about 1
percent of the population) German Jewish community. This pogrom,
called *Kristallnacht,* resulted in the deaths of more than 1,000 Jews and
the arrest of another 30,000. German fascism's violent, anti-Semitic out-
bursts proved to be merely a prelude to the concentration camps and
the systematic extermination of Europe's Jews during World War II.

Nazi foreign policy was an active one, seeking two goals: the destruction of the Treaty of Versailles and the expansion of Germany's boundaries, or the quest for living room *(Lebensraum),* as Hitler characterized
it. With much of Europe deeply mired in the Depression and paralyzed

by memories of World War I, Hitler achieved a series of diplomatic triumphs that seemed to confirm his self-proclaimed infallibility. In rapid succession he withdrew Germany from the League of Nations (1933), commenced rearmament (1935), remilitarized the Rhineland (1936), intervened in the Spanish Civil War (1936–1939), annexed Austria (the Anschluss) (1938), and destroyed Czechoslovakia with the acquiescence of the western democracies at the Munich Conference (1938). Only when he invaded Poland in September 1939 did he overreach himself. The error proved to be fatal. In inaugurating the European phase of World War II, Hitler set in motion forces that eventually brought him down and destroyed fascist Germany in the process.

INTERPRETIVE ESSAY
George P. Blum

Fascism as a dominant force burst quite suddenly upon the European scene in the aftermath of World War I. Next to communism, fascism has been one of the most problematic phenomena of the twentieth century, and historians have offered various explanations of its origins and its political, economic, social, cultural, and international impact. Originally the term *fascism* referred to the movement that Benito Mussolini organized in 1919 and turned into Italy's ruling regime three years later. Since the 1930s the term has also been applied to other extreme nationalist authoritarian movements and regimes such as National Socialism or Nazism in Germany, the Falange in Francisco Franco's Spain, the Arrow Cross in Hungary, and the Iron Guard in Romania.

Fascist movements promoted intense nationalism with expansionistic territorial aspirations. They were vehemently antisocialist and anti-Marxist, and they aimed to destroy working-class parties and organizations. They rejected liberalism and democracy, and once in power they eliminated nonfascist political parties and emasculated parliamentary institutions. In their place, they established an authoritarian regime, whose center was a political party embracing fascist ideology, led by a single charismatic leader, and legitimized by plebiscites. Ruthless repression and terror without respect for the law crushed any opposition. Militarism, war, and conquests were glorified, and uniforms, military rituals, and parades were used to generate a spirit of unity among the fascist militants and the people. Controlled mass propaganda imparted the aims of the movement to the people and kept them psychologically attuned to the leader's designs. Racism and anti-Semitism were primarily characteristic of the National Socialist movement. Italian fascism embraced anti-Semitism only after Italy became an ally of Nazi Germany on the eve of World War II.

Italian Fascism had its formal beginning in Milan, when Benito Mussolini formed the first *Fasci di Combattimento* (fighting units) in March 1919. Made up of dissident socialists, syndicalists, and nationalist war veterans, the Fascists were united in their patriotism and their demand for social and political change. Fascist participation in electoral politics brought at first nothing but disappointment. However, new opportunities arose when Fascist *squadristi* (armed bands dressed in black shirts) fanned out into the countryside and offered their services to large landowners as a private police force against peasants. This alliance between landed wealth and Fascist bands came about when landowners felt threatened by peasant leagues organized on socialist lines. Similar cooperation between property and Fascism occurred in some urban areas, where industrialists paid *squadristi* to raid the offices of left-wing newspapers, socialist headquarters, and even Catholic trade unions.

Mussolini's propaganda skillfully used patriotic and anti-Bolshevik themes, playing on the fears of the broader populace. The Fascist movement attracted support from the lower middle class, small shopkeepers, clerical workers, artisans, and also intellectuals and professionals who faced a chronic shortage of white-collar jobs. Lastly, Mussolini gained the respect of the middle class, which was becoming more and more insecure.

The economic and social disarray following the war, including the return to a civilian economy that threw 2.5 million demobilized soldiers onto the labor market, greatly exacerbated Italy's political problems. The physical hardship of unemployment and inflation was added to the Italian public's psychological disappointment over the peace settlement. The legend arose that the arrogant allied peacemakers and the unassertive liberal Italian politicians at the peace conference had "mutilated" Italy's victory by denying Italy promised annexations.

By the summer of 1922, many Italian politicians had determined that Mussolini and his Fascists had to be taken into the government if stability was to be restored in the country. It was hoped that once the Fascists shared governmental responsibilities, they would be tamed and desist from violence. Mussolini encouraged this view by softening his earlier anti-republican stance and by showing receptiveness to liberal economic policies and to a possible accommodation with the Catholic

Church. However, he also threatened an insurrectionary "march on Rome."

Though Mussolini gathered 17,000 or so *squadristi* ready to descend on Rome, the government had more than enough military force to suppress a Fascist insurrection. But neither the government nor the king nor the army leadership mustered the will to resist the Fascists. King Victor Emmanuel III backed off from declaring martial law, and on October 30, 1922, appointed Mussolini prime minister. Mussolini formed a fourteen-member coalition government consisting of Fascists, nationalists, liberals, democrats, and Catholic Popolari. He reserved the most important ministerial posts for his party, adding the foreign and interior ministries to his prime ministership. The Italian strongman then received a vote of confidence from the parliament and was given temporary authority to rule by decree. In the words of historian Alan Cassels, Mussolini's takeover of government "could hardly be called a coup d'état because the authorities surrendered before a blow could be struck."

The Fascists held less than 10 percent of the seats in the Chamber of Deputies. Even a formal union with the Nationalists in 1923 increased their representation only minimally. To improve their position, the Fascists initiated a new electoral law to give the party that received the most votes in a national election two-thirds of the seats in parliament so long as that party attained at least a quarter of the total votes cast. In the 1924 election, Mussolini's list received 65 percent of the votes, giving him a secure parliamentary majority even without the new law.

Mussolini faced a major crisis in 1924 when several Fascists murdered Giacomo Matteotti, a socialist leader who had protested Fascist violence during the elections. Despite public and parliamentary outcry, Mussolini retained the support of the king who, together with conservatives and the Church, feared the socialists if Mussolini were removed. After months of wavering, early in 1925 the Fascist leader assumed moral responsibility for Matteotti's death but also ominously declared, "Italy wants peace and quiet . . . this we shall giver her, by love if possible, by force if need be."

Within two years, the coalition government was ended and the cabinet made fully Fascist. The Socialist Party, the Catholic Popolari, and labor unions were banned. The parliament was further weakened when Mussolini obtained virtual permanent authority to rule by decree and the principle of ministerial responsibility to parliament was abolished. The suppression of the press silenced all public opposition, and a newly formed secret police combatted antifascist activity. A Special Tribunal for the Defense of the State passed arbitrary and sometimes secret sentences, though never on a scale equal to the Nazi or Soviet abuse of justice. Only a small number of death sentences were passed and no more than 10,000 persons imprisoned. To be sure, Fascist jails were often wretched places for political prisoners, and penal colonies were notoriously brutal, claiming the lives of unknown numbers. However, Mussolini's rule never became an absolute dictatorship comparable to Hitler's or Stalin's regime. Hannah Arendt, in *The Origins of Totalitarianism*, characterizes Fascist Italy as "not totalitarian, but just an ordinary national dictatorship."

Mussolini had to work within a governmental structure that retained an independent monarchy and military. Even though in 1928 the legislative authority to nominate a premier was transferred from the king to the Grand Council of Fascism, the ruling committee of the party, the king remained the legal commander-in-chief until Italy's entry into World War II in 1940. Many Italian aristocrats, civil servants, and military officers continued to give their first allegiance to the monarchy. The Catholic Church also asserted an independent role in Italian life, which was strengthened rather than weakened by the Lateran Accords of 1929 with the Fascist government. The Duce, Mussolini's favored title as party leader, managed to control the bureaucracy, but not the army or the Church. It was striking how in the face of military defeat the king, the army leadership, and even the Grand Council of Fascism turned against Mussolini and deposed him in 1943.

Nazism, the German version of fascism, seemed to have a better prepared base in the antidemocratic traditions of the authoritarian German Empire than did fascism in the nineteenth-century Italian movement for unity and liberalism. Germany acquired democracy in the wake of military defeat, and many Germans viewed it as a foreign imposition. Throughout much of its life, the Weimar Republic remained a political system supported by a minority of people, struggling in the aftermath of World War I with an economic slump, foreign occupation, unprecedented hyperinflation, and reparations. Yet the first German republic managed to weather these crises and the persistent challenges to parliamentary democracy by opponents from the right and the left ten years longer than Italy under its constitutional monarchy. As German economic conditions improved after the mid-1920s, in part with foreign credits, so did the prospects of parliamentary democracy. Quite likely, it would have survived in Germany and Nazism would have remained but a noisy fringe movement if the Great Depression had not cut short prosperity.

The early traces of National Socialism can be found in various small pan-German and anti-Semitic political associations that appeared in the Austro-Hungarian Empire around the turn of the century. It was an off-shoot of these fringe organizations, the recently organized German Workers' Party in Munich, that Adolf Hitler joined in 1919. A product of an Austrian lower-middle-class family, Hitler drifted aimlessly before volunteering for the German army at the outset of World War I. Hitler found comradeship and direction for his life in the trenches on the Western Front, where he served bravely throughout the war. Bitterly disappointed by Germany's defeat, he decided to become a politician. Due to his oratorical talent, he became the principal propagandist of the fledgling Munich party and, by 1921, the dictatorial leader, the Führer, of the newly named National Socialist German Workers' (Nazi) Party.

The tenets of the Nazi Party reflected many of the prejudices and ideas that Hitler had embraced in prewar Vienna: vehement German racial nationalism, including imperial aspirations for *Lebensraum*, anti-Semitism, hostility to liberal democracy, and, especially, hatred of Marxism. Nazi propaganda attacked the "November criminals," that is, Jews, socialists, communists, and liberals who allegedly had brought down the imperial government in the revolution of 1918. It condemned the "dictate" of the Versailles Treaty and perpetuated the legend that the German front-line soldiers had held off the enemy, but had been "stabbed in the back" by the home front. At first the Nazi Party remained concentrated in Bavaria. In 1923 Hitler felt confident enough to stage the Beer Hall Putsch, trying to seize power in Munich, the capital of Bavaria, in preparation for a march on Berlin in imitation of Mussolini; but he failed ingloriously. He was arrested and his party temporarily outlawed.

But in due time the Nazi movement recovered. When tried on charges of treason, Hitler turned the proceedings into a propaganda triumph, charging that the socialist president of the Weimar Republic and those in government were the real traitors. After his release from prison in 1924, he showed considerable organizational talent in the reconstruction of his party. By the end of the decade, worsening socioeconomic conditions gave him and his party the opportunity to gain wide support among the masses.

One major effect of the severe economic conditions of the Great Depression, with its attendant social hardships, was deep political polarization of the German electorate. When unemployment reached 3 million in 1930, many of the workers began to support the communists. Members of the middle and lower middle class, many of whom had suffered in the hyperinflation of 1923, saw this trend as a threat to the established order. They flocked to the Nazis, who claimed to be a bulwark against revolution. In the 1930 Reichstag election, the Nazis increased their representation from 12 to 107 seats and became the largest party in Germany next to the Social Democrats. Increasingly, the Weimar president had to use constitutional emergency provisions to govern the country, which meant that the democratically elected parliamentary based cabinet was replaced with a presidentially appointed cabinet. In short, democracy ceased to function in Germany several years before Hitler came to power.

In 1932, when unemployment peaked at 6.5 million, three successive national elections gave Hitler a unique opportunity to engage in mass agitation. His bitter attacks on political opponents and his emotional appeals for the restoration of Germany's greatness impressed voters of all social classes. He was also the first to use the airplane to reach more cities and audiences, thereby revolutionizing the style of campaigning. The Nazi Party emerged as Germany's largest party with 37 percent of the vote in July 1932. As the leader of the largest party, Hitler held out for the office of chancellor. Intrigue by conservative nationalist politicians like Franz von Papen and Kurt von Schleicher as well as Hitler's shrewd calculations brought his appointment as chancellor by a reluctant President Paul von Hindenburg on January 30, 1933.

Hitler presided over a coalition cabinet containing only a handful of Nazis, but they held important positions. He moved quickly to consolidate his dictatorial powers. A Reichstag fire, which allegedly portended a communist uprising, was used as a pretext to suspend constitutional guarantees. Communists and some Social Democrats were arrested and soon incarcerated in permanent concentration camps. After gaining an increased plurality of 43.9 percent—but not a majority—in the March Reichstag election, Hitler masterminded the adoption of the Enabling Act, which gave him dictatorial powers. Between May and July, he dissolved the trade unions and political parties, replacing them with Nazi-directed mass organizations in a process called *Gleichschaltung*, or coordination. One year later, in June 1934, he violently purged the leadership of the paramilitary Storm Troopers (SA) under Ernst Röhm in order to mollify the army leadership, the only force that might have challenged him on his road to absolute dictatorship. When President von Hindenburg died in August, the army leaders accepted the merger of the offices of president and chancellor, with Hitler taking the titles of Führer and *Reichskanzler*. He thereby became the supreme commander of all the Reich's armed forces, and officers and soldiers were required to swear an oath of personal allegiance to Hitler.

Whereas Mussolini's regime retained aspects of a semipluralistic state based on law, the Nazi *Führerstaat* was a complex, one-man dictatorship over the state administration, army, big business, and industry. In the Hitler regime the party or its affiliated organizations, such as the elite SS (*Schutzstaffel* or guard echelon), which carried out police, state security, intelligence, and in World War II also military functions, commanded a prominent and powerful place. This was in contrast to Mussolini's Italy, where the party enjoyed little autonomy and was subordinate to the state bureaucracy.

The rise of fascism in Italy and Germany stimulated radical national politics in many European countries and resulted in the formation of sometimes competing fascist parties. None of them produced a lasting strong leader. The absence of a charismatic personality and the presence of authoritarian and nationalist movements and parties inhibited—if they did not prevent—the establishment of fascist regimes. Though most European states developed some totalitarian groups or parties, it will be helpful to look briefly at the particular experience of Spain, Hungary, and Romania, all of which showed significant variations of fascism.

Spanish fascism emerged from several radical right-wing factions in the late 1920s and early 1930s, and became consolidated with the establishment of the *Falange Española* in 1933 under the leadership of José Antonio de Rivera. He and his Falangists were antiliberal, antiparliamentary, and authoritarian. They also evinced an interest in socialism. After General Francisco Franco, a conservative military commander, rebelled against the Spanish Republic, he merged the reactionary Catholic Carlists, the *Requeté,* with the Falange in 1937. As Falange leader Franco, now also the head of state, kept the revolutionary aspirations of the Old Falangists in check and manipulated the party to his own ends. Franco was never a fascist, neither during the Civil War nor during his long rule as *Caudillo* (leader); but he based his conservative dictatorship on the army, the Catholic Church, the upper class, and segments of the middle class.

In Hungary and Romania fascism and reactionary politics were intertwined. Between 1920 and 1944, Hungary was under the regency of Admiral Miklos Horthy, a reactionary who hoped to see the large Hungarian realm of earlier centuries restored. Fascist movements, inspired by German National Socialism, appeared in the early 1930s. They flourished under the profascist, anti-Semitic prime minister Gyula Gömbös. In 1935 most fascist factions were united in the Arrow Cross Party under the leadership of Ferenc Szálasi, a former general staff officer. During World War II, the Arrow Cross leader plotted to overthrow the reactionary Horthy regime. He succeeded only in 1944, after Horthy had fallen out of favor with Hitler, and presided over a short-lived fascist regime that collaborated with the Nazis in the killing of Hungary's Jews.

A peculiar form of fascism appeared in Romania in 1927 with the formation of the Legion of the Archangel Michael, soon better known as the Romanian Iron Guard. C. Z. Codreanu, the founder of this movement, was a religious mystic, and the Legionaries advanced their own interpretation of Romanian Orthodoxy, aspiring to attain national salvation for the Romanian people or "race." They appealed to radical nationalist youth and the peasantry, professed a strident anti-Semitism, engaged in violence and murder at times, and maintained a rigidly hierarchical internal organization with a paramilitary external form. In 1940 General Ion Antonescu, a conservative favorite of the fascists, formed a right-wing coalition government that included the Iron Guard. When the latter staged a coup against him in the following year, Antonescu liquidated the Iron Guard with the encouragement of Hitler, who wanted to preserve stability in Romania to protect his oil supplies.

Fascist regimes, intent on exercising utmost power, subordinated economic policies to their domestic and external objectives. Private property was not abolished, as under communism, but it was subjected to regulatory or racial restrictions and occasional political meddling. Economic planning was instituted haphazardly during peacetime and more rigorously during war. Fascists attacked economic liberalism because it advocated individual self-interest, and socialism because it caused conflicts between labor and capital that undermined national unity. In order to eliminate antagonism between workers and employers, the fascists prohibited labor unions and strikes, and formed associations or corporations that included both workers and employers.

In Fascist Italy much attention was devoted to the idea of corporativism. Mussolini's propaganda touted it as an alternative "third way" between capitalism and socialism. Corporativism aimed to restore social cohesion by encompassing labor and capital in corporations. The basis for the Fascist corporative state was laid in 1925, when the Italian General Confederation of Industry (*Confindustria*) and the Confederation of Fascist Trade Unions recognized each other as respective spokesmen of capital and labor. Soon a law designated several branches of economic activity, for example, industry, agriculture, banking, and commerce, as appropriate for corporations. However, it was not until 1934 that mixed corporations of employers and employees were actually established. The capstone of the corporate structure was put in place in 1939 when the

Chamber of Fasces and Corporations, consisting of elected and appointed members of corporations, replaced the Italian parliament.

Fascist corporative theory had the potential of innovation in economic
life, but in practice corporativism failed to effect convincing results. It
was difficult to establish a workable relationship among business, labor,
the Fascist Party, and the Duce's dictatorship. Overall, Fascist economic
policies favored the interests of commerce and industry. They increased
national income only modestly at best, ballooned the public debt, and
thanks to falling wages and rising prices, left the poor poorer and the
rich richer.

In contrast to less developed Italy, Germany boasted rich natural and
industrial resources. Hitler understood that Germany's recovery from the
Depression was a prerequisite for rearmament and the attainment of
economic self-sufficiency, or autarky. He enacted pragmatic policies that
poured larger and larger funds into public works projects: roads, canals,
public buildings, bridges, and the popular program of constructing mo-
tor highways, the *Autobahnen.* In addition, tax breaks allowed industries
to expand. These dynamic economic activities absorbed many unemployed; other young men were taken into the voluntary, later compulsory, labor service and the expanding army. The unemployment figures
fell from 6 million in 1932, to 4.5 million in 1933, 1.7 million in 1935, and
less than half a million in 1937. At the same time, rearmament expenditures rose dramatically from 1 billion Reichsmarks in 1933 to 30 billion
in 1939, requiring enormous deficit spending in addition to ordinary tax
levies. The condition of workers improved moderately, though real
wages began to decline toward the end of the decade with the production of more guns and less butter.

Quite early the German government faced an unfavorable balance of
payments, since it lacked foreign exchange to pay for increasing imports
of raw materials to feed rearmament. Greater state control was imposed,
and in 1936 the Four-Year Plan was instituted to spur German production of raw materials to achieve autarky. In pursuing its economic policies, Nazi Germany did not adopt the tortuous process of corporativism
but instead operated with programs that were partial to big business and
industry. From the start, Hitler intended to solve most of Germany's
economic problems by *Lebensraum,* or the acquisition of territory, which
of course required gearing the German economic engine for eventual
war.

For dictators like Mussolini and Hitler, the control of government and
coordination of economic life were only some of the prerequisites for the

achievement of absolute power. Another very major objective was the creation of a national community in which every member internalized the aims of fascist ideology. Both regimes tried to silence prestigious intellectual, scientific, and artistic figures who were known to reject fascism. In Italy this forced the historian Gaetano Salvemini, the physicist Enrico Fermi, and the conductor Arturo Toscanini to become expatriates. In Nazi Germany the novelist Thomas Mann and the physicist Albert Einstein, together with many other luminaries, suffered the same fate. Joseph Goebbels, the Nazi minister of public enlightenment and propaganda, publicly burned the works of Karl Marx, Sigmund Freud, and many others. In Mussolini's Italy, where repression was less brutal and arbitrary, such incidents did not occur, but intellectuals and artists either had to remain silent on political matters or compromise with the regime.

Radio, film, newspapers, and publications were controlled in both fascist societies. Goebbels, who was in charge of all the media and the arts, showed considerable ingenuity in the effort to keep the German populace attuned to Nazi aims and psychologically receptive to the regime's message. He saw to it that newspaper editors followed his ministry's daily guidelines and received foreign news only from the German Press Agency. Keenly aware of popular culture's effectiveness, the Third Reich's propaganda master particularly promoted films. Since he realized that continuous Nazi propaganda films would turn audiences off, he encouraged the production of entertaining films to provide viewers with plenty of escapist experience, especially during the war.

The fascist regimes regulated public education from elementary to university levels. However, they placed their major hope for shaping the attitudes and character of the youth along ideological lines in youth organizations: the Fascist youth cadres, which encompassed Italian boys from age eight to twenty-one, and the Hitler Youth, which included ten- to eighteen-year-olds. Comparable but separate formations reached girls. Males in their late teens were inducted into the Italian army or into the *Wehrmacht*, or German army, after spending a short term in the labor service.

Adults in both societies belonged to organizations directly affiliated with the party or under party control. In Italy the largest and most active organization for working adults was the *Depolavora*, through which the Fascist regime influenced the social and leisuretime activities of the urban masses. These activities emphasized uplift and self-improvement less than the comparable Nazi organization Strength Through Joy, an arm of the German Labor Front designed to coordinate the free time of the working class. In addition to the SS for the elite and the SA for many other males, the Nazis maintained a great variety of party-affiliated professional organizations as control mechanisms, ranging from the National Socialist Physicians' League to the National Socialist Stenographers' League. Women and mothers especially were urged to belong to the National Socialist Women's League. Both Fascist Italy and Nazi Germany emphasized a traditional role for women that placed them in the home, divided between the kitchen and the bedroom. Official policies and differential wages discriminated against women in the professions and in the ordinary workplace.

In retrospect, it is evident that social policies failed to transform Italian society in the image of the fascist personality and community. The collapse of the regime during World War II allowed reconstruction to proceed along lines indicated before the advent of Mussolini. In Germany the consequences of Nazi social policies were more complex. The intention of primarily transforming the belief systems rather than effecting a social revolution miscarried. What Hitler and the Nazis achieved in their blind pursuit of rearmament, war, and racial empire was, however, the destruction of some major pillars of the old order: the German aristocracy and the Prussian army leadership. They also significantly weakened the rigidity of the traditional social structure. These developments made possible the remodeling of western Germany and, since the reunification, of eastern Germany as well, in the image of a revised capitalist socioeconomic system with liberal democratic values.

Fascist efforts to unite the nation through sociopsychological changes were not ends in themselves; rather, they were designed to ready the people for the achievement of greatness through imperial expansion. A basic principle in Italian Fascism and German Nazism was the idea that nations (and races, according to Nazism) were engaged in a perpetual struggle for self-assertion and survival. The early Fascist movement was boosted in the public's eye when Mussolini promised that he would end the submission of Italy to the stronger powers, which was evident in the peace settlement of World War I that supposedly denied Italy its justly earned territorial rewards. Similarly, Hitler's party capitalized on the German perception of the harshness of the "dictate" of Versailles and pledged to restore Germany's greatness as a nation. Even under the Weimar Republic, Germany pressed for a revision of the peace settlement by negotiation. Under the domination of ideologically aggressive regimes, Italy and Germany became a perpetual threat to international peace because they were prepared to go to war.

Within a year after becoming prime minister, Mussolini found a pretext to seize the Greek island of Corfu and soon thereafter to occupy

Fiume, whose status was under dispute with Yugoslavia. He was rebuffed on Corfu, but won a compromise settlement on Fiume largely because Britain and France, Italy's wartime allies, raised no serious objections. Until the mid-1930s, Fascist foreign policy balanced precariously between Italy's alliance with Britain and France, and a rapprochement with Germany. After Hitler's advent to power, the Duce wanted both to ensure continuous revisionism and to check excessive pan-German aspirations. In July 1934, the Austrian Nazis attempted to seize power in Vienna in preparation for Austria's unification with Germany. However, the effort collapsed when Mussolini announced that he was sending Italian forces to the Brenner Pass.

What changed the cool relationship with Hitler to an alliance was Mussolini's decision to pursue colonial schemes in Africa. His attempt to gain control of the Mediterranean—the *mare nostrum* reminiscent of ancient Roman days—and the acquisition of Ethiopia were but the first steps in his ambitious plan for expansion. It seems to have been undertaken, in part, as an alternative to domestic social reform. The British and French governments appeared at first ready to make territorial concessions to Italy in Ethiopia, but public opinion induced them to back weak League of Nations sanctions against Italy. Mussolini now moved closer to an alliance with Hitler, establishing the Rome-Berlin Axis in 1936. He acquiesced to Hitler's annexation of Austria in 1938, while becoming a junior partner in what Hitler later called "the brutal friendship" with Italy.

Many scholars believe that Nazi foreign objectives were outlined in Hitler's *Mein Kampf,* which he wrote in the mid-1920s. In implementing his decisions, however, Hitler demonstrated singular opportunism in the means and timing of his actions, and remarkable skill in exploiting the weaknesses of the democracies. In 1935 and 1936, he ostentatiously violated the Treaty of Versailles and the Locarno Pact by announcing full rearmament of Germany and occupying the demilitarized Rhineland. British and French appeasement encouraged Hitler to make even bolder moves, convinced that the Allies would not fight. The annexation of Austria was followed by the destruction of Czechoslovakia as an independent state, and finally an attack on Poland in September 1939, which unleashed World War II in Europe. A nonaggression pact with the Soviet Union, concluded only days before the strike against Poland, was envisaged as a temporary maneuver by Hitler.

After blitzkrieg strikes brought unprecedented German military successes in Poland, Norway, and France, Hitler was ready to invade Soviet Russia in 1941, even though Britain, by refusing to give in, presented him with his first strategic deadlock. Hitler's decision to attack the USSR was his fatal error. The lure of living space and the attainment of territorial hegemony in Europe from the Atlantic to the depths of Russia blinded him to the military and political realities that thwarted the realization of these aims. Germany's (and Italy's) unilateral declaration of war on the United States after Japan attacked Pearl Harbor in December 1941 (a step not necessitated by the alliance with Italy and Japan) pointed to Hitler's increasing irrationality in the pursuit of his all or nothing designs and in time brought disaster and ultimate defeat.

A good idea of the nature of the Nazi New Order can be gained from the occupation regime that the Germans imposed on European territories under their control during the war. Whereas the Italian Fascist conquerors followed a fairly typical military occupation policy in France and in the Balkans, the Nazi treatment of occupied people was largely based on ideological principles. In addition to exploiting the economic and human resources of conquered areas for Germany's war effort, Nazi authorities applied racial criteria to occupied populaces. For vast numbers of Europeans, especially from eastern Europe, this brought enslavement as "racially inferior" masses. Millions of them were deported to different areas of Europe or brought to Germany and used as slave labor. The persecution of Jews in prewar Germany was but a harsh prelude to the destruction of millions of Jews and others as parasitic subhumans under Hitler's Final Solution. Hitler's New Order in Europe was composed of an empire of concentration camps under the infamous head of the SS, Heinrich Himmler, and, after 1941, extermination camps in Poland as well. Mechanized racial genocide became the very last end of Nazi policy.

Fascism in Europe came to an abrupt end in spring 1945 with the total defeat of Nazi Germany by the Allies and Adolf Hitler's suicide on April 30. Shortly before that, Benito Mussolini had been captured by antifascist Italian partisans and summarily shot. After the collapse of Fascist Italy in 1943, he had been ordered by Hitler to head a new Fascist regime in German-occupied northern Italy.

Being closely tied to the personalities of Hitler and Mussolini, fascism as an ideology and a political system was a European phenomenon, if not principally a German and Italian phenomenon. Outside Germany and Italy it made only a limited impact on countries like Spain, Hungary, and Romania, becoming submerged in the political ambitions of fairly traditional military dictators. The legacy of fascism, especially vehement Nazism, was a vast sea of material destruction, the loss of tens of millions of human lives, and the horror of unprecedented dehumanization. Until recently, Germany and Europe remained deeply divided and dominated by two ideologically antagonistic powers as a stark reminder of fascism's defeat. Today it is fairly easy to discern fascist elements in other political regimes—both right-wing authoritarian and left-wing socialist or communist. However, it is not likely that another fascist regime of the magnitude of Nazi Germany or Fascist Italy will arise in Europe. For that to happen would require a unique combination of a seductive nationalist ideology, a mass party led by a charismatic leader, and a society under severe socioeconomic stress, making its populace receptive to the all or nothing solutions of a future ruthless dictator.

SELECTED BIBLIOGRAPHY

Allen, William S. *The Nazi Seizure of Power: The Experience of a Single Town 1922–1945.* Rev. ed. New York: Franklin Watts, 1984. Classic study of the takeover of a town by the Nazis and their impact on the community.

Arendt, Hannah. *The Origins of Totalitarianism.* Rev. ed. New York: Harcourt, Brace and World, 1966. An important study of totalitarianism's antecedents and its significance for the twentieth century.

Bracher, Karl Dietrich. *The German Dictatorship: The Origins, Structure, and Effects of National Socialism.* Translated by Jean Steinberg. New York: Praeger, 1970. The best scholarly account of the Nazi regime by a distinguished German historian.

Bullock, Alan. *Hitler: A Study in Tyranny.* Rev. ed. New York: Harper and Row, 1964. This remains the best scholarly account of Hitler as the man and historical actor.

Carsten, F. L. *The Rise of Fascism.* Berkeley: University of California Press, 1967. A very good overview of the formative period of fascism in Italy, Germany, and other European countries.

Cassels, Alan. *Fascism.* New York: Thomas Crowell, 1974. A lucid comparative study of Italian Fascism, German National Socialism, and other European fascist movements.

Deakin, Frederick William. *The Brutal Friendship: Mussolini, Hitler, and the Fall of Italian Fascism.* New York: Harper and Row, 1962. An interesting study of the decline of Mussolini's power and regime.

Fest, Joachim C. *The Face of the Third Reich: Portraits of the Nazi Leadership.* Translated by Michael Bullock. New York: Pantheon, 1977. Good short biographies of Hitler's close associates.

Fleming, Gerald. *Hitler and the Final Solution.* Berkeley: University of California Press, 1984. Elucidates Hitler's role in instigating the destruction of the European Jews.

Haffner, Sebastian. *The Meaning of Hitler.* Translated by Ewald Osers. Cambridge, MA: Harvard University Press, 1979. A very readable account of Hitler as a modern dictator with a relentless penchant for all or nothing actions.

Kershaw, Ian. *Hitler.* New York: Longman, 1991. Excellent short account of how Hitler acquired, maintained, and expanded his power.

Kirkpatrick, Ivone. *Mussolini: A Study in Power.* New York: Hawthorne Books, 1964. One of the best biographies in English of the Duce.

Kitchen, Martin. *Fascism.* London: Macmillan, 1976. A brief introduction to the major theories of fascism before the 1970s.

Mack Smith, Denis. *Mussolini.* New York: Alfred A. Knopf, 1982. An authoritative, concise biography of the Italian dictator.

Payne, Stanley G. *Falange.* Stanford: Stanford University Press, 1961. Standard work on the subject.

———. *Fascism: Comparison and Definition.* Madison: University of Wisconsin Press, 1980. An excellent comparative survey of fascist movements and regimes in Europe and a brief consideration outside Europe, offering a typology of fascism.

Schoenbaum, David. *Hitler's Social Revolution: Class and Status in Nazi Germany, 1933–1939.* Garden City, NY: Doubleday, 1966. A study of the impact of Nazism on German society before World War II.

Sugar, Peter, ed. *Native Fascism in the Successor States.* Santa Barbara: ABC-Clio, 1971. Short accounts of fascist fronts and movements in central and eastern Europe.

Tannenbaum, Edward R. *The Fascist Experience: Italian Society and Culture, 1922–1945.* New York: Basic Books, 1972. An informative examination of popular culture, literature, and intellectual and cultural life concentrating on the 1920s and 1930s.

Woolf, S. J., ed. *Fascism in Europe.* New York: Methuen, 1981. First published in 1968, this expanded edition analyzes the political, economic, and social conditions that produced fascist movements.

Migrant laborers seeking work in California's Imperial Valley (1936). The Great Depression brought unemployment, hunger, and despair. (Photographic Archives, University of Louisville)

4

The Great Depression, 1929–c.1939

INTRODUCTION

An economic depression is a period of substantially decreased business activity usually accompanied by high unemployment, falling wages, and declining prices. While depressions were not an uncommon occurrence (there were major depressions in 1873–1878 and 1893–1897), the one that began in 1929 was so severe, long-lasting, and global in nature that it earned the name the Great Depression.

After the debilitating economic upheaval caused by World War I, the world warmly welcomed the return of prosperity in the early 1920s. However, the glow of prosperity, which lasted until 1929, masked some significant economic problems. For a start, not all the world shared in this prosperity. During the 1920s, global agriculture underwent a profound crisis. Encouraged by increased demand during World War I, when much of Europe's agricultural capacity was in limbo, farmers in such countries as the United States, Canada, Argentina, and Australia had gone deeply into debt in order to expand their operations. It is estimated that during the war 33 million new acres were put under plow. With the war's end and the resumption of normal agricultural activity in Europe, demand slumped and production grew. Above average global harvests from 1925 to 1928 aggravated the resultant overproduction. By the late 1920s, debt-ridden farmers everywhere were going bankrupt, agrarian purchasing power had virtually disappeared, the world agricultural price index, which registered 226 in 1919, now stood at 134, and the price of a bushel of wheat in terms of gold was the lowest it had been in 400 years.

Furthermore, the prosperity of the late 1920s clearly rested on the export of U.S. capital and the strength of U.S. import markets. Europe was especially dependent upon the United States. Beginning in 1924, a huge infusion of U.S. capital jump-started the German economy, whose improvement subsequently sparked a general European economic upturn. Nevertheless, even before 1929 the European economy showed signs of weakening as U.S. investors shifted their resources from Europe back to the United States in order to take advantage of the unprecedented boom in the American stock market. However, the stock market surge was not a permanent one and, in fact, it ended abruptly. On Thursday, October 24, 1929, the U.S. stock market collapsed, setting off a spectacular panic that ultimately brought about the Great Depression.

By the end of November 1929, the average share of stock had lost 40 percent of its pre-crash value; over the next few years the average share would lose another 40 percent of its value. Between 1929 and 1932, the Dow Jones Industrial Average plunged from a high of 381 to a low of 41. Five thousand American banks were forced to close.

Shaken by the stock market's collapse, U.S. investors who had overextended themselves now called in their loans and liquidated their investments. Germany, more dependent upon American capital than any other country, suffered accordingly. As the German economy slowed to a standstill, the rest of Europe, itself heavily dependent upon German reparations payments from World War I and closely integrated with the German economy as a whole, started to grind to a halt. Furthermore, as the downturn in the United States spread to the industrial sector of the economy, American markets—which the rest of the world had relied on for the export of their goods—began to dry up. The 1930 Smoot-Hawley Tariff, which raised already high protective duties on imported goods, only aggravated matters. Unemployment rose dramatically. In this fashion, the collapse of the U.S. stock market created a ripple effect that swept over the world economy with devastating consequences.

The crisis deepened perceptibly when the most important bank in Vienna, the Credit-Anstalt, collapsed on May 11, 1931. The failure of the Credit-Anstalt caused a major financial panic. Worried investors withdrew funds from banks everywhere and moved them about in a desperate attempt to find a haven for their wealth. Numerous banks simply failed, leaving depositors in the lurch. The world banking system teetered on the brink of collapse.

Many investors made their way to London, where they sought to exchange pounds sterling for gold. This "flight from the pound" reached gigantic proportions, and on September 19, 1931, it forced the British government to abandon the gold standard. Henceforth, the Bank of England would no longer sell gold for pounds. This decision, which spelled the end of the post–World War I attempt to recreate an international banking system based on gold, brought chaos to international trade and further intensified the Depression.

The worst of the Depression came in 1932. It is estimated that world production declined by 38 percent between 1929 and 1932, and that world trade dropped by more than 66 percent. Reported global unemployment reached 30 million, and millions of others, especially in the non-Western world, worked only sporadically. With so many people unemployed or underemployed, demand plummeted, causing additional layoffs and business closings. A vicious downward economic spiral gripped the globe.

Quite naturally, the universal misery spawned by the Great Depression sparked calls for action. However, most governments refused to implement radical policies and confined themselves to modest relief measures designed to alleviate human suffering. The principle of classical, or liberal, economics dictated this essentially passive response. According to classical economic theory, which prevailed at that time, business activity is cyclical. Periods of prosperity will inevitably be followed by slumps, which in turn will inevitably be followed by periods of prosperity. When slumps come, as they must, the government response should be to refrain from action and wait for the business cycle to run its course. If governments wish to speed up the cycle, they should adopt deflationary measures such as balanced budgets and reduced governmental expenditures in order to restore business confidence more rapidly. While these steps may hurt some people, the pain will be temporary. Once business confidence is restored, investment and economic expansion will resume, unemployment will decline, demand will increase, and prosperity will return.

Even though the ideas of classical economics dominated conventional wisdom at the time, the cataclysmic nature of the Great Depression motivated others to seek different solutions. A handful of socialists turned for inspiration to the Soviet Union, where Karl Marx's dictum about the collective ownership of the means of production was being implemented and Joseph Stalin was introducing his planned economy. However, most people recoiled from the Soviet model because it was too radical.

The concept of corporatism, which predated the Great Depression, found some enthusiastic adherents, especially in the business community. Under corporatism, each branch of a nation's economy would be organized into corporations resembling cartels or trusts. The corporations would be dominated by businessmen with, perhaps, representatives of the government and labor sitting in. These units would then regulate and manage the economy to the presumed benefit of all. Among other things, the corporations would set prices, control wages, and determine production and distribution.

The British economist John Maynard Keynes offered a different solution. For Keynes, the fundamental cause of the Great Depression was inadequate demand rather than excessive supply. Deflationary steps only aggravated the problem. In his 1936 book, *General Theory of Employment, Interest, and Money,* Keynes advised governments to step in and stimulate the economy by increasing the money supply, undertaking public works, and redistributing income through tax policy. He argued that government intervention designed to put the unemployed back to work and to put more money in the pockets of more people would bring increased demand and a general revival of economic activity. This would be a much desired result, even if it required the government to run a deficit rather than balance its budget. Although Keynes' ideas would become popular after World War II, during the Depression most governments followed the dictates of classical economics.

Typical of the commitment to classical economics were the actions of successive British governments. The Labour Party, led by Prime Minister Ramsay MacDonald, held power when the Depression began. After tepid and unsuccessful attempts to stimulate the economy, in 1931 MacDonald's wing of the Labour Party broke away and formed a coalition government with the Conservatives under Stanley Baldwin. Dominated by the Conservatives, the so-called National Government initiated deflationary policies. Government expenditures were reduced, welfare payments were cut, protectionist tariffs were introduced, and businessmen were left to their own devices. The results were disappointing. Great Britain, which had never really shared in the prosperity of the 1920s, recovered from the Depression, only gradually, if at all. Unemployment, which stood at 1.2 million in 1929, soared to 2.7 million (or 22 percent of the work force) in 1932, and remained above 2 million until 1936. In 1938 the unemployment figure was 1.8 million.

The Great Depression arrived in France later and less suddenly than in other countries. As late as 1930, France continued to exceed its pre–World War I industrial production level by at least 40 percent. However, when the slump hit, it lasted longer in France than elsewhere. By 1938 recovery was nowhere in sight. Industrial production remained below 1930 and 1931 figures, and unemployment stood at historically high levels. Reacting to the economic downturn, a series of unstable coalition governments applied deflationary measures, including a reduction of civil servants' salaries. French governments vigorously resisted any proposals to stimulate the economy. In 1936 a coalition socialist government under the leadership of Léon Blum attempted to reinflate the French economy. The Blum experiment was short-lived, due in part to French conservatives' implacable hostility to any program devised by socialists.

In the United States, the Great Depression took a heavy toll. By 1932 U.S. industrial production was just barely half of what it had been in 1929, more than 12 million Americans were unemployed, and national income had dropped by more than 50 percent. President Herbert Hoover refused to depart significantly from traditional classical economic doctrine and consequently was defeated in the election of 1932. Although the new president, Franklin D. Roosevelt, had run on the promise of further deflationary policies, once in office he instituted a number of measures designed to reinflate the American economy. In this manner Roosevelt's New Deal somewhat resembled Keynes' ideas. However, despite this flurry of government activity and Roosevelt's immense personal popularity, the U.S. economy remained in the doldrums. Although national income had risen dramatically from its low point in 1932, by 1938 it still fell short of the 1929 level.

The Great Depression in Germany not only wrecked that country's economy, but also destroyed Germany's fragile republic and cleared the way for the Nazi dictatorship. Devastated by the loss of American capital in the wake of the stock market crash, Germany experienced a precipitous economic slide that by 1932 resulted in more than 6 million unemployed (about 35 percent of the work force) and a decrease in industrial production of about 50 percent. After the collapse of the ruling socialist government in 1930, a shaky conservative coalition under the leadership of Heinrich Brüning governed Germany. Following classical economic precepts, the Brüning government strove to balance the budget by reducing state expenditures, cutting wages, and slashing unemployment benefits. This course of action simply exacerbated an impossible situation, increasing economic misery for millions of Germans and causing the electorate to seek solace in the political extremes.

A major beneficiary of this misguided policy was Adolf Hitler, who came to power on January 30, 1933, and quickly turned Germany into a Nazi dictatorship. Following the advice of financial wizard Hjalmar Schacht, the Nazi state actively intervened in Germany's economic life. It made huge investments in public works, especially road building and arms production. This policy, combined with strong government controls over both business and labor, and a determination to achieve autarky, or economic self-sufficiency, helped to pull Germany out of the Depression. By 1936 German unemployment had dropped markedly and a miraculous economic recovery appeared to be under way. By 1938 Germany's economy was booming and German purchasing power had regained its 1929 level.

It is hard to gauge the effects of the Great Depression in Italy since that country's economy was—even by 1929—not fully developed. As a result, unemployment levels and the amount that national income decreased are difficult to determine. Furthermore, Benito Mussolini's fascist dictatorship set up a smoke screen of propaganda about its grandiose development projects in order to obscure the effects of the Depression. Nevertheless, there can be no doubt that Italy suffered an economic decline.

In response to the Great Depression, Mussolini's regime, which had already experimented with corporatism, developed its version of that concept more fully. In practice this meant turning essential control of the country's economy over to the Italian business community, although the government intervened when necessary to bail out enterprises that appeared ready to go bankrupt. As a consequence, the Italian government sometimes found itself owning a controlling interest in a business or industry. Nevertheless, the government usually left decision making for those industries in the hands of the industrialists, preferring the support of the Italian business community to the exercise of absolute power over the Italian economy.

The course of the Great Depression varied from country to country. By 1938 some countries had virtually recovered their economic vitality, while others continued to lag behind or languished in economic disarray. Nevertheless, as important as the Great Depression was, the outbreak of World War II was about to overshadow it.

INTERPRETIVE ESSAY
Lowell J. Satre

The Great Depression is historically overshadowed by other traumatic events of the twentieth century, particularly the two world wars and the savage brutality of the Nazi and Stalinist regimes. The Great Depression itself, however, proved to be the longest sustained economic depression of the modern world, and helped to create feelings of utter despair that destroyed what appeared to be the orderly and prosperous world of the late 1920s. Indeed, the collapse of the industrialized economies of the Western world not only led to long-term mass unemployment, but ultimately transformed social relationships, destroyed established governments, brought the Nazis to power, and helped to cause international diplomatic complications that led to World War II. Moreover, the impact of the Great Depression was truly worldwide, as the peoples of the non-European world also found their economies and societies transformed.

The United States had become, by the 1920s, the dominant economic force in the world. American manufactured goods, along with coal and oil, serviced much of the world, and American loans to Europe helped to restore a modicum of material and political stability to an area still recovering from the ravages of the Great War. Just as the world prospered with the United States, so it also suffered as the U.S. economy plunged into its greatest crisis. While the crisis began dramatically with the New York stock market crash of October 1929, the economies of the United States and the European nations had begun slowing down earlier. Prices of agricultural products had collapsed, and wages for large numbers of the labor force, so important as consumers of manufactured goods, were exceptionally low.

The Great Depression was effectively two interrelated problems: a financial crisis with international consequences, and a downturn in production that caused massive unemployment and accompanying social and political problems. Governments generally focused initially on overcoming the financial crisis; unfortunately, steps taken to deal with that crisis all too often created even greater unemployment.

The collapse of stock prices in the United States forced American banks, which had overinvested in the heady atmosphere of the stock market bonanza of the late 1920s, to raise money to cover their investments, which were often only partially paid for. Banks refused to extend short-term loans as they became due. Banking houses in Germany and Austria were especially harmed, as they had been major recipients of American loans. This massive movement of dollars and gold from Europe to the United States, which had commenced in the 1920s as investors were attracted by the promise of high or quick financial gain in the U.S. stock market, would continue well into the 1930s. In fact, U.S. prosperity in the 1920s created international economic problems. The United States, with its massive production base, imported relatively few finished goods and maintained a healthy balance of payments. Other nations, because they were unable to sell goods to the United States, were also unable to purchase U.S. goods. A shortage of capital in Europe in turn curtailed capital investment in manufacturing facilities, which likewise led to the laying off of workers.

The financial crisis peaked in 1931. Credit-Anstalt, the largest Vienna bank and a major holder of foreign funds, went broke in May. This failure precipitated a crisis of confidence in German banks. President Herbert Hoover's call for a moratorium on the payment of war debts and reparations failed to stop the hemorrhaging of funds. Investors, looking for security, turned to the British pound sterling, which in turn came under pressure. The culminating event occurred on September 19, 1931, when the British government announced that it was pulling the pound from the gold standard. Britain's Commonwealth associates followed Britain off the gold standard, as did several other European nations. The United States followed suit in 1933. The international exchange mechanism, so painfully rebuilt following World War I, had effectively ceased to exist.

While the financial and stock markets were collapsing, consumption of goods fell off, manufacturing dramatically slowed down, and unemployment mounted. By 1932 unemployment in Europe, excluding the Soviet Union, amounted to 15 million, with 6 million in Germany alone. How did the governments react? All of them, to a greater or lesser degree, took steps to cope with the economic crisis. Ultimately, government intervention in the economy became a significant hallmark of the Great Depression.

Compared to many other European nations, Britain's relatively weak economy of the 1920s meant that it had not developed overproduction. British banks and stock exchanges were not as severely affected, and while unemployment was high in older industries like coal, cotton textiles, and shipbuilding, newer industries were relatively healthy, as was home construction. Britain shed its free trade policy and instituted a protective tariff in 1931. Orthodox financial responses called for curtailing government spending as revenue decreased; as a result, relief payments were reduced. In spite of the suffering of the unemployed, extremist political ideologies gained relatively little support in Britain.

The Scandinavian countries were more successful than other nations at dealing with the Depression. While these northern states suffered high unemployment because their economies were tied to foreign trade, reformist Social Democratic parties took steps to alleviate the problems and to direct the economy toward recovery. The Swedish government, unlike other European governments, increased expenditures via deficit spending to encourage economic recovery. The government also aided in the expansion of consumer and production cooperatives, expanded social services, and early on provided relief work for the unemployed and developed an extensive public works program.

France, which did not significantly feel the effects of the Depression until 1932, was ultimately one of the hardest hit. Until 1936 the French government, rent by political divisions, remained wedded to orthodox economic policy and did not attempt to aid the economy with government spending. In 1936 Léon Blum led a left-of-center coalition, the Popular Front, in a New Deal–style program providing for wage increases, labor union recognition for collective bargaining, a forty-hour work week and paid vacation, increased public spending, and devaluation of the franc, making French products more competitive in the world market. Blum's government, however, lasted but a short time, and the politically and socially divided nation had not recovered from the ravages of the Depression when World War II erupted in 1939.

In Germany, the conservative governments of the Weimar Republic bowed to the enormous pressure of the industrialists and large landowning interests to curtail government spending, especially on social measures, and to reduce the taxes on employers and increase them on laborers. When the Reichstag refused to approve this program, the government resorted to emergency executive powers and ruled by decree. Government policy only worsened the Depression, and the inability of the government to deal meaningfully with the crisis was a key ingredient in Adolf Hitler's attaining power in January 1933.

Hitler's government wielded more control over the economy than that of any other European nation except the Soviet Union. On the whole, Hitler did not curtail the power of large companies, and businesses remained under private ownership; a hybrid system of planning was imposed on a capitalist economic structure. Hitler's initial program called for large public works projects to provide relief for the huge numbers of unemployed. In November 1934, the government oriented the economy to rearmament and military preparation. This was paid for by increased taxes and deficit spending, and by restricting private investment in the manufacture of consumer goods. The policy did bring a quick end to unemployment.

Benito Mussolini's fascist Italian government attempted to direct the economy through corporations of employers and workers, but in fact real power was increasingly concentrated in the hands of industrialists and Fascist Party officials. The government did come to the rescue of several basic industries by investing in them, thus providing for limited government ownership.

The government of the Soviet Union exercised the greatest control over any one nation's economy; this had begun before the onset of the Depression with the massive movement for the collectivization of agriculture and the forced development of a huge industrial base. While the Soviet Union could satisfy most of its own needs internally, it continued to trade with the noncommunist world throughout the 1930s, exporting grain—despite a shortage of it in the nation and a deliberately planned famine that took the lives of millions—at a greater rate than at any time since the 1917 Russian Revolution in order to procure goods needed for manufacturing.

Nations of eastern Europe, already struggling for survival, were particularly hard hit by the Great Depression. These nations had recently emerged from the ruins of World War I and the disintegration of the Habsburg, Romanov, and Ottoman empires. The new nations were saddled with long-standing nationality conflicts while struggling to develop their political institutions and their economies, which generally lacked diversity or natural resources. With some exceptions, these nations exported agricultural products or raw materials. Unfortunately, the price on the world market for foodstuffs and raw materials had dropped over 50 percent by 1938. Many of these nations were unable to generate the funds needed to import manufactured articles or to repay international loans contracted in the 1920s, not only because of the price collapse of their chief export items, but also because neighboring trading partners had taken steps to protect their own agricultural interests, as in the case of Germany's powerful Prussian landholding Junkers.

Even before Hitler's rise to power, however, some Germans had advocated economic integration and cooperation between Germany and nations in the Danube River basin. But these economies were not sufficiently complementary to make economic union a reality, as all had a strong agricultural component. The German state, under the Nazi regime, did successfully negotiate goods-exchange agreements with these nations. In the case of Bulgaria, Turkey, Yugoslavia, and Hungary, most of their foreign trade was with Germany, making them economically dependent on their more powerful neighbor.

Meanwhile, eastern and central European nations faced a major economic and social crisis. Both large and small landholding farmers were destroyed; peasants were unable to purchase manufactured goods. Members of the middle class and civil servants were thrown out of work. Anti-Semitism, long present in the area, intensified as people sought an explanation for their collapsed material world and focused on those from whom they held loans—often Jews. Nationalities, artificially merged after the war in states such as Yugoslavia and Czechoslovakia, blamed each other for the crisis. Home-bred right-wing political movements, loosely patterned after the Fascist and Nazi parties, emerged.

While the impact of the Great Depression on politics and financial policy is relatively easy to follow, the tremendous upheaval the prolonged economic crisis caused in society is less easy to measure. Millions lost employment and found their standard of living greatly reduced; as a result, many suffered acute physical and social problems. Family employment patterns altered, as women and occasionally young adults replaced the elder male as the chief breadwinner. Class hatred was often exacerbated, as those at the bottom of the economic ladder despised the wealthy, who, in spite of their own occasionally reduced incomes, continued to enjoy an exceptionally comfortable material life.

In Germany, as in many other countries, youngsters completing school were faced with little or no chance of employment. These German students were often supporters of National Socialism, which attracted them by its promises of dynamic change and by criticism of the prevailing economic order. Yet, one must not assume that despair was all-encompassing. In Great Britain, indeed, leisure activities continued to grow and be enjoyed by great numbers of people who took advantage of the mobility provided by the automobile or flocked to incredibly popular cinema halls.

Disillusionment with the breakdown of normal or anticipated lifestyles was especially noticeable in the literature of the period, where writers graphically questioned and criticized the prevailing social order and political structure, and called for a more just society. In Great Britain, George Orwell particularly expressed this despair in several works, including *The Road to Wigan Pier* (1937), where he examined the desperate plight of the English coal miners. Walter Greenwood, in his novel *Love on the Dole* (1933), follows the trials of the young in England's industrial north, who were unable to gain meaningful employment and all too often attached themselves to the corrupt elements in society in order to gain social recognition or economic support. A similar German novel, Hans Fallada's *Little Man, What Now?* (1933), portrays a young married couple and their baby struggling to survive in the vicious atmosphere of Berlin in the early 1930s.

The fiscal crisis caused by the Great Depression initiated a series of international meetings to attempt to solve the monetary problems facing the United States and Europe. The matter was particularly complex because it involved not only economic issues, but also very sensitive political considerations. World War I had left in its wake the complicated issue of war debts and reparations. Germany, deemed the primary guilty party in the war, was required by the victors to make substantial payments toward the rebuilding of war-ravaged Europe, particularly to France and Belgium, the scene of much fighting on the Western Front. At the same time, the victor nations were expected to repay their loans to the United States, from which they had borrowed heavily during the war. The Dawes Plan of 1924 had established a workable reparations plan for Germany, aided by substantial loans from the United States. Further changes were made by the Young Plan in 1929. Debt repayment by France and Britain to the United States depended at least partially on receiving reparations payments from Germany. The Great Depression curtailed loans from the United States to Europe and put these repayment schemes in jeopardy. President Herbert Hoover's call on June 20, 1931, for a one-year moratorium on payments of war debts and other international obligations was approved by European nations on July 6, 1931, too late to stem the German financial crisis. In June 1932, a conference in Lausanne, Switzerland, effectively ended war debt payments almost by default.

While governments met to attempt to solve some aspects of the Great Depression, they individually took steps that ultimately hindered economic recovery. Economic nationalism was a common response to mounting unemployment and sagging sales. The already high U.S. tariffs were significantly raised in 1930 with the passage of the Smoot-Hawley Tariff Act. This in turn led to a series of retaliatory tariffs by other nations. One of the problems with the Smoot-Hawley Tariff, in addition to its direct economic impact, was that it gave the impression that the United States was providing no leadership in the crisis. The World Economic Conference held in London in 1933 failed to resolve the gold currency issue or to reduce tariffs, partly because of steps taken by Franklin D. Roosevelt, recently elected president of the United States.

This conference marked the last major collective attempt to solve the problems of the Great Depression; thereafter economic nationalism was in the forefront.

While the Great Depression was not the only factor in bringing Hitler to power, it was certainly a key ingredient. With Hitler in power, the diplomatic affairs of Europe were dramatically altered and Europe drifted toward World War II. Preoccupation with Depression-induced economic or fiscal problems detracted from England and France's willingness to concentrate on the dangers of aggressive nations such as Germany or Japan. Great Britain, for example, was struggling politically over its budget and the gold standard when Japan invaded Manchuria in September 1931. France, whose fractured economy caused turmoil in its political life, was going through a series of weak governments when Hitler illegally remilitarized the Rhineland in March 1936.

The Great Depression caused a crisis in politics, especially in central and eastern Europe, where governments still recovering from the terrible disruptions of the Great War were unable to solve the economic crisis. International cooperation, long preached as a means of resolving issues, had failed. These nations not only turned toward their own internal resources, but began arming themselves in an attempt to solve the crisis by aggressive international action. Ironically, preparation for war through the expansion of military personnel and the manufacturing of weapons was to a great extent responsible for significantly reducing unemployment and pulling nations, including Germany, Britain, and the United States, out of the Depression.

The impact of the Great Depression on the world outside of the United States and Europe varied rather considerably. Generally, those areas with close economic ties to the Western trading nations found that their international trade collapsed, while countries with peasant-based or subsistence-level economies were rather slightly affected. One key factor in the response of the various countries to the Depression was their own political power; colonies had no choice but to follow the dictates of their mother country, while independent nations had a greater possibility of shaping their own economy.

Most primary producing countries, that is, those producing basic agricultural goods such as rice, coffee, sugar, and cotton, and raw materials such as minerals, ores, and rubber, all normally important trading items, were very adversely affected by the Depression. In fact, many of these producers faced major economic problems in the 1920s, long before the onset of the Great Depression. A.J.H. Latham, in *The Depression and the Developing World* (1981), argues that developing countries helped cause the Depression by expanding production of basic goods, especially food-stuffs, during the 1920s. An overabundance of grains from Canada, the United States, Australia, and Argentina, combined with a restored European agricultural base, coincided with overproduction in the East, especially in the rice culture of Asia. These surpluses dramatically depressed agricultural prices worldwide, which remained low throughout much of the 1930s. Economic recovery throughout the world was slow partly because the income of farmers, who were a very large portion of the spending public, remained low.

Primary producing countries found their economies hurt in several ways. While income from exports dropped dramatically, the cost of imports, while also declining, remained relatively high. Since nations could not afford to continue importing these goods—often manufactured—they either went without or began producing them themselves. But these countries were also affected by the startling drop in foreign investment, especially by the largest investors, the United States and Great Britain. New foreign investment by the United States declined from $1.15 billion in 1929 to $2.4 million in 1937, while British foreign investment for the same period fell from $720 million to $96.4 million. As examples, United States investment in Asia and Oceania plummeted from $137 million in 1928 to nil in 1932, while that in Latin America dropped from $331 million to nil for the same period.

Chile and Brazil were two Latin American nations whose economies shifted from commodities toward industrial goods. Chile's cotton fabric production increased over fivefold between 1929 and 1937, providing for 50 percent of the domestic market by the latter year. In Brazil, production of steel and cement showed large increases. As a result, neither nation was as dependent on its primary commodities, coffee for Brazil and nitrates for Chile. Latin American governments—playing a growing role in directing the economy and in the process transforming society—took various steps to develop their own manufacturing. Argentina and Brazil had both begun industrialization during World War I when they were unable to purchase manufactured goods from foreign sources. These nations, often imposing protective tariffs in the 1930s, were thus able to expand on a manufacturing base that had been established earlier. Politics in many of these nations, and specifically in Argentina and Brazil, followed a worldwide trend toward more authoritarian governments. In spite of a more diversified economy, life for the poor in Latin America remained extremely difficult.

The Latin American nations, as a whole, probably took more decisive steps than any other countries to reorient their economies. But some other countries showed similar moves, including Egypt, which suffered initially from a sharp drop in the price of exported raw cotton. Employment in manufacturing increased 66 percent between 1927 and 1937, and production mushroomed in many sectors, including cement, petroleum goods, and especially mechanically woven cloth.

The shift from a rural to an urban economy could be seen in parts of India, as in the southern area of Madras, with implications for the social order. Peasants there traditionally borrowed money from the large landowners, who not only had the financial resources but could also hold grain off the market until prices rose. The seemingly permanent drop in the price of grain was hard not only on the peasants but also on the large landowners, who could not sustain the traditional loans and often found themselves in bankruptcy. Members of some landholding families, in order to survive, had to find work outside the traditional family occupation. When some landowners/creditors attempted to corner the market to drive up prices, food riots ensued. Peasants also successfully organized against payment of unreasonable rent to the *zamindari*, or estate owners, whose privileged social and economic positions in the community were permanently altered during the Depression.

As southern Madras's agricultural economy deteriorated, its urban economy developed more fully. Those who had financial interests in both rural and urban areas shifted their focus to the latter, partly because industrial prices in India declined less than agricultural prices. In urban areas, capital was increasingly invested in agricultural processing, heavy industries like electricity and cement, and financial institutions like banking and insurance. In spite of these economic shifts, India's economy and society remained predominantly agricultural. While it is true that peasant India was far more directly affected by the famine of 1918 than by the Great Depression, the country's overall economic growth was particularly slow throughout the 1930s.

China, like India, had a primarily agricultural economy. While China's foreign trade, including silk and silk-related products, cotton cloth, tea, tobacco, and handicraft goods made by peasants, was markedly reduced by the Depression, the factories—Chinese or foreign-owned—located on the coast and tied to international markets were the most directly affected. Peasants often responded to the drop in prices for cash crops by returning to the cultivation of more traditional grains. Probably no more than 3 percent of the peasants were involved in export-based commodities; peasants consumed most of their own agricultural products, and those marketed were sold locally. A case can be made that the Chinese economy was not adversely affected by the Great Depression. While poverty, even famine, occurred in some provinces, these were a part of the normal Chinese economy, and resulted from natural catastrophes as well as banditry and the rule of warlords. In 1931, for example, the great Yangtze flood took as many as 2 million lives and left a trail of destruction and disease in its wake. One historian estimates that China's economy, both agricultural and manufacturing, continued to expand throughout the period, even excluding development in Manchuria. A primary cause of this was that China's huge domestic market dictated the direction and production of the economy. External trade, which did decline, was a small and relatively unimportant part of the economy.

Japan suffered more initially from the Depression than most nations. Farmers were hardest hit because the already weak international markets for raw silk and rice collapsed. Unemployment in Japan's export-oriented manufacturing sector skyrocketed, as companies cut back sharply on production. The initial government reaction to the Depression was to do nothing and wait for the economy to right itself. Government inaction and growing distress led to social unrest and violence, including the assassination of the prime minister.

Yet Japan was the first nation to recover from the Depression, and government policy was to a great extent responsible. Under Finance Minister Takahashi Korekiyo, Japan undertook an aggressive investment plan to increase demand. While spending on the military expanded, even more important to recovery were the public works relief programs for rural areas, where farmers switched from production of silk cocoons to wheat and potatoes. Certain home industries were protected by tariffs, and incentives and subsidies were provided for industries such as shipbuilding and automobiles, all aided by a devalued yen. Industry became even more efficient by reducing already low labor costs and by developing better machines. The *zaibatsu,* or financial combines, which had sufficient capital to survive the Depression, especially benefited from government policy. By 1931, recovery was under way in Japan.

In spite of Japan's early economic recovery, the Depression played an important role in the antidemocratic, authoritarian military gaining control over the government. Japanese politics during the 1920s had been a contest between civilian political parties and military leaders. After 1929 this balance tilted decisively to the military elite and helped lead to policies that culminated in World War II. Blame for Japan's economic ills fell especially on the political parties and the bureaucracy that had sought prosperity through cooperation and trade with other nations. Some military leaders believed that the military could better deal with economic problems, especially in view of the tariff barriers raised by other nations to stem the influx of Japanese goods. It was believed that military expansion and the creation of an empire would help provide the needed raw materials and markets. The success of the Japanese military in Manchuria beginning in 1931 and the open warfare in China after 1937 helped to point Japan in the direction of a military-dominated government. The rise of authoritarian regimes in Germany and Italy, and the frustrations and problems associated with the Depression and a weak civilian government, reinforced the movement toward authoritarian government.

The Philippines did not suffer particularly from the Depression, mainly because its sugar-producing sector, which employed about 6 million workers, enjoyed a protected market in the United States. In contrast to the situation in many other primary producing countries, industrialization did not accelerate in the Philippines during the 1930s. The landholding elite, whose livelihood appeared safeguarded by the guaranteed sugar market in the United States, was not interested in reorienting the economy. Moreover, since the United States controlled the colony, its government did not have the power to institute tariffs that would protect industry from manufactured goods flowing in from the United States and Japan.

Africa was unique in that virtually all of the countries were under the control of various European nations. However, the Union of South Africa, although formally under British rule, was essentially self-governing by this time. Except for the early part of the Depression, South Africa's economy expanded considerably during the 1930s as capital flowed in to help expand the gold-mining industry, which benefited from a substantial rise in the price of gold during the decade. Iron and steel were also produced for the first time in Pretoria, and farming remained viable because of the need to feed the growing urban population. Not all mining in Africa flourished; markets for copper and diamonds, for example, were depressed, and unemployment mounted. While native labor was needed in the gold mines, especially in South Africa, Southern Rhodesia, and the Gold Coast, wages remained depressed and few benefits such as education were extended. Not only was there a huge pool of available native labor, but colonial governments, working hard to strengthen export-based companies, helped to discipline workers who struck over low wages or poor working conditions. While natives often gained little from the healthy mining industry, skilled whites such as engineers thrived as mining districts bid for their services. The white-black earnings ratio in Northern Rhodesia was about thirty to one.

Farmers producing goods destined for export, such as coffee, were

hard hit by the Depression. Many were European settlers whose mon-
oculture estates were particularly vulnerable. While the government
aided them by reducing taxes and by loans, many could not survive; in
Kenya about one in five went bankrupt. Revenues for many African colonies, based on foreign trade, shrank. British colonial governments found
themselves increasingly dependent on the natives for their tax base and
they maintained taxes on households and individuals as much as possible. In fact, colonial governments such as Kenya's found that native
farmers were often more efficient and adaptable than their European
settler counterparts. The British colonial governments were expected to
balance their budgets, and payments had to be made to overseas credi-
tors who had lent substantial funds for work on infrastructure such as
roads in the 1920s. In the case of the Gold Coast, import duties on certain
goods were raised, some officials were required to retire early, and
spending on public works was slashed. Generally, the British were not
effective at providing public works for relief measures. The French government, attempting to develop an economically self-sufficient empire,
was more inclined to aid colonies through loans and protective measures.

Some colonial-based European companies did very well during the
Depression. In West Africa, while many small exporting businesses went
under, huge ones like Unilever, with greater capital bases, were able to
thrive because they could cut expenses and buy out weaker competitors.
Aided by friendly governments, large companies could also control competition and reduce prices for basic commodities by establishing a commodities pool from which all large purchases would be made.

How did the native Africans respond to the Depression, which so often
altered their lives and brought economic deprivation? In certain parts of
British West Africa, some Africans took their wealth out of the increasingly insecure land and invested it in education and urban institutions.
In French West Africa, peasants drifted to towns, where few opportunities existed, and became part of the urban poor. Workers occasionally
attempted to unionize and to strike. Riots in several colonies helped to
reduce taxes. In places the Depression also led to the radicalization of
native politics, as was the case with the Kikuyu in central Kenya. The
Kikuyu proved relatively successful at overcoming the Depression, some
becoming shopkeepers and others independent farmers who competed
successfully with European settlers. The Kikuyu Central Association protested government and settler activities that discriminated against the
indigenous people, aided a series of strikes in the late 1930s, and gained
political support outside its own tribe. The economic success and polit-

ical involvement of the Kikuyu would lead them onto a collision course with the European community in the post–World War II era.

Government leaders were not prepared politically or intellectually to cope with the all-pervading crisis caused by the Great Depression. Governments did respond, however. After a flurry of ineffective international meetings to try to solve the currency and gold standard problems, nations turned increasingly to national responses. They abandoned gold, raised tariffs, and created monopolies. This was ironic, for over the previous several decades trade had become far more international and interdependent, even though that trend had been temporarily interrupted by the Great War. This nationalistic response was eventually accompanied—worldwide and not simply in the better-known cases of Nazi Germany and Fascist Italy—by increasingly authoritarian regimes that acted as activist governments pledged to solve economic and social problems. The Great Depression caused enormous personal suffering through the loss of jobs and self-esteem, decline in income, and deprivation of material goods, and led to greater class friction. The Depression, by encouraging the rise of vicious nationalism exemplified by a rapid growth in racialism and anti-Semitism and by aggressive military action, was a major cause of the catastrophic World War II.

SELECTED BIBLIOGRAPHY

Baker, Christopher J. "Debt and Depression in Madras, 1929–1936." In *The Imperial Impact: Studies in the Economic History of Africa and India*, pp. 233–242. Edited by Clive Dewey and A. G. Hopkins. London: Athlone Press, 1978. Examines impact of the Depression on the Indian agricultural sector and its society.

Beyan, Amos. "The Development of Kikuyu Politics During the Depression, 1930–1939." *Journal of Third World Politics* 6 (Spring 1989): 29–47. Shows how the Depression helped radicalize African politics.

Brown, Ian, ed. *The Economies of Africa and Asia in the Inter-war Depression.* New York: Routledge, 1989. Revisionist writers questioning some of the accepted interpretations of the Depression.

Davis, Joseph. *The World Between the Wars, 1919–39: An Economist's View.* Baltimore: Johns Hopkins University Press, 1975. Detailed economy-oriented account of extended period.

Fallada, Hans. *Little Man, What Now?* New York: Simon and Schuster, 1933. Novel set in Germany during the Depression.

Galbraith, John Kenneth. *The Great Crash, 1929.* 3rd ed. Boston: Houghton Mifflin, 1972; first published 1954. Brief classic account oriented toward the United States.

Garraty, John A. *The Great Depression.* New York: Harcourt Brace Jovanovich, 1986. Excellent on social impact of the Depression in the United States and

Europe, and an interesting chapter comparing the New Deal and Nazi responses to the Depression.

Gray, Nigel. *The Worst of Times.* Totowa, NJ: Barnes and Noble, 1985. An oral history of British working-class life during the Depression.

"The Great Depression." *Journal of Contemporary History* 4 (October 1969). Outstanding resource; entire issue devoted to the Depression, with separate articles on each of the major European nations and on eastern Europe, and one on the primary producing countries.

Greenwood, Walter. *Love on the Dole.* London: Penguin, 1969; first published 1933. Depression novel set in England.

Jewsiewicki, B. "The Great Depression and the Making of the Colonial Economic System in the Belgian Congo." *African Economic History* 4 (Fall 1977): 153–176. Sees the Great Depression as leading to the development of a highly controlled, exploiting, European-dominated economic system.

Kindleberger, Charles P. *The World in Depression 1929–1939.* London: Penguin Press, 1973. Scholarly account of causes and course of the Depression, especially governments' fiscal policies.

Latham, A.J.H. *The Depression and the Developing World, 1914–1939.* Totowa, NJ: Croom Helm, 1981. Sees overproduction of commodities in the developing world as an important cause of the Depression.

Orwell, George. *The Road to Wigan Pier.* New York: Harcourt, Brace, 1958; first published 1937. Classic study of the unemployed in industrial England.

Rees, Goronwy. *The Great Slump: Capitalism in Crisis, 1929–1933.* New York: Harper and Row, 1970. United States and Europe during the crisis; especially good on politics.

Roberts, A. D., ed. *The Cambridge History of Africa. Volume 7: From 1905 to 1940.* Cambridge, England: Cambridge University Press, 1986. Decent coverage of the Depression, especially in regard to policy of the Europeans over their colonies.

Thorp, Rosemary, ed. *Latin America in the 1930s: The Role of the Periphery in World Crisis.* London: Macmillan, 1984. Specialist-oriented; includes formulas, statistics, and excellent case studies of various economies.

Tomlinson, B. R. *The Political Economy of the Raj 1914–1947.* London: Macmillan, 1979. Scholarly detail of impact of the Depression on India and on the economic relationship between India and Britain.

Van der Wee, Herman. *The Great Depression Revisited.* The Hague: Martinus Nijhoff, 1972. This interesting collection contains both broad and specific articles on a variety of issues.

5

World War II, 1939–1945

INTRODUCTION

The origins of World War II are rooted in such causes as aggressive nationalism, expansionistic imperialism, virulent Social Darwinism, bitter resentment of the Treaty of Versailles that concluded World War I, and the global power vacuum that World War I helped to create. The first instance of violence associated with World War II occurred in 1931, when a belligerent, militaristic Japan seized the Chinese province of Manchuria. Despite condemnation by the League of Nations, the international body created after World War I to maintain global peace and security, Japan continued to press China throughout the 1930s. Finally, in 1937 Japan launched a full-scale attack on China. During their offensive, the Japanese captured the city of Nanking, setting off a seven-week-long orgy of looting, rape, and murder that took the lives of perhaps 200,000 Chinese.

In Europe, Adolf Hitler's rise to power in Germany in 1933 foreshadowed the end of what proved to be a precarious peace. Intent on solidifying his hold on Germany, Hitler at first moved slowly in international affairs. Nevertheless, by early 1936 he had withdrawn Germany from the League of Nations, sponsored a failed coup d'état in Austria, and an-

U.S. troops wade ashore in the South Pacific. A truly global conflict, World War II ended fascist regimes in Europe and Asia, but failed to achieve genuine peace. (Photographic Archives, University of Louisville)

nounced the rearmament of Germany in violation of the Treaty of Versailles.

Beginning in 1936, Hitler increasingly turned his attention to foreign affairs. In March of that year he remilitarized the Rhineland in defiance of the Treaty of Versailles. He also intervened on the side of the Spanish fascists in the Spanish Civil War, which began in 1936. In March 1938, again in defiance of the Treaty of Versailles, he annexed the independent Austrian state to his Third Reich.

The Anschluss, as the annexation of Austria was called, brought scant response from Great Britain and France, the chief guarantors of Versailles. Mired in the depth of the Great Depression and haunted by gruesome memories of World War I, the French and especially the British had determined to follow a policy of appeasement in their relations with Hitler's Germany. According to the architects of appeasement such as British prime minister Neville Chamberlain, war could be avoided by giving in to legitimate and limited German demands. Unfortunately, Hitler's demands were both illegitimate and unlimited, although for a long time Western statesmen refused to acknowledge this.

The height of appeasement occurred in September 1938 at the Munich Conference. There France and Great Britain disgracefully reneged on their real and implied commitments to Czechoslovakia and permitted Hitler to annex the Sudetenland, or that part of Czechoslovakia that bordered Germany. Appeasement died only in 1939 when Hitler broke his solemn promise and absorbed what was left of the Czech state. Shortly thereafter, Hitler began to threaten Poland. The Poles, relying nervously on promises of support from Great Britain and France, resisted.

World War II in Europe began on September 1, 1939, when Nazi Germany invaded Poland. Using a tactic called blitzkrieg, or "lightning war," the Germans soon overwhelmed the hapless Poles. Blitzkrieg called for massed mobile units having enormous firepower to punch a hole in the enemy lines and then race to the enemy's rear, cutting lines of communication and creating chaos. Two days after the invasion, Poland's allies, Great Britain and France, declared war on Germany. Meanwhile, Joseph Stalin's Soviet Union, which had signed a nonaggression pact with Germany on August 23, 1939, also attacked Poland and annexed the eastern portion of that country. This proved to be the prelude to the Soviet seizure of Estonia, Latvia, and Lithuania in the summer of 1940. During 1939–1940, the USSR also fought a short war with Finland, the so-called Winter War, bringing the Soviets additional territory. After the conquest of Poland, military activity virtually ceased until the following spring, when Hitler turned his attention to western Europe.

Beginning with the invasion and conquest of Denmark and Norway, Hitler moved against the Netherlands, Belgium, and Luxembourg, and attacked the important nation of France on May 10, 1940. Hitler's victory over France was unexpectedly easy. France, suing for peace on June 22, 1940, was divided between an army of German occupation in the north and a puppet regime called Vichy France in the south. Henri Pétain, a World War I French war hero, and Pierre Laval, a prewar politician, administered Vichy France. These two collaborators were often referred to as "quislings," a term of scorn derived from Vidkun Quisling, the Nazi puppet who oversaw conquered Norway. Eventually, a vigorous resistance movement called the Free French, led by Charles de Gaulle, a French officer who had fled the Nazis, challenged both Vichy France's legitimacy and the Nazi occupation. As France fell, the British army, which had helped to defend France, barely escaped to Britain from encirclement on the French beaches at Dunkirk. Benito Mussolini, fascist dictator of Italy, had also joined his ally Hitler in the attack on France and was preparing an attack on Greece. Germany and Italy, the Axis powers, were experiencing great success.

Having defeated France, Hitler now turned his attention to Britain, where he faced a new leader, the resolute Winston Churchill, who had been named prime minister in May 1940. During the Battle of Britain in the fall of 1940, Hitler unsuccessfully tried to bomb the British into submission by striking at civilian as well as military targets.

In 1941 the course of the war in Europe entered a new phase when Hitler launched a surprise attack on his erstwhile ally, the Soviet Union, after having achieved additional military success in the Balkans. In December 1941 the German armies reached the gates of Leningrad and Moscow before their offensive bogged down and Soviet resistance stiffened.

Meanwhile, on the other side of the globe Germany's ally Japan pursued a policy of conquest. Having occupied much of China as well as the French colony of Indochina, Japan now challenged the United States. In response to a surprise attack on its fleet at Pearl Harbor in December 1941, the United States declared war on Japan. In a matter of days, Germany and Italy declared war on the United States. Great Britain, the USSR, and the United States now found themselves aligned against Germany, Italy, and Japan. The former countries soon formed what came to be known as the Grand Alliance and made the strategic decision to dedicate the bulk of their resources to achieving victory in Europe.

The high-water mark for the Axis powers came in December 1941, but the next three and one-half years witnessed a slow but steady erosion of their position. During 1942 the British, under General Bernard Montgomery, first stopped the Axis advance in North Africa at the Battle of El Alamein, and then successfully counterattacked. By the spring of 1943, British and American units had cleared North Africa of Axis forces.

The African victories set the stage for the invasion of Sicily and then the Italian mainland, which occurred later in 1943. The Allied triumph in Sicily led to the overthrow of Mussolini and the opening of armistice negotiations between the Italian army and the Allies in July 1943. However, the Germans intervened, rescued the captured Mussolini, reestablished his dictatorship, and, most important, occupied Rome and proceeded to mount a staunch defense of their position on the Italian peninsula.

Perhaps the most consequential battle of the war took place on the Eastern Front during the winter of 1942–1943. At the city of Stalingrad (now Volgograd) on the banks of the Volga, Russia's most important river, the Soviet, or Red, Army under the leadership of Generals Vasily Chuikov and Georgi Zhukov surrounded and annihilated its German opponents. The victorious Soviet army lost more men at Stalingrad than the United States lost in combat during the entire war. In July 1943 the Soviets followed up their victory at Stalingrad by defeating the Germans at the Battle of Kursk, World War II's largest tank battle. These two crushing defeats broke the back of the German army and forced it to commence its slow and bitter retreat to Berlin.

Meanwhile, during 1942 the United States, with help from its British allies, stopped the Japanese onslaught in the Pacific theater of operations. After defeating the Japanese navy at the battles of Midway and the Coral Sea, the United States adopted a strategy of "island hopping," which called for Allied forces to move toward the Japanese heartland one island at a time. Repulsing the Japanese at Guadalcanal and ousting them from the Gilbert, Marshall, Caroline, and Mariana islands, U.S. forces under General Douglas MacArthur and Admiral Chester Nimitz moved steadily closer to Japan's home islands. In October 1944 the United States destroyed the remnants of Japan's fleet at the Battle of Leyte Gulf and liberated the Philippines.

During the latter part of 1943, Anglo-American units became bogged down in Italy while the Red Army gradually but decisively defeated the Germans on the Eastern Front. It was not until June 6, 1944, that the Western allies finally launched a much anticipated cross-channel invasion when they went ashore at Normandy in France and opened the long-awaited "second front." D-day, as the invasion was known, proved to be a great success. Under the leadership of the American general

Dwight D. Eisenhower, the Western allies cleared the Nazis from France. Paris was liberated on August 24, 1944.

By the start of 1944, the Red Army had expelled the Germans from Soviet soil and was beginning to move against Germany's allies in eastern Europe and the Balkans. The Soviets defeated Romania and Bulgaria, invaded Hungary and Slovakia, and liberated parts of Yugoslavia, including the capital, Belgrade. By late 1944 the Red Army had crossed into East Prussia, thereby bringing the war to German soil.

The Soviet triumphs in eastern Europe alarmed some Westerners who had never trusted Joseph Stalin and who regarded his communist regime almost as distastefully as they regarded Hitler's Nazi state. However, the Western leaders, Winston Churchill and the U.S. president, Franklin D. Roosevelt, early on had agreed not to ask Stalin tough questions about the nature of a postwar Europe for fear that Stalin might abandon the alliance and seek a separate peace with the Germans. Consequently, Allied wartime diplomacy tended to focus on other issues.

Even before American entry into the war, Churchill and Roosevelt met at sea off the coast of Newfoundland in August 1941 and signed the Atlantic Charter, which set forth a series of liberal principles to guide the postwar world. Almost a year earlier, Roosevelt defied isolationist sentiment at home and gave the hard-pressed British fifty aged but serviceable destroyers in return for ninety-nine-year leases on several British bases in the western Atlantic and the Caribbean. In March 1941 Roosevelt persuaded the U.S. Congress to approve his policy of Lend-Lease, whereby the United States lent or leased to its allies billions of dollars worth of supplies with the understanding that they would be returned or paid for after the war. Originally designed to supply Great Britain, Lend-Lease was extended to include the Soviet Union once it entered the war.

Roosevelt and Churchill met again at Casablanca in January 1943. The Casablanca Conference resulted in a pledge to continue hostilities until Germany surrendered unconditionally. The next meeting took place at Teheran, Iran, in December 1943. With Stalin participating for the first time, the three allies discussed the occupation and demilitarization of a conquered Germany. They also discussed Roosevelt's proposal to create an international body designed to maintain global peace.

In October 1944 Churchill, ignoring Roosevelt's belief that Stalin was manageable, and growing ever more worried about the expanding Soviet presence in eastern Europe, traveled to Moscow. The British leader sought to determine Stalin's intentions for the lands liberated by the Red

Army. The result of Churchill's trip was an old-fashioned division of eastern Europe into well-defined spheres of influence. However, postwar events rendered this agreement virtually worthless.

The last major wartime diplomatic conference convened in February 1945 at Yalta in the Soviet Union. Topics on the agenda included the disposition of Poland and, by extension, the rest of eastern Europe, the future of Germany, Soviet participation in the war against Japan, and Roosevelt's international organization, the United Nations.

Yalta took place against a backdrop of stunning Allied victories. After a December 1944 setback at the Battle of the Bulge, the British and the Americans, now joined by units of liberated France's army, pushed forward into Germany, crossing the Rhine River in March 1945. At the same time Soviet forces captured Warsaw, Budapest, Vienna, Danzig, and Königsberg, expelled the Germans from Poland, and pushed farther into Germany proper from the east.

In the course of reclaiming captured territory from the Germans, the Allies discovered a number of concentration camps where the Nazis had interned Jews, "undesirables" such as communists and homosexuals, and prisoners of war. At infamous camps such as Auschwitz, Treblinka, and Maidanek, millions of innocent people were put to death. Especially horrendous was the systematic murder of Europe's Jews, the "Final Solution" that Hitler applied to what he termed the "Jewish problem." Of the approximately 12 million who died in the camps, 6 million were Jews.

In late April 1945, with the war's end drawing near, Mussolini was captured and executed by Italian partisans. A few days later, on April 30, 1945, Hitler committed suicide in his besieged bunker in Berlin. On May 7, 1945, representatives of the German military surrendered to Eisenhower. One day later, the act of surrender was repeated at Russian headquarters in the fallen German capital.

All that remained was to wrap up the war in the Pacific. Japan, which had lost Saipan in 1944, and Iwo Jima and Okinawa early in 1945, now faced a horrible new weapon of mass destruction. On August 6, 1945, the United States dropped the world's first atomic bomb on Hiroshima; three days later Nagasaki suffered the same fate. Meanwhile, on August 8, 1945, in keeping with agreements reached at Yalta, the USSR entered the war against Japan. A formal announcement of surrender by the emperor was read to the Japanese people on August 15, 1945; on September 2 formal surrender ceremonies took place on the U.S. battleship *Missouri,* anchored in Tokyo Bay. World War II had finally ended.

INTERPRETIVE ESSAY
Larry Thornton

More destructive than any other conflict, World War II dominates twentieth-century world history. The forces that produced the war occupied center stage for much of the preceding twenty years, and the ramifications of the changes wrought by this war continue to affect the world today. For an entire generation—as well as the following generations influenced by that generation—World War II was and remains the defining mark by which all subsequent conflicts are measured.

Strictly speaking, World War II was two separate but coterminous wars that had little relationship to each other. In Asia, Japan waged a war of conquest against China and the British, French, Dutch, and American empires. The European war pitted Germany, Italy, and their junior allies—Bulgaria, Hungary, and Romania—against the Soviet Union and several of the same states Japan was battling. Nominally allies, Germany and Japan made little pretense of coordinating their military plans.

Thus, for example, when Germany launched Operation Barbarossa (the 1941 invasion of the Soviet Union), no corresponding Japanese campaign was launched from Asia, even though Soviet and Japanese forces had repeatedly clashed along the Soviet-Manchurian frontier since 1937. German and Japanese imperial interests went in completely different directions. The enemies of Germany and Japan did a better job of coordinating their efforts in the two theaters simply because they had to determine priorities (Europe had the higher priority) in order to allocate resources.

Each major power had an ideological rationale to support its war efforts. The Japanese proclaimed a Greater East Asia Co-Prosperity Sphere, which promised Asia for the Asians under Japanese leadership. The Nazis believed that Germany needed *Lebensraum,* or "living space," to survive the Darwinian struggle among the races. Germany would conquer substantial sections of eastern Europe and make room for future generations of Germans by reducing the indigenous populations.

In June 1941 the states aligned against Germany signed the Inter-Allied Declaration, pledging to work for "a world in which, relieved of the menace of aggression, all may enjoy economic and social security." In August 1941, the British and the Americans announced their war aims in the Atlantic Charter, which promised a postwar world safe and secure for all people. These sentiments were reiterated on January 1, 1942, in the so-called United Nations Declaration.

The contrast between war aims is quite manifest. The Germans and the Japanese sought conquest, plain and simple. Despite their claims of liberating the oppressed from Stalinism or Western domination, the brutal occupation policies followed by the Germans and the Japanese convinced the conquered peoples of just the opposite. These unfortunates had simply changed masters, and the new ones were, in many ways, more ruthless and demanding. On the other hand, the idealistic war aims espoused by the Allies were frequently unattainable, which at times made the Allies appear deceitful.

At its peak, World War II involved military forces from fifty-six nations (not including colonies or imperial territories). The war raged throughout Asia, Africa, and Europe as well as above, on, and beneath the surface of the Atlantic and Pacific oceans. World War II was also total war. Although the term total war had been used during the French revolutionary wars and during World War I, there is no comparison between these efforts and World War II.

Waging total war required mobilizing a society's human and technical resources. Just as a nation drafts its young men, so it must also organize its economy for the war effort. Inherent in thoroughgoing mobilization is the tendency toward compulsion. Total war conscripts every resource; it utilizes the entire society.

Governments requisitioned property, registered and directed labor, controlled industry, allocated the distribution of raw materials, rationed or cut production of consumer goods, and limited civilian consumption. Germany was slower to mobilize its economy fully, striving to supply both guns and butter. When Albert Speer became minister for armaments and production in 1942, Germany successfully moved to a total war economy, thereby prolonging the war by one to two years. Germany and Japan never grasped the inherent contradiction between their efforts to wage unlimited war and their limited resources and production capacity. In this sense their campaigns were doomed to fail when they engaged opponents with superior economies.

In addition to mobilizing their economies earlier, the Allies had greater industrial capacity and capital resources than the Axis powers. Claiming to be the "Arsenal of Democracy," the United States alone supplied $50 billion worth of arms and equipment to its allies. In contrast to Germany and Japan, the combined American, British, and Soviet industrial capacity could support total war.

Nations also mobilized their human resources. Obviously military conscription became the order of the day, but total war required more than uniformed warriors. Civilians also had to be enlisted in the war effort. In most countries men between the ages of eighteen and sixty carried out work considered vital to the war effort. Most societies also recruited women to replace the men who had marched off to the front. Great Britain decreed the compulsory employment in war work of women between the ages of nineteen and forty, while "Rosie the Riveter" and her counterparts became war heroines working to build tanks or other vital goods for the United States, the Soviet Union, and other states.

World War II also fostered the roots of what Dwight D. Eisenhower, in the 1950s, called the military-industrial complex through the mobilization of the scientific, academic, and technical communities. Over 30,000 scientists and engineers were part of the war effort in the United States alone. Governments financed research projects and sought expert advice on the adaptation of inventions and discoveries for military purposes. Although the United States' Manhattan Project (the development of the atomic bomb) is the most dramatic example of this mobilization of science and technology, the list of new or improved weapons is long and impressive, including radar, sonar, magnetic mines, proximity fuses, rockets, missiles, and jet planes. In addition to the development of new weapons, war-related research also led to new products and procedures with nonmilitary applications, such as quinine, DDT, the cyclotron, and the first blue baby operation.

Research and development was one of several areas where the Allies had a distinct advantage over the Axis powers. Virtually all nonmilitary achievements were the prerogatives of the Allies, who had the industrial, financial, intellectual, and moral resources to engage in major research and development beyond the immediate demands of the war. By comparison, the Axis states realized no significant nonmilitary achievements because they could not spare the resources and their values did not impel them in this direction.

Beyond compulsion or coercion, every state found propaganda quite useful to instill commitment, to maintain morale, and to promote sacrifice. German propaganda, which Joseph Goebbels, Germany's minister of propaganda, considered as important as the army in the field, appealed to patriotism, stressed elements of Nazi ideology and, to a lesser extent, used racist images to diminish the humanity of the supposedly inferior peoples. Japanese propaganda also stressed inherent differences between the purity of its cause and the tainted qualities of its opponents.

The Soviet propaganda effort evolved from early emphasis on vigorous defense of the revolution and socialism to the defense of Mother Russia; the conflict became the Great Patriotic War as the Nazis joined the evil pantheon that included the Mongols, the Tartars, the Turks, and Napoleon. To reinforce this theme, Soviet propaganda emphasized elements of both classic and popular culture. With themes of perseverance and victory, Sergei Eisenstein's film *Alexander Nevsky*, Leo Tolstoy's *War and Peace*, and Dmitri Shostakovich's *Leningrad* Symphony received considerable attention. Popular arts also joined the war effort. In the first four days of the war over 100 songs were composed in Moscow. During the war, professionals and amateurs alike composed thousands of songs for state- or party-sponsored contests and festivals, or for their own amusement and expression. Soviet propaganda also stressed vengeance against the "gray-green slugs" and promised to shed a pool of blood for every drop of Soviet blood, or to blind two eyes for every blinded Soviet eye.

In the United States, Hollywood joined the war effort, producing the Why We Fight series, seven films initially made to educate servicemen and women and subsequently shown to the general population. Even Bugs Bunny, Daffy Duck, and other cartoon characters went to war, and Spike Jones' City Slickers mocked the Nazis in their hit song "Der Fuehrer's Face." American propaganda was not always so lighthearted, though, as evidenced by the regular portrayal of Japanese leaders and soldiers as monkeys or apes.

In many ways, one can argue that World War II as total war represented the logical application of modern rationality to war. After defining victory as the desired end or goal, officials set out to devise the most efficient means to realize that goal. The extent of organization and technological sophistication required to produce the desired goal was unparalleled. It may seem odd to characterize destruction of this magnitude as the culmination of rationality, but lucid men and women, for the most part, made the organizational and operational decisions and formulated the tactics and strategies. Without advanced industrialized, technical, mechanical societies, which require rational officials, total war is not possible.

The human toll remains the most obvious measure of the success of modern rationality—the cold, mechanical harnessing of vast amounts of talent, energy, and resources resulting in the most destructive war in history. Statistics overwhelm one's capacity to comprehend. Estimates of the total death toll reach as high as 57 million. In the Soviet Union, which bore the brunt of the European war, perhaps one out of every eight or nine people died. Fifteen percent of the Polish population was killed. About 4 million Germans and at least 2 million Japanese perished.

War consciously and intentionally waged against civilians distinguished the violence of World War II. Civilian deaths accounted for approximately 50 percent of the total casualties (compared to 5 percent in World War I). Civilians were constantly targeted, as bombs fell on cities like Shanghai and Warsaw at the start of the war and on Berlin and Tokyo at the very end. The Japanese conquest of Nanking, late in 1937, set off an unprecedented seven-week wave of mass murder, rape, torture, and pillage in which over 200,000 Chinese died. In spite of his public statements that Germany did not wage war against women and children, Hitler's forces everywhere attacked civilian populations. The Allies also carried the war to their opponents' homelands.

However, the Axis powers engaged in unparalleled atrocities. Rooted in the desire to exploit fully their conquered territories and in assumptions of inherent racial superiority, these states imposed occupation policies that brooked no opposition and harshly retaliated against manifestations of resistance. While the Japanese viciously retaliated against their opponents, attempted to cow the conquered peoples, mistreated and starved prisoners of war, conducted brutal experiments of dubious medical value, and forcibly recruited Korean and other women to serve as prostitutes or "comfort girls," they never matched Germany's systematic violence.

Germany established new standards of violence and horror as Nazis sought to rearrange Europe's demographic composition. The Nazis were ruthlessly determined to apply Darwin's principle of natural selection, as they understood it, to human society. This meant that "races," or ethnic groups, were considered superior or inferior organisms shaped by nature through a struggle in which only the fittest survived. Since nature's law was kill or die, no moral or humanitarian constraints could sway the Nazis from their self-appointed task to build up the superior Germanic or Aryan "race" in its war against the inferior peoples. Bolstered by this ideology, the Nazis had few qualms about administering their conquered territories with ruthless abandon. The Nazis focused their primary efforts against what they perceived as the most immediate threats: the Jews and the Soviet Union.

In what was euphemistically called the "Final Solution to the Jewish Question," the Nazis attempted to kill every Jew in Europe, and they were more successful at this than at any other endeavor. About two-thirds of Europe's Jews died at the hands of the Nazis; this amounted to some 5.8 million people. In the Soviet Union, more than 7 million soldiers died, almost half as a result of starvation after surrender. Nazi administrators ruthlessly went about reducing the population of the occupied Soviet territory by about two-thirds; this accounted for a significant portion of the estimated 15 million Soviet civilian casualties. Orders were issued to kill immediately all members of the Communist Party, and the Nazis executed hundreds more in retaliation for each act of sabotage, resistance, or assassination.

Other Nazi programs operated on a smaller scale, but were less murderous only by degree. An effort was made to eliminate every vestige of Polish leadership by killing priests, trade union leaders, professors, and other prominent people. The infamous *Nacht und Nebel* order provided for the disappearance without any explanation into the "night and fog" of anyone considered a threat to the Nazi Reich. Concentration camp inmates were subjected to brutal medical and pseudoscientific experiments where no consideration was given to their willingness or to their well-being before, during, or after the procedures. In addition, many people across Europe starved as a result of the Nazi policy of exporting foodstuffs to Germany.

All across Europe and Asia people suffered because of forced labor. Workers were forcibly recruited and sent off to work in factories supplying the German or Japanese war efforts. Tens of thousands of forced laborers perished because of long hours, starvation diets, unmerciful discipline, and inhumane living conditions. This policy was counterproductive because output was low and replacement difficult, at the very time that German and Japanese industrial production increasingly lagged behind that of the United States and the Soviet Union.

The most serious charges of systematic brutality leveled against any of the Allies pale by comparison, although some Soviet policies provoked considerable embarrassment. To many, the 1939 Nazi-Soviet Pact and subsequent occupation of eastern Poland, the 1939–1940 Winter War against Finland, and the occupation of the Baltic states and the Romanian province of Bessarabia challenged the ideals of the Atlantic Charter and the United Nations Declaration. Worse still, approximately 10,000 Polish army officers perished at the hands of Stalin's NKVD security forces (ironically, in 1943 the Germans discovered and exposed their graves in Katyn Forest near Smolensk). Many observers were also shocked by the disorderly behavior of the Red Army once it entered Germany and by interference in the internal affairs of the states occupied by the Red Army.

The incarceration of Japanese Americans and Japanese Canadians was another noteworthy manifestation of Allied brutality. Out of fear and racism in the aftermath of the Japanese attack on Pearl Harbor, the U.S. and Canadian governments authorized the forcible removal of more than 110,000 citizens of Japanese descent from the western states and provinces. Placed in isolated, prisonlike internment camps for the duration of the war, these people, who had displayed no disloyalty, suffered considerable deprivation and humiliation as well as the loss of their homes, farms, and businesses.

In terms of horror or scale of violence, one must look back hundreds of years to find other periods that, while lacking modern means of destruction, might match World War II in reckless and shameless abandon: to the Thirty Years' War (1618–1648), which depopulated entire regions of the German states through the ravages of war and the accompanying blights of starvation, disease, and economic disruption, or to the thirteenth-century Mongol invasion. However, these examples, once standards, dim by comparison. Nothing in history matches World War II.

Beyond this, the end of World War II presented immediate problems and altered the shape of the world over the next two generations. Much as when a child knocks down a pile of building blocks, one of the most immediate and vexing problems was how to put it all back together again. However, the war so altered the countries, cultures, and societies it touched that restoration of the status quo ante bellum was not feasible in many cases. New power relationships emerged from the war, bringing new perspectives to world politics and complicating the process of drawing new maps and making the peace. Unfortunately, in many places the end of the war did not bring peace or even an end to the shooting.

Foremost among the immediate problems presented by the end of the war was the human problem. In one way or another, the war had uprooted millions of people: forced laborers, concentration camp inmates, refugees, collaborators, and others labeled displaced persons (DPs). Many wanted to return home, but for others home no longer existed; and most of the survivors of concentration camps or forced labor were so physically debilitated that they were incapable of setting off for home. The war's destructiveness in Europe made moving people around very difficult because few trains ran, few bridges stood, and little road transportation existed.

In addition to the DPs, all of whom faced immediate problems, three other groups experienced unique difficulties. Many Soviets who found themselves in regions controlled by the Western Allies did not want to return to the Soviet Union, where the security forces assumed that any-

one who survived Nazi captivity had betrayed the Soviet state and deserved punishment. Unfortunately, the Western Allies had earlier agreed
to Stalin's demand that all Soviets be repatriated, which meant, in some
cases, that fixed bayonets and pointed guns were used to force people
onto trains headed east.

Another great tragedy befell many Jews who outlasted the Nazis. It
became abundantly clear to many that they were not welcome in their
old communities and even in their old homes. After the Jews had been
deported, their possessions were often seized by their former neighbors,
who were not eager to see the rightful owners return. In the seven
months after the war, at least 350 Polish Jews who tried to return home
were murdered. The worst incident took place in Kielce on July 4, 1946.
After a Polish boy claimed to have escaped imminent death at the hands
of two Jews, a mob killed forty-two Jews. Following this pogrom, about
100,000 Polish Jews, more than half of those who survived the Nazis, left
Poland. Prompted by the Nazi effort to slaughter all of them and by
postwar anti-Semitism, many Jews left for Palestine, soon to become Israel, or for the Western Hemisphere.

Germans living outside the postwar boundaries of Germany also suffered. As former German territory was absorbed into the Soviet Union
or Poland, the Allies agreed to the expulsion to Germany of those resi-
dents who were ethnic Germans. Following this precedent, Czechoslovakia and Hungary also deported the German minorities living within
their frontiers. Altogether, between 12 and 13 million expelled ethnic
Germans arrived in Germany, most penniless and competing with other
Germans for shelter, food, and jobs, all of which were in short supply.
Frequently those expelling the Germans took advantage of the opportunity for vengeance or profit and robbed, raped, harassed, and murdered them (some estimates put this death toll near 2 million). The
process of expulsion often marked the end of German communities that
had flourished for centuries in eastern Europe.

For millions of people in both Asia and Europe, the end of the war
did not mean the end of suffering. The populations in the defeated states
and in many other devastated regions faced an ongoing struggle to survive. Economies collapsed, money ceased to have value, jobs and materials did not exist, food and fuel were scarce. In many places cigarettes
became the only functioning currency and the occupying armies the only
source for cigarettes. Without the black market, basic goods such as soap
or glass or coffee were impossible to get. Recovery and reconstruction
appeared improbable in the foreseeable future. The victorious armies

found themselves responsible for the populations that had recently been their enemies. No other agencies existed that could provide basic maintenance or reconstruction assistance.

The victors also attempted to do away with those forces they thought had caused the war and to punish responsible individuals. In Germany the powers conducted denazification campaigns in their respective zones of occupation. The campaigns differed and reflected each state's emphasis on the roots of Nazi ideology. The Soviets took swift and drastic action against some 45,000 individuals who had occupied prominent positions in the pre-1945 economy or politics. Industrialists, landowners, military officers, civil servants, and Nazi Party officials were punished as active Nazis, which meant that they lost their positions and property; in addition, many were sent to Soviet labor camps. The Americans distributed about 12 million questionnaires that, when completed, would identify Nazis who could then be subjected to judicial proceedings. Initial estimates called for trials for about 3 million Germans, but the demands of reconstruction and the pressures of the Cold War meant lenient treatment for many offenders whose skills were needed in the new Germanies. In all four occupation zones, reeducation campaigns were instituted to instill antifascist values as a foundation for new political and social systems.

In both Germany and Japan, the Allies also indicted individuals and organizations for crimes against peace, conspiracy to wage aggressive war, war crimes, and crimes against humanity. Using captured documents and witnesses, the prosecution argued that the atrocities were so offensive that civilization demanded accountability. After months of testimony, most of the defendants were found guilty and given sentences ranging from death to imprisonment. Subsequently, thousands of Nazis and Japanese were tried in international tribunals as well as in the courts of Germany, the United States, the Soviet Union, Poland, Czechoslovakia, Israel, Hong Kong, Singapore, and Borneo. Even so, many people accused of committing horrific atrocities managed to escape prosecution.

Continuing the fighting long past the time when the military outcome was determined significantly shaped the politics of a postwar world in ways that none of the combatants had anticipated. The United States and the Soviet Union imposed a peace upon Europe that preserved the postwar status quo for more than forty years. No dominating force imposed its will on Asia. Since the Japanese had driven out the Westerners and then withdrawn after their defeat, a vacuum existed. With the door open, many different nationalist conflicts and revolutions followed.

Germany ceased to exist for all practical purposes until the occupying powers returned sovereignty to the defeated Germans (Germany did not reappear in a complete sense until its stunning reunification in 1990). Similarly, Poland did not regain its national independence, lost first to the Germans and then to the Soviets, until the end of the 1980s. The crushing German victory over France in 1940 meant that the restoration of French power and prominence depended on states more powerful than France. Acknowledged as one of the so-called Big Four and given a permanent seat on the United Nations Security Council and an occupation zone in Germany, France assumed these perquisites of rank less from its own efforts than through the beneficence of its allies. Great Britain, still weakened from World War I, suffered apparently irreversible national exhaustion. As a primary result of Germany's destruction, the diminution of both France and Britain, and the overshadowing power of the United States and the Soviet Union, Europe could no longer politically dominate the world as it had for centuries.

Japan also ceased to exist for all practical purposes. However, in 1947 the United States imposed a new constitution on Japan, and in 1951 a formal peace treaty was signed. Meanwhile, in China civil war resumed. Waging a type of "undeclared peace" during World War II, Chiang Kai-shek's China had attempted to spend as few of its resources as possible against Japan in anticipation of the postwar resumption of hostilities with Chinese communist forces. With this strategy, China retained enough of its nominal Great Power status to warrant a permanent seat on the UN's Security Council; but Chiang's government did not survive the battle with Mao Zedong's communist forces. In 1949 Mao's army drove Chiang's Kuomintang army from the mainland to the island of Taiwan.

When the imperial powers attempted to reassert authority over their prewar colonies, many of which were in Asia, they faced increased opposition, growing expectations for independence, and, in some cases, armed resistance. U.S. support of decolonization added further impetus to this drive and, starting with the Philippines in 1946, the ranks of independent states expanded over the next two decades. Although the former imperial powers managed to restore their economic power in the decade after the war, their political influence never returned to prewar levels.

After World War II, new conflicts, wars, and revolutions broke out around the world. In addition to China, Greece fought a civil war that pitted Greek royalists, who had fled before the Nazis, against Greek communists, who had played a significant role in the anti-Nazi resistance. Ho Chi Minh declared Vietnamese independence and led forces that had battled against the Japanese against the returning French colonials. From 1948 to 1959 the British fought a communist-led insurrection in Malaya. Other serious conflicts in the late 1940s pitted the Dutch against Indonesian nationalists, Arabs against Israelis, and Indians against Pakistanis. In the aftermath of a war that disrupted the status quo for much of the world, the process of shaping a new, global status quo was long, contentious, and frequently bloody.

Perhaps the postwar changes most affected the status of the two clearest victors, the Soviet Union and the United States. For the Soviet Union, the victory over Hitler's Germany allowed—at a devastating cost—the projection of Soviet influence and power into eastern and central Europe, and gave Stalin's communism legitimacy as a viable alternative to liberal democracy. In addition, the success of the Chinese communist revolution and the turmoil throughout the Third World offered opportunities for further expansion of Soviet influence. Nevertheless, as impressive as it seemed at the time, Soviet success proved temporary.

For the United States, the only power to emerge largely unscathed and considerably stronger than before the war, victory brought increased postwar responsibilities that could not be ignored. In many ways, the decision to locate the headquarters of the United Nations in New York City reflected the recognition of the United States' dominant position and U.S. acceptance of its leading economic and political role in the world. American policy makers faced the dilemma of deciding what part of the prewar status quo to preserve, what to rebuild, and what to change. The United States also shouldered the burden of supporting reconstruction through loans, grants, investments, and security costs. Of course, this increased economic role also meant an increased political role, since the United States expected a voice in shaping the processes it funded.

Reflecting the heightened power and prestige of both the Soviet Union and the United States and the diminished stature of several of the traditional Great Powers, the postwar political system developed into a kind of bipolarity. The two superpowers, each with its own distinct ideological foundation, struggled to promote their own security and political agenda while limiting the other's successes. This struggle came to be known as the Cold War. Each superpower emphasized the self-evidence of its own ideology and attempted to persuade any who would listen that the other's efforts amounted to malevolence. In the late 1950s, bipolarity gave way to multipolarity through the Non-Aligned Movement, an organization of smaller states that sought to avoid exclusive association with either superpower in an effort to chart their own courses and exert influence on political and economic questions before the United

Nations or other forums. After the mid-1960s, global power was more diffuse than it had ever been.

Efforts were made to achieve collective security in the postwar world through the auspices of the United Nations. Even before the war ended, Allied representatives met to discuss the new UN organization. In 1945 the UN Charter was drafted and ratified, taking effect on October 24 of that year. Specific powers to investigate any situation that might lead to conflict between members were vested in the Security Council. Since the war, the United Nations has sponsored peacekeeping forces, negotiations, and wide-ranging humanitarian programs. While its record has been spotty, the organization has developed an effectiveness that its predecessor, the League of Nations, never had.

Although the guns have been silent for fifty years, the legacy of World War II is still very much with us. Both academic and popular culture attest to its continuing fascination. With the dissolution of the Soviet empire and of the Soviet Union itself, the world may see the war's last chapters being written as the century ends. Ironically, Asia, the site of substantial nationalist and revolutionary turmoil in the decade after the war, appears to have attained a semblance of stability, while parts of Europe, so long locked into the stability imposed by the Cold War, teeter on the brink of an abyss. It is now clear that many forces held in check by the postwar settlement, including virulent nationalism and neo-Nazism, have surfaced. No matter how these ramifications of World War II play out, the world has never seen anything like it before or since.

SELECTED BIBLIOGRAPHY

Barnhart, Michael. *Japan Prepares for Total War: The Search for Economic Security, 1919–1941.* Ithaca, NY: Cornell University Press, 1987. An account of the outbreak of the war in Asia, this work focuses on Japan's efforts to overcome its economic vulnerabilities.

Calder, Angus. *The People's War: Britain, 1939–1945.* New York: Pantheon, 1969. A good discussion of the British home front during the war.

Clausen, Henry C., and Bruce Lee. *Pearl Harbor: Final Judgement.* New York: Crown, 1992. A thorough account of who was responsible for this debacle.

Dallin, Alexander. *German Rule in Russia, 1941–1945.* London: Macmillan, 1957. This is the standard account of Nazi occupation policies in the USSR.

Dower, John W. *War Without Mercy: Race and Power in the Pacific War.* New York: Pantheon Books, 1986. In one of the most important books on the war, the author compares how race was invoked by the Japanese and the Americans.

Dziewanowski, M. K. *War at Any Price: World War II in Europe, 1939–1945.* Englewood Cliffs, NJ: Prentice-Hall, 1987. A concise survey of the war in Europe.

Fussell, Paul. *Wartime: Understanding and Behavior in the Second World War.* New York: Oxford University Press, 1989. In this follow-up to his highly acclaimed study on World War I, Fussell continues his examination of the culture of war.

Hilberg, Raul. *The Destruction of the European Jews.* Chicago: Quadrangle, 1967. One of the standard studies of the Holocaust.

Hough, Richard. *The Longest Battle: The War at Sea, 1939–1945.* New York: Morrow, 1986. A general survey of the naval aspects of the war, with some excellent battle maps.

Ienaga, Saburo. *The Pacific War, 1931–1945: A Critical Perspective of Japan's Role in World War II.* New York: Pantheon Books, 1978. Ienaga has written a penetrating analysis of the war against Japan.

Jones, F. C. *Japan's New Order in East Asia, 1937–1945.* London: Oxford University Press, 1954. This is one of the best accounts of the way Japan governed its empire.

Presseisen, E. L. *Germany and Japan: A Study in Totalitarian Diplomacy.* The Hague: Martinus Nijhoff, 1958. Presseisen has written a clear description of the relationship between these two powers.

Taylor, A.J.P. *The Origins of the Second World War.* New York: Atheneum, 1961. Taylor's controversial study attacks the standard view that Hitler was solely responsible for the coming of war.

Terkel, Studs. *"The Good War": An Oral History of World War II.* New York: Pantheon, 1984. Terkel lets a variety of Americans tell stories of their experiences at the battlefront as well as the home front.

Toland, John. *The Rising Sun: The Decline and Fall of the Japanese Empire, 1936–1945.* New York: Random House, 1970. A fine popular history.

Trunk, Isaiah. *Judenrat: The Jewish Councils in Eastern Europe under Nazi Occupation.* New York: Macmillan, 1972. Trunk examines the validity of the accusation that Jewish officials collaborated, willingly or unwillingly, with the Nazis.

Werth, Alexander. *Russia at War, 1941–1945.* New York: Dutton, 1964. Werth's book is the standard account of World War II on Europe's Eastern Front.

Willmott, H. P. *The Great Crusade: A New Complete History of the Second World War.* London: M. Joseph, 1989. One of the best single-volume accounts of the war, with considerable interpretation as well as narrative.

Wright, Gordon. *The Ordeal of Total War, 1939–1945.* New York: Harper and Row, 1968. Part of the magnificent Rise of Modern Europe series, Wright's book focuses on the war's economic and social aspects as well as its military and political ones.

6

The Cold War, c. 1946–1991

INTRODUCTION

The Cold War dominated international relations during the latter portion of the twentieth century. It featured an intense and unrelenting rivalry between the United States and its allies on one hand and the Soviet Union and its supporters on the other hand. Cold War competition touched every facet of human activity. The Cold War influenced and in many instances drove politics, economics, diplomacy, culture, and technology. Despite several near misses, the animosity between the two prime antagonists never escalated into an armed clash, hence the term "Cold War."

The origins of the Cold War remain a source of great controversy. Prior to World War II, many Western leaders viewed the Marxist regime in Russia with a mixture of fear and hatred. Conversely, the Soviet Union of Vladimir Lenin and Joseph Stalin regarded the capitalistic West as its mortal enemy. Although the West and East eventually allied during World War II in a successful military struggle against Nazi Germany, in many ways the wartime experience served to confirm rather than allay prewar suspicions. Almost immediately after the Nazis surrendered in May 1945, the alliance began to break apart. Increasing Soviet domination of Poland—the country Great Britain and France originally went to

U.S. Vice President Richard M. Nixon confronts Soviet leader Nikita S. Khrushchev during the famous "Kitchen Debate" at the U.S. exhibition in Moscow, July 1959. The defining event of the post–World War II era, the Cold War pitted the democratic and capitalist West against the communist bloc. (Reproduced from the Collections of the Library of Congress)

war to defend—disturbed the West; U.S. president Harry Truman's un-expected decision in May 1945 to end Lend-Lease aid to the USSR upset the Soviets. An acrimonious quarrel soon developed.

Initially the Cold War focused on war-torn Europe. It was there that sides were first chosen and a sort of ground rules for the conflict emerged. A major point of disagreement was how to handle defeated and occupied Germany. The issue of reparations presented a serious problem. The Soviets, citing the extensive damage done to their country by the invading German armies, demanded that much of Germany's industrial infrastructure be dismantled and shipped to the USSR. The West, not wanting to support an economically destroyed Germany, and fearing that the Soviets wished to cripple the German economy in order to bring about a communist takeover, refused. In short order, the joint administration of occupied Germany broke down and each side began to formulate its own plan for Germany's future.

Meanwhile, the Soviet Union continued to integrate formerly inde-pendent countries such as Estonia, Latvia, and Lithuania into the USSR, and steadily consolidated its hold over Poland, Czechoslovakia, Hun-gary, Romania, and Bulgaria, countries its Red Army had recently lib-erated. These actions, together with its German policy and Stalin's belligerent February 1946 speech citing the threat capitalism posed to Soviet security, caused former British prime minister Winston Churchill to declare in a March 1946 speech, "From Stettin in the Baltic to Trieste in the Adriatic, an iron curtain has descended across the continent."

The pivotal year 1947 opened with Great Britain informing the United States that it could no longer continue to support either Turkey or the conservative Greek government that was then fighting a communist in-surgency. The implication was clear: Britain was abandoning its position in the eastern Mediterranean. Without much hesitation, the United States moved into the vacuum, replacing Britain as chief supplier to the Turks and the embattled Greeks. On March 12, 1947, Truman delivered a speech to the U.S. Congress in which he enunciated what became known as the Truman Doctrine. The U.S. promised to "support free peoples who are resisting attempted subjugation by armed minorities or outside pres-sures." The Truman Doctrine became a cornerstone of U.S. policy during the Cold War.

The Truman Doctrine was greatly influenced by the work of American diplomat George F. Kennan and several other American statesmen who at this time formulated the policy of "containment." Containment pos-tulated that the best response to perceived communist expansionism was to strengthen existing Western institutions in order to deny communism an opportunity to take root, to oppose (chiefly by economic measures) communist attempts to threaten the West's vital interests, and to wait patiently yet vigilantly until the insecure Soviet regime changed for the better or, as was the case, collapsed under the weight of its own short-comings.

Implementation of the containment policy also led to the Marshall Plan, named for U.S. Secretary of State George C. Marshall, which followed quickly on the heels of the Truman Doctrine. Offering exceptional amounts of American aid to devastated Europe, the Marshall Plan proved instrumental in rebuilding the shattered economies of Western Europe. However, Stalin and his allies denounced the Marshall Plan as an insidious American trick to gain economic hegemony over Europe. The USSR refused to participate in the plan and ordered its satellites to do likewise. In order to secure congressional approval of the Marshall Plan, the Truman administration portrayed it as an effective way to combat communist expansion in Europe.

In the wake of the Marshall Plan, in September 1947 the Soviets established the Communist Information Bureau, or Cominform, which, like the prewar Communist International (Comintern), served to bring the global communist movement under Moscow's close control and to turn that movement aggressively against the West. Following the Soviet lead, communist parties in Western Europe, particularly France and Italy, railed against the Marshall Plan and used their influence, especially with the working class, to try to disrupt normal life.

In February 1948, the communists masterminded a coup d'état in Czechoslovakia that replaced a coalition government with one completely subservient to Moscow. Angered by events in Czechoslovakia, the West took steps to create a military alliance and also signaled its intention to form an independent West German state. Stalin retaliated by initiating the Berlin Blockade, one of the most dangerous crises of the Cold War. In June, Stalin cut off Western access to Berlin, the divided German capital located deep within the Soviet zone of occupation. Through something of a logistical miracle, the West managed to supply its portion of Berlin by air for almost a year. Stalin called off the blockade in May 1949, but by that time the West had already committed itself to the establishment of a German state closely allied to the West, and to the North Atlantic Treaty Organization, a military alliance aimed against the USSR. Stalin responded by establishing an East German state tied to the Soviet Union and an opposing military alliance, the Warsaw Pact.

Although initially centered on Europe, the Cold War soon became global in nature. As early as 1946, the United States and the USSR squabbled over the latter's claims to share control over the entrance to the Black Sea with Turkey and to establish a sphere of influence in northern Iran. On both issues the Americans took a tough stance. However, the USSR scored what appeared to be a major victory in 1949 when the Chinese communists under Mao Zedong defeated the American client Chiang Kai-shek and gained control over the most populous country in the world. It was almost universally assumed that Mao would do the Soviet Union's bidding.

In the following year, the Cold War actually heated up. On June 25, 1950, the communist government of North Korea under Kim Il-sung invaded South Korea. Responding to this invasion, the United Nations, the site of seemingly interminable East-West wrangling since its inception, became involved. Taking advantage of the Soviet delegation's boycott of the UN Security Council, the United States managed to have the UN brand North Korea as the aggressor and to enter the conflict on the side of South Korea. Three years later the parties to the Korean War signed a truce, but not before China had joined the fray on the side of North Korea and some American commanders had unsuccessfully urged the use of nuclear weapons.

With the truce in Korea and the death of Stalin in 1953, the Cold War's intensity slackened a bit, and East-West relations entered a phase of alternating periods of rapprochement and crisis that prevailed until the end of the struggle. The Cold War had become institutionalized.

By 1955 Nikita Khrushchev had emerged as Stalin's successor in the USSR, and he embarked on a policy of "peaceful coexistence" whereby East and West were to continue their competition, but in a less confrontational manner. Propaganda blasts were interspersed with periodic summit meetings during which Soviet and U.S. leaders sometimes amicably discussed the international situation. Positive steps such as the 1955 Austrian State Treaty, which provided for the end of Austria's occupation and the establishment of a sovereign but neutral Austrian state, were matched by negative steps such as a series of nerve-racking crises over Berlin, culminating in the 1961 construction of the Berlin Wall, which physically divided the already politically divided former German capital.

A truly terrifying arms race was another central feature of the Cold War. Both the United States and the USSR amassed huge arsenals of the most destructive thermonuclear weapons. Moreover, the two rivals also developed a myriad of systems including intercontinental ballistic missiles (ICBMs) with which to rain down a nuclear holocaust upon each other. In this respect the sides appeared to be evenly matched, leading to a stalemate sometimes described as "the balance of terror." Both sides subscribed to the MAD doctrine (Mutual Assured Destruction), and in a macabre way MAD served to restrain the competing superpowers. In fact, from the early 1960s onward, a growing realization of the dangerous nature of the arms race led to a series of nuclear arms agreements.

This realization was hastened by the 1962 Cuban Missile Crisis, which almost exploded into nuclear conflict. Disturbed by the behavior of Fidel Castro, the successful Cuban revolutionary who identified with Marxism, in 1961 the United States backed an invasion of Cuba by anti-Castro elements that ended in disaster. The failed Bay of Pigs invasion prompted Castro to move clearly into the Soviet orbit. Eighteen months later, upon discovering that the USSR was placing missiles in Cuba that could easily reach the United States, President John F. Kennedy issued an ultimatum to Khrushchev to remove the missiles or face dire consequences. Although Castro was ready for a nuclear showdown, Khrushchev was not. The Soviets removed their missiles and a nuclear war was narrowly averted.

Beginning in the 1970s, the policy of detente appeared to offer a possible end to the Cold War. Detente seemed an unlikely development at the time. The United States was still mired in Vietnam, fighting what it believed was a Moscow-inspired attempt to spread communism. The Soviet Union had only recently brutally repressed Czechoslovakia's attempt to achieve "socialism with a human face," a move that gave rise to the Brezhnev Doctrine whereby the Soviet leader, Leonid Brezhnev, claimed for the Soviet Union the right to intervene in any "socialist" country in order to preserve socialism. Nevertheless, under detente the United States, led by President Richard Nixon and his chief foreign policy advisor, Henry Kissinger, and Brezhnev's USSR tried to relax tensions in their relationship and to find common ground on a number of issues of mutual interest. High points of detente included the 1972 Strategic Arms Limitation Agreement (SALT I), which set limits on the number of offensive weapons the United States and the Soviet Union could produce and restricted each country's antiballistic missile defense system. In 1975, thirty-five nations including the United States and the USSR signed the Helsinki Agreements, a set of international accords that legitimized the post–World War II boundaries in Europe and also committed the signatories to honor their citizens' human rights and to expand cultural and trade relations.

Detente, however, was short-lived. In the West, numerous critics attacked detente as little more than thinly veiled appeasement. Their criticism appeared well founded when the USSR cracked down on Soviet dissidents despite a pledge at Helsinki to respect human rights, and expanded its military might at an alarming rate. When the Soviets invaded Afghanistan in December 1979 and crushed the independent trade union Solidarity in Poland two years later, detente was dead. In 1980 Ronald Reagan, a strident anticommunist, was elected U.S. president. Within months of his inauguration, Reagan was publicly denouncing the Soviet Union as an "evil empire." The coldest days of the Cold War had returned.

The Cold War also saw both the United States and the USSR attract and retain clients who frequently served as surrogates for the superpowers. This was particularly true of the Third World, or those countries that emerged from colonialism after the end of World War II. Quite often these clients had nothing to commend themselves to their masters other than a willingness to be bought. More dangerous was the fact that some clients tended to subvert or ignore their master's wishes, pursuing independent and sometimes perilous courses. Many Third World leaders became adept at playing off one superpower against the other in order to further their own aims.

In 1985 Mikhail Gorbachev came to power in the Soviet Union and, unexpectedly, the Cold War began to wind down. Realizing that the USSR faced massive economic problems, Gorbachev initiated a policy of reform known by the code words *glasnost* (openness) and *perestroika* (restructuring). He also sought better relations with the West. Real achievements in lessening East-West tensions were soon overshadowed as the reform process within the USSR spun out of control. When the Soviet Union officially disintegrated in December 1991, the Cold War was over.

INTERPRETIVE ESSAY
Thomas Philip Wolf

When World War II ended, optimism prevailed. Allied forces had triumphed over fascism in Japan and Germany, whose brutality, including the near annihilation of European Jewry, shocked the world. The victors agreed to punish the guilty and created an organization to address international problems, a successor to the League of Nations called the United Nations. Nations could now concentrate on creating a better world, one in which Allied promises of prosperity and freedom would be realized. That rosy outlook soon dissolved.

No single factor explains the emergence of the Cold War. In part it was due to Soviet actions; in part it was due to Western, particularly U.S., responses to those actions. Mutual mistrust was a compelling factor. Even before the war ended in the Pacific, signs of a troublesome peace emerged. At the Potsdam Conference the new U.S. president, Harry Truman, and the British prime minister, Clement Attlee, who had recently succeeded Winston Churchill, encountered the demanding and inflexible Soviet head of state, Joseph Stalin. Soviet attitudes, reflected in Stalin's behavior, had diverse roots. Although most Americans were unaware of it, the Soviets endured by far the heaviest losses in the war. Conservative estimates put the Soviet death toll at 20 million. In Soviet eyes, these losses were aggravated by the British and American delay in mounting a second front in Western Europe to alleviate German military pressure on the Soviet Union. Soviet leaders were also skeptical of U.S. intentions since the U.S. government had earlier intervened in the Russian civil war on the side of the anticommunist forces and had refused to grant the USSR diplomatic recognition until 1933. When one adds to these factors traditional Russian paranoia, derived from centuries of invasion by their Western neighbors, it is understandable that the Soviets sought a buffer zone on their western border. Soviet expansionism could also be viewed as a continuation of the historic Russian desire to extend the nation's borders to the Pacific and to control a warm water outlet such as the Bosporus Straits. Another element of Soviet conduct greatly contributed to Western distrust. Communist Party commissars accompanied Soviet armies as they moved west, turning back the German forces. Following Stalin's orders, these commissars established regimes abjectly subservient to Moscow.

Largely ignorant of Russian history and Soviet sacrifices during the war, most Americans attributed Soviet expansionism to a worldwide communist conspiracy rather than Russian nationalism. Although West Europeans were less convinced of the conspiracy interpretation, in the aftermath of the war they had little choice but to accept American leadership. Nevertheless, the conspiracy view had merit. In addition to territory they had directly conquered, in Eastern Europe the Soviets used the threat of military intervention to compel noncommunist leaders to yield to indigenous communists. They also sought an enhanced presence in Western Europe and in the Far East, where they had played only a minor role in the war effort, and they aided communist movements seeking to gain control by force, as in China. Soviet propaganda, disseminated worldwide by radio and print, heightened Western suspicions and reinforced the West's belief in the existence of an international communist conspiracy.

How should the United States respond to this situation? If it followed the precedent of the 1920s, it would promptly disarm and disengage from Europe. Initially it demobilized much of its military capacity and turned inward, but soon a policy known as containment evolved.

President Truman, a student of history, was acutely sensitive not only to the transgressions of recent dictators but also to others over the centuries. For his generation, the primary lesson of World War II was that it could have been prevented if the democracies had opposed Hitler sooner. In particular, the outcome of the 1938 Munich Conference was widely accepted as reason for democratic nations to defend their collective security. Many concluded that at the end of World War II one expansionist totalitarian foe had been replaced by another, and Truman saw no choice but to oppose this new threat. Moreover, the weapons developed during the war, notably the atomic bomb, were so destructive that the United States could not wait until future hostilities began to rearm. To do so would ensure defeat.

Truman's secretaries of state, General George C. Marshall and Dean Acheson, concurred in his assessment. With their economies in disrepair, Western European nations needed American economic aid if they were to resist the communist threat. And, along with many American businessmen, the Truman administration concluded that the nation's economy would not prosper unless world markets, particularly in Europe, were revived.

Especially in Europe, the Cold War fomented espionage and counter-espionage on a large scale. Berlin became a notable site for these activities. The United States created its first peacetime intelligence agency, the Central Intelligence Agency (CIA), a successor to the wartime Office of Strategic Services (OSS). The need for this apparatus was confirmed by the defections to the Soviet Union of Guy Burgess and Donald Maclean, British foreign office officials and longtime spies for the Soviets.

Soviet espionage agencies produced more comprehensive information than did their Western counterparts since Soviet agents operated in open societies in which information was relatively easy to obtain. Comparable data were off limits to even citizens of the communist nations. Realizing that it lacked full information, the CIA and other Western intelligence entities assumed that the communist nations were more formidable than they actually were. However, if communism endangered the very existence of Western civilization, it behooved the West to err on the side of caution. To do otherwise was irresponsible.

To implement the multifaceted containment policy, Truman had to overstate the magnitude of the Soviet challenge, otherwise the U.S. Congress would not have provided the funds to build and maintain the most expensive military apparatus in the history of the world or to help Western Europe reconstruct its economy. Persuading the American people to approve this policy was more difficult than persuading Congress. It was desirable that public support be created without producing hysteria; yet the public had to be convinced to accept the burdens of world leadership indefinitely. The effort to achieve a balance between avoiding anticommunist paranoia and obtaining long-term commitment was only partially successful. For example, the American public never fully endorsed foreign aid; but the Truman administration adopted that policy, and subsequent presidents continued it.

The specter of Soviet expansion had a marked impact on the American public, whose reaction was often emotional, based as it was on both incomplete facts and faulty assessment of them. Politicians eager to exploit the communist threat also impaired the public's ability to understand the situation.

Anxiety about communism fanned suspicions about Soviet agents infiltrating the U.S. government. That anxiety was used to promote political careers. Republican Congressman Richard Nixon of California grabbed headlines as a member of a congressional committee investigating allegations that a key ex–State Department official was a Soviet spy. In September 1949 the startling announcement that the Soviets had created an atomic bomb deepened concern about the Soviet threat. In 1951 American courts found Julius and Ethel Rosenberg guilty of transmitting nuclear secrets to the Soviets. The Rosenbergs were subsequently executed.

The most prominent politician to play upon American fears of communist infiltration was Republican Senator Joseph McCarthy of Wisconsin. McCarthy and others of his ilk launched a number of congressional investigations. The advent of television magnified the impact of these exercises. Although these hearings were not judicial proceedings, statements by witnesses could be used in subsequent trials, and witnesses could be found in contempt of Congress. With McCarthy encouraging public condemnation of witnesses, the constitutional safeguard of the Fifth Amendment that protects one from self-incrimination was frequently invoked but largely ineffective in persuading the public that a witness was not guilty. Eventually McCarthy overstepped his bounds, and his Senate colleagues censured him in 1954.

Individuals were fired from government agencies, universities, and the entertainment industry. Others were blacklisted or never told why they were dismissed or not hired. Some employers consulted with persons or organizations that maintained lists of persons whose patriotism was deemed questionable. In addition to the U.S. attorney general's list of suspect organizations, others circulated covertly. Generally, the alleged act of disloyalty was membership in an organization in the 1930s or early 1940s when that group was legal and reputable.

Unquestionably Soviet agents were active in the United States, but anticommunist hysteria in the postwar decade exaggerated the actual threat and appeared ready to sacrifice the liberties that distinguish constitutional governments from authoritarian ones. The underlying consequence of McCarthyism, red-baiting, and other emotional responses to "godless communism" was to place in jeopardy the fundamental principles of a free society. In particular, freedom of speech and freedom of association were in danger of being sacrificed to combat communism on the home front. Thus a subtheme of the Cold War was the struggle to avoid diluting constitutional principles while maintaining national security.

Not all Americans accepted the proposition that containment was the proper response to the Soviet Union. Former Vice President Henry A. Wallace headed a Progressive Party in 1948 that urged a less hostile posture toward the USSR, but his candidacy failed badly at the polls. A few scholars, entertainers, and others continued to advocate a moderate approach toward the Soviets, but their view never appealed to more than a small minority in the United States.

Preoccupation with the communist threat dominated presidential election campaigns throughout the next four decades. For example, in the 1960 campaign two prominent issues were the commitment of the United States to protect two islands occupied by Chinese nationalist troops off the shore of mainland China, and John F. Kennedy's charge that there was a "missile gap" in favor of the USSR. After the election, the Kennedy administration announced that it had discovered there was no missile gap, and the offshore islands were never heard of again. The elections of 1960 and 1964 brought Democrats to the White House. Since Republican candidates were generally judged to be more anticommunist than their Democratic opponents, the successful Democrats—John Kennedy and Lyndon Johnson—were determined not to appear weak when confronted with a communist challenge.

Initially, international events seemed to confirm the fear of an imminent communist seizure of the world. A pattern of provocation and reaction developed as illustrated by the 1948 Soviet blockade of Berlin. The Soviets would mount deliberate actions to provoke the Western powers, who in turn would respond without using military force. This scenario was repeated on several occasions, including the East Berlin uprising of 1953 and the Hungarian Revolution of 1956. As long as neither side employed military power against the other, a "cold war," as presidential advisor Bernard Baruch termed it in 1947, existed.

Sometimes the West made the first move in this game of international chess. Six years after the United States initiated the North Atlantic Treaty Organization (NATO), the Soviet bloc nations created its mirror image in the Warsaw Pact. The Soviet response to the Marshall Plan was the Council for Mutual Economic Assistance (Comecon), an organization originally composed of the USSR and five other communist nations within the Soviet sphere whose economies were dominated by Moscow.

Diplomatically, one side would offer a proposal and the other side would make a counterproposal. The communists offered the Rapacki Plan to create a weapons-free zone in Europe, while President Dwight D. Eisenhower suggested an "open skies" policy whereby each side would permit a limited number of flights over its sovereign territories to ensure that no sneak attack was being prepared. Western objections torpedoed the Rapacki Plan, and the Soviet Union rejected "open skies."

Domestic pressure dictated that the United States deny the existence, at least diplomatically, of some communist governments. For the most devoted anticommunists, any normal contact with communist regimes was immoral. This explains the U.S. policy toward the People's Republic of China for nearly a quarter of a century. Influenced by outspoken members of Congress who were unstinting in their support of the deposed Generalissimo Chiang Kai-shek, the United States refused to extend diplomatic recognition to the world's most populous nation. Critics of the Truman administration claimed that it had "lost China," which presumed that somehow the United States possessed, or at least could control, that nation until it fell to the communists. The Soviets also used the nonrecognition tactic, for instance with Israel and the Republic of South Africa.

Why didn't the Cold War continue as it had under Truman and Stalin? There were several reasons, the most dramatic being Stalin's death. After that, the Soviet Union showed signs of greater flexibility, both internally and externally. While there was not a steady, even process toward less rigidity, changes occurred that were inconceivable under Stalin.

Among the more notable events were Nikita Khrushchev's denunciation of Stalin at the Twentieth Congress of the Communist Party of the Soviet Union (1956), the release of *The New Class* by the Yugoslav Milovan Djilas, in which he claimed that communism had merely replaced one exploitive group with another (1957), and the writings of Boris Pasternak, Alexander Solzhenitsyn, and Yevgeny Yevtushenko, dissidents who publicly criticized the Soviet hard line. In contrast to Stalinist practice, none of these Russian authors was imprisoned or executed for his publications.

Cultural and diplomatic exchanges also brought warmer relations. In 1959 the visit of Vice President Richard Nixon to the USSR and Khrushchev's tour of the United States mitigated the view of the superpowers as ogres. The rhetoric was still inflammatory, but threats to break diplomatic ties or declare war disappeared. In the arts and athletics, personal interactions increased awareness on each side of the other's lifestyle and created lasting friendships.

Gradually, the United States perceived that some communist states did not take orders from Moscow. Yugoslavia, Albania, and, most important, China demonstrated their independence of Soviet directives. And there were other signs, although not as clear-cut, that the Iron Curtain nations did not agree on all issues. After 1968, the communist parties of Western Europe tended to move away from Moscow, a development called Eurocommunism.

American leaders saw the cost of the arms race escalating. President Eisenhower responded by placing greater reliance on nuclear weapons than conventional military forces, a strategy that required developing more powerful bombs and long-range delivery systems. However, weapons research also created new health hazards, which led to Soviet-U.S. treaties to control that danger. Eventually, both sides admitted the impracticality of nuclear war and sought ways to avoid either accidental or intentional hostilities.

The economic impact of the Cold War was considerable. For four decades, the United States was locked in an arms race that challenged its economic vitality but also provided many jobs in the military, in defense industries, and in research activities at universities and think tanks. Major contractors such as Boeing, Martin-Marietta, General Electric, and General Motors were awarded defense contracts on a "cost plus fixed profit" basis, which meant that those firms could not lose money. They were assured of a profit even if contract costs ran over budget, as they often did. One could contend that the Cold War justified a kind of welfare system for American industry, including smaller enterprises that received subcontracts from major corporations.

American communities vied with one another to be the sites of defense plants and military bases. Military installations brought employment, not only on site, but in the surrounding communities that provided services and goods for military personnel. Public schools near military bases were

awarded federal funds to cover the additional costs of teaching the children of military personnel. The total indirect economic benefits of wartime readiness were diffuse and difficult to track, but significant.

Universities, especially major ones, received billions of federal government dollars to conduct research across a vast spectrum of topics. Independent research institutes appeared as well. The upshot was an
expansion of higher education and intellectual activity to an unprecedented level.

The 1957 Soviet launch of the first space satellite, Sputnik, shocked the
United States, which until then believed that Soviet technological break-
throughs resulted from stealing the West's secrets; however, Sputnik
could not be explained thus, since the free world did not yet have the
ability to put objects into space. The United States now regrouped to put
greater emphasis on science and engineering, but the passage of the National Defense Education Act provided support for college students in
other fields as well.

Sputnik had profound military implications. If a satellite could orbit
the earth, it could be used for global reconnaissance. More important, it
could deliver bombs from long distances. This prospect stirred American
presidents to shift space and missile research into high gear, culminating
in the moon landing of 1969.

Although the prospect of nuclear war was ominous, not everyone
thought it was hopeless. Henry Kissinger, a Harvard political scientist,
contended in his book *Nuclear Weapons and Foreign Policy* that nuclear
warfare, at least on a limited scale, was not unthinkable but rational.
Meanwhile, American school children learned drills to follow in case of
nuclear attack, and in the early 1960s civil defense preparations expanded.

At first glance, this response seemed reasonable, but it came to reflect
a profound misunderstanding of the key security link between the two
superpowers: Mutual Assured Destruction (MAD). MAD assumed that
a nuclear attack by either the United States or the USSR would result in
a response that would leave both nations destroyed. U.S. civil defense
measures, and community shelters such as subways in the USSR, were
potential abrogations of MAD. Even more significant was President Ronald Reagan's Strategic Defense Initiative ("Star Wars"). If one side could
perfect a foolproof defense, it could then attack the other without for-
feiting its own safety.

The Cold War mentality tended to impose misleading interpretations
on events. Three examples illustrate this proclivity to misinterpret and
oversimplify. First is the charge that at the February 1945 Yalta Confer-

ence Franklin Roosevelt gave Eastern Europe to the Soviets. Actually, the USSR had conquered that territory as it repelled the German military. Only by employing comparable force, a clearly unacceptable option, could the United States dislodge the Soviets.

A second case is the Korean War. For Americans, that war, although unpopular, demonstrated that military might could halt communist aggression. It also reinforced the view of an international communist conspiracy. This reasoning ignored three fundamental factors: first, that independent of communist ideology, China could not tolerate hostile military forces on its border; second, that East Asia was the obvious primary sphere of influence for China, the largest and most dominant Asian nation for centuries; and third, that many Asians saw the U.S. military in the Far East as another instance of Western imperialism, justifying China's armed response.

Similarly, construction of the Berlin Wall in 1961, separating West Berlin from East Berlin, was widely condemned in the West as a cruel provocation. For East Germany, the Wall stopped the loss of scientists and engineers, who were fleeing through West Berlin by the thousands. While the Wall was a personal tragedy for many, it halted the "brain drain" from East Germany and stabilized that country. The most highly educated and ambitious East Germans now had to make the best of life in that country.

Without the cooperation of governments in Western Europe, American efforts to make that region a bulwark against communism would fail. Support for U.S. policy was diverse. The British Labour Party, despite a faltering economy and a tradition of pacifism until 1939, committed itself to the burden of rearmament under the forceful leadership of Foreign Secretary Ernest Bevin. Robert Schuman, a frequent member of France's coalition cabinets, was a preeminent spokesman for European integration, an explicit principle of U.S. economic aid. Chancellor Konrad Adenauer of West Germany was a fervent anticommunist and devotee of the multinational response to the Soviet threat.

Adenauer, a devout Catholic, was also a leading figure in Europe's Christian Democracy, which was staunchly anticommunist. In France, Christian Democracy was represented first by the Popular Republicans (MRP), a fixture in the cabinets of the Fourth Republic, and later by the Gaullists. Italy's Christian Democrats were automatic cabinet leaders for five decades. Paradoxically, Italy and France, the most Catholic nations in Western Europe, also had the two largest communist parties in the free world.

While the initial focus of the Cold War was Europe, it assumed global dimensions, spreading to Latin America, the Middle East, and, most violently, Asia. Both blocs—that led by the Soviets and that led by the Americans—sought to create alliances with Third World nations and to subvert those friendly to the other side.

Cold War considerations drove the global policies of both the United States and the Soviet Union. For many years, the United States regarded any nation not critical of the Soviets as unfriendly, and saw any nation, no matter how corrupt, that was anticommunist as deserving of American favor. The Soviet views were the mirror opposite of these. As a result, both Soviet and U.S. foreign aid often had a greater military component than an economic one, as the protagonists worked to keep their clients in power. Arms sales became a major offshoot of the Cold War. The two superpowers became the major purveyors of arms worldwide, sales that were supplemented by those of their respective allies such as Czechoslovakia and France.

If deemed necessary, the United States used direct military power to intervene in Third World nations that appeared to be succumbing to Marxism. At other times the CIA orchestrated the overthrow of popularly endorsed governments, as it did in Iran and Guatemala in the 1950s and in Chile in the 1970s.

The United Nations, intended to be a forum for resolving international problems, became another Cold War arena. The United States and the Soviet Union were at odds on nearly every major issue. Ordinarily, each labored diligently to line up backers, especially in the General Assembly. Early on, the United States had the upper hand, but gradually, as more Third World nations joined, the membership majority assumed a more independent posture, reflecting its detachment from the Great Power struggle and its concentration on issues of direct concern to its members.

The drive for self-determination within the Cold War context presented the United States, and often Great Britain and France, with a dilemma. How could these governments that proclaimed popular sovereignty oppose independence? But the Soviets and Chinese supported Third World independence movements. Whether in Africa, Asia, or Latin America, the typical leaders of independence movements were labeled communists, and in fact often received aid from communist regimes. U.S. administrations were reluctant to endorse independence movements since strident anticommunist domestic foes would condemn this.

In Vietnam, the twin forces of containment and anticolonialism clashed. Why did containment fail in Southeast Asia? Unlike Europe and Korea, the anticommunist regime in Vietnam did not maintain popular backing. Its cruelty and corruption were compounded by the fact that its members were largely Catholic in a society that was overwhelmingly Buddhist. For the first time, television brought the brutality of warfare into American homes daily. European allies that endorsed U.S. policy confronted vocal domestic opposition. Young American adults increasingly opposed the war. The Vietnam struggle also underscored the American public's reluctance to support containment indefinitely if that involved heavy loss of American lives.

By the late 1950s, Western Europe was reassessing its Cold War posture for several reasons. First, Soviet nuclear warheads could readily reach European targets, but were not a direct threat to the United States. This proximate danger became a concern for Western Europe. Second, while they had no choice in the late 1940s but to follow American leadership, their economies were now strong enough to permit more independence from the United States. Third, by the 1960s, young adults in Europe had little memory of World War II and the birth of the Cold War. Those events were remote for them, but the prospect of military service and televised reports from Southeast Asia were not.

In Britain, efforts to modify U.S. policy arose from the left and the right. The members of a grass-roots movement, the Campaign for Nuclear Disarmament (CND), would rather "be Red than dead," preferring unilateral disarmament. This issue split the Labour Party for decades. Even British politicians committed to American leadership sought to mediate between the two superpowers. Prime Minister Harold Macmillan worked for years to arrange a summit conference, but met with failure when the 1960 Paris conference was canceled in the aftermath of the downed American U-2 spy flight over Soviet territory.

Reaction to the Vietnam War brought sit-ins, demonstrations, and bombings across Western Europe. These movements were joined to other causes that threatened the stability of democratic governments, notably the May 1968 student demonstrations in France.

Independence from American leadership in the Cold War was also manifested by European statesmen, particularly Charles de Gaulle. As France's president, he endorsed the American position on the U-2 overflights, but later pulled all French forces from NATO and frequently criticized U.S. policy in Southeast Asia.

It is easy to forget that even in its early years containment was flexible. For example, despite the common view of communism as an international monolith, the United States aided Yugoslavia in 1948 so that that state could remain beyond the Soviet orbit. Yet for many, especially in the United States, the Cold War simplified the world. The "good guys," the United States and its allies, confronted the "bad guys," the Soviets and their "stooges," both foreign and domestic. However, this vision became increasingly obsolete. Of many examples, one stands out: Richard Nixon's 1972 visit to China. This U.S. president, who had made his reputation as a relentless foe of communism, added de facto recognition of Red China to his previous approval of grain sales to the Soviet Union. Perhaps his China visit was motivated partially by reelection considerations, but it was the key step in abandoning the myth that Chiang Kai-shek's Taiwan represented China.

The Cold War ended unexpectedly. Two structural factors hastened the collapse of the Soviet Union. One was heavy Soviet expenditures for national defense, which drew massive resources away from the consumer sector. According to one estimate for the mid-1980s, the Soviets were allocating 15 percent of their gross domestic product to military purposes, and about 2 percent of their work force was under arms, as compared to U.S. figures of 7 percent and 1 percent, respectively. A second factor was the increased awareness of the relative opulence of noncommunist nations. Much of this perception filtered through East Germany and other Iron Curtain nations that received television broadcasts from West Germany. This broadcasting, which was not part of any special Western propaganda effort but, rather the same fare that Europeans received, expanded in the 1980s as efforts to jam those broadcasts decreased.

As important as these factors were, they probably would have been insufficient to end the Cold War had the Soviet leadership continued in its Stalinist pattern. Certainly, the Soviet economy was no worse than in 1945–1946. The crucial figure was Mikhail Gorbachev. With more formal education than his predecessors, he represented a new generation seeking to free the Soviet people from the economic stagnation generated by an inefficient system of production and distribution, as well as inordinate defense expenditures. Putting his supporters in key posts, Gorbachev transformed the top levels of Soviet decision making while reassuring the West that his changes were genuine. By the late 1980s, his power was slipping, having miscalculated the impact of the trends he had unleashed. Before he was pushed aside, however, he pressured the governments of Eastern Europe to moderate their oppressive rule. The most dramatic event occurred when East Germany opened the Berlin Wall, an act that symbolically marked the end of the Cold War.

For the United States, the Cold War had extensive consequences. Reaction to the Vietnam War, especially antiwar demonstrations, tore at the very fabric of American society, while the more general threat of confrontation with the Soviet Union justified a larger and more intrusive role for the government. The Cold War also had a marked economic effect. From 1965 to 1990, U.S. Department of Defense expenditures totaled 5 to 8 percent of gross national product, with the military establishment employing a similar portion of the labor force. In the mid-1980s, more than 30,000 companies were involved in military production. Combined with the challenge presented by such international competitors as Japan, the United States faced a wrenching adjustment of its economy as it drew down its Cold War arsenal.

Some results of the Cold War must be speculative. Without it, it is highly unlikely that the United States would have been as devoted to rebuilding the German and Japanese economies. It probably would have adopted a more self-interested, isolationist posture, as it did after World War I. It is also unlikely that the United States and the Soviet Union would have pursued space research as actively as they did, and without the emphasis on space it is inconceivable that its scientific offshoots, such as miniaturization, would have been achieved as quickly. Even with the Cold War, once the moon landing was accomplished the American public showed declining interest in financing space programs.

The Cold War's impact on Europe is also speculative. One might assume that the Christian Democrats' doctrinaire anticommunism enabled them to dominate some Western European governments for decades. Undoubtedly the Cold War greatly enhanced U.S. influence in Western Europe. It also generated a sense of urgency among Western Europeans that otherwise they might not have felt, and this sense of urgency furthered the cause of European unification.

What is certain is that the end of the Soviet-U.S. struggle left a far more fragmented, complex world than that which had prevailed for nearly half a century. The breakup of the Soviet empire and its collateral nations, such as Yugoslavia, unleashed nationalistic aspirations that communist leaders had suppressed. Of course, these efforts to combine ethnic identity with national sovereignty probably would have erupted decades before if not suppressed by communist rule.

Despite decades of indoctrination, ideology retained little importance in the former Iron Curtain regimes. Nationalism held a higher priority than ideology, as it did in noncommunist nations. Arguably, anticommunist ideology in the United States proved more durable than Marxist-Leninist instruction in the European communist regimes.

As much as anything, the Cold War suggests the primacy of leadership. Stalin and Truman in the 1940s and Gorbachev later shaped the world to fit their vision. Differences in governmental institutions are important, but individuals can have a monumental impact, as the career of F. W. de Klerk in South Africa demonstrates.

With the end of the Cold War there will be many postmortems, but it is evident that despite some setbacks, containment was effective in defeating the communist challenge. It did not, of course, resolve the underlying problems that have beset mankind throughout history: hunger, disease, poverty, and ethnic animosity.

SELECTED BIBLIOGRAPHY

Beschloss, Michael R., and Stuart Talbott. *At the Highest Levels: The Inside Story of the End of the Cold War.* Boston: Little, Brown, 1993. This work traces the final days of the Cold War.

Brinkley, Douglas. *Dean Acheson: The Cold War Years, 1953–1971.* New Haven: Yale University Press, 1993. This documents the persistence of an architect of the containment policy.

Calvocoressi, Peter. *World Politics since 1945.* 6th ed. London: Longman, 1991. First published in 1968, this book examines the Cold War struggle and its impact in five regions of the world.

Feis, Herbert. *From Trust to Terror: The Onset of the Cold War, 1945–1950.* New York: W. W. Norton, 1970. Close examination of this period, with a useful listing of prominent participants in key events.

Gaddis, John Lewis. *The Long Peace: Inquiries into the History of the Cold War.* New York: Oxford University Press, 1987. Eight essays that explore different dimensions of the Cold War.

Graebner, Norman A., ed. *The Cold War: A Conflict of Ideology and Power.* 2nd ed. Lexington, MA: D. C. Heath, 1976. Fifteen essays, by both supporters and foes of U.S. policy.

Hyland, William G. *The Cold War: Fifty Years of Conflict.* Originally published as *The Cold War Is Over.* New York: Random House, 1991. The author argues that the Cold War began with the Molotov-Ribbentrop Nonaggression Pact of 1939.

Isaacson, Walter, and Evan Thomas. *The Wise Men: Six Friends and the World They Made.* New York: Simon and Schuster, 1986. Detailed account of the backgrounds and roles of several American officials who fashioned post–World War II U.S. foreign and defense policy.

Kofsky, Frank. *Harry S. Truman and the War Scare of 1948: A Successful Campaign to Deceive the Nation.* New York: St. Martin's Press, 1993. A negative assessment of Truman, George C. Marshall, and others who advocated a strong military posture toward the USSR.

LaFeber, Walter. *America, Russia, and the Cold War, 1945–1990.* 6th ed. New York: McGraw-Hill, 1991. This is a standard treatment of the key events in the Cold War.

Lukacs, John. *A New History of the Cold War.* 3rd ed. Garden City, NY: Doubleday, 1966. Useful account of the first twenty years of the Cold War and its origins.

Maddox, Robert James. *The New Left and the Origins of the Cold War.* Princeton: Princeton University Press, 1974. Seven prominent scholarly dissenters critique American Cold War policy.

Maier, Charles S., ed. *The Cold War in Europe: Era of a Divided Continent.* Rev. ed. Princeton: Markus Weiner, 1993. Set of essays addressing the major issues and figures in the Cold War.

May, Ernest R., ed. *American Cold War Strategy: Interpreting NSC 68.* New York: Bedford Books, 1993. Includes the text of the document that formally stated U.S. containment policy.

McClellan, David S. *The Cold War in Transition.* New York: Macmillan, 1966. An analytic rather than historical examination that notes the dilemma that military intervention in Southeast Asia presented to the United States.

Purifoy, Lewis McCarroll. *Harry Truman's China Policy: McCarthyism and the Diplomacy of Hysteria, 1947–1951.* New York: Franklin Watts, 1976. Critical of U.S. policy in the Far East, this book blames McCarthyism for those errors.

Rees, David. *The Age of Containment: The Cold War, 1945–1965.* New York: St. Martin's Press, 1968. A British scholar looks at the Cold War from the differing perspectives of U.S. containment and Marxist support of revolutionary efforts around the world.

Spanier, John W. *American Foreign Policy since WWII.* 11th ed. Washington: Congressional Quarterly Press, 1988. An excellent synthesis of events, motives, and forces in the Cold War years.

Thompson, Kenneth W. *Cold War Theories.* Vol. 1: *World Polarization, 1943–1953.* Baton Rouge: Louisiana State University Press, 1981. This is an excellent examination and commentary on the background and early years of the Cold War.

———. *Interpreters and Critics of the Cold War.* Washington, DC: University Press of America, 1978. Examines the views of Reinhold Neibuhr, Hans Morgenthau, George Kennan, Walter Lippmann, and others.

Young, John W. *The Longman Companion to Cold War and Detente, 1941–1991.* London: Longman, 1993. Detailed chronology, brief biographies of major figures, and an extensive bibliography are features of this reference source.

Chou En-lai, Liu Shao-chi, and Mao Zedong at the Peking airport in March 1964. Mao's victory in the Chinese civil war brought the world's most populous nation under communist control. (Reproduced from the Collections of the Library of Congress)

7

The Chinese Revolution, 1911–1949

INTRODUCTION

China, the world's most populous country, has spent much of the twentieth century in a state of almost continual revolutionary upheaval. The origins of China's turmoil date to the nineteenth century, when the antiquated Chinese Empire came under relentless pressure from a technologically more advanced Western world. These pressures eventually shattered the Chinese status quo and ushered in the era of revolution.

By 1839 the Qing dynasty had ruled China for almost 300 years. However, it had grown old and brittle, and in the nineteenth century it showed clear signs of exhaustion. The Qing faced increasing discontent, manifesting itself in open rebellions that the rulers had difficulty repressing. Even more ominous for the Qing, aggressive European states had turned their attention to China.

In 1839 China and Great Britain went to war over the issue of free trade. Great Britain demanded that China accommodate British trading interests, especially the continued importation into China of opium from India. When the Chinese refused, war broke out. This First Opium War ended in 1842 with the Treaty of Nanjing, but it was soon followed by a Second Opium War that ended in 1858 with the Treaty of Tianjin. In both conflicts the Europeans (France had joined Great Britain in the Second Opium War) administered humiliating defeats to the Chinese. The result of the European victories was the so-called treaty system, a series of agreements that reduced Chinese sovereignty and extended to the Europeans and Americans special privileges such as extraterritoriality, a quasi-legal device that exempted foreigners in China from Chinese legal jurisdiction. The message of China's weakness was driven home in 1860 when an Anglo-French expedition marched to Beijing, the Chinese capital, and burned the emperor's summer palace to the ground.

Simultaneously, the Qing faced a major domestic crisis. The Taiping Rebellion began in 1850 and dragged on for fourteen years. It drained the central government of what meager resources it possessed and contributed greatly to the breakdown of central authority. It was only with the help of foreigners that the Qing ended the Taiping Rebellion, but the dynasty now found itself more beholden to those foreigners than ever before, while at home its authority in many regions had virtually disappeared.

Taking advantage of China's weakness, other powers enriched themselves at its expense. For example, Great Britain claimed Hong Kong, France encroached in what was to become French Indochina, and in 1860 Russia forced China to surrender its claims to the lands north of the Amur River and east of the Ussuri River. This huge area became Russia's Maritime province, where the Russians then founded the city of Vladivostok.

During the latter part of the nineteenth century, the Qing grip on power continued to weaken. Toward the end of the century, the dynasty experimented with reform in an effort to revitalize its decrepit state. Copying their Japanese neighbors (whom they despised), the Chinese hoped to foster both Western technology and efficiency in order to defeat those very same Westerners and to restore Chinese pride and sovereignty. While these efforts never really got off the ground, they did alarm the imperialists, who feared that a revived China would thwart their ambitions. The result was a wild scramble for control over bits and pieces of China.

War with Japan in 1894–1895 ended in yet another humiliating defeat for the Chinese, all the more galling this time because of their hatred of the Japanese and the fact that Japan, an Oriental state, had successfully copied the Western model in order to defeat China, another Oriental state. Although Japan was forced to relinquish many of its gains from the 1895 Treaty of Shimonoseki that ended the war, the defeat revealed China's utter helplessness. In a short time, Germany, Russia, France, and

Great Britain staked out claims for themselves on China's prosperous east coast.

In their rush to fill the vacuum created by China's disintegration, the imperial powers sometimes collided with each other. The most spectacular collision resulted in the Russo-Japanese War of 1904–1905. The Japanese were victorious once again, and Japan's sphere of influence in East Asia expanded accordingly; however, Japan's victory held additional significance. For the first time in modern history, a nonwhite country had defeated a major European state. This event's significance was not lost on the other victims of European imperialism, including China. While these victims condemned Japan's imitation of European imperialism, they could not help but notice that Japan had made itself a formidable power by copying the West.

Among educated Chinese, the spectacle of their proud empire being devoured piecemeal intensified their desire for change. Not only did they passionately hate the imperialists, they also despised the Qing dynasty, which they viewed as either incompetent or traitorous or a combination of both. Secret societies proliferated and, in the case of the Boxers, launched deadly attacks on foreigners that prompted only further Western intervention in China.

In 1911 the dam of pent-up frustration burst. Revolution broke out and the Qing dynasty was quickly overthrown. Dr. Sun Yat-sen, a leading opponent of the old regime, proclaimed a Chinese Republic. However, the revolution was only a partial success. Although the Qing had been toppled, a stable national government did not emerge. Sun's republic was stillborn, and the country plunged into acute anarchy characterized by the rise of warlords, individuals who commanded military detachments and who ruled in regions or provinces without any recourse to a national government. Eventually, a nominal government formed in the north at Peking while Sun remained strong in the south; but in fact central authority had disappeared, and the bulk of China was dominated by freebooting warlords.

In January 1915, Japan took advantage of Western preoccupation with World War I to expand its influence in China once again. Japan presented to the Peking government its Twenty-One Demands, a set of proposals that would have given Japan even greater sway over China's land and commerce than it already enjoyed. China at first resisted these demands, receiving support from the United States, which sought to safeguard its own interests. However, China eventually acquiesced to most of what Japan wanted, and Japan replaced Germany as the dominant foreign power in Shandong province and gained virtual control over Manchuria.

In 1917 China entered World War I on the side of the Allies. As was the case with many other exploited peoples, Chinese intellectuals were stirred by the ideals and ideas of U.S. president Woodrow Wilson, and they looked forward to the Paris Peace Conference with great anticipation in the hopes of ending the treaty system and regaining full sovereignty. However, their hopes were shattered when the Paris conferees ignored China and instead confirmed Japan in its possession of Germany's former concession at Shandong, thereby validating Japan's increasing domination of China.

The shabby treatment accorded the Chinese gave rise to the May 4th Movement—named for the date in 1919 of the first of many demonstrations against the decisions of the Paris Peace Conference. The May 4th Movement galvanized the country; Chinese from all walks of life protested against foreign, but especially Japanese, interference in China. They pledged themselves to a course of revitalization and national unity. So significant was the May 4th Movement that noted historian Theodore Von Laue refers to it as "the first stirring of patriotic mass politics in China."

In the course of the 1911 Revolution and the turmoil that followed, Sun Yat-sen, who strongly supported the May 4th Movement, emerged as the most important Chinese leader. Although Sun's movement, the Kuomintang (KMT) or Chinese nationalists, failed to supplant the Qing dynasty, he worked to extend its authority from its stronghold in the south and to bring the entire country under KMT control. Sun saw this as a first step toward achieving his twin goals of modernizing China and terminating all special privileges for foreigners. Sun's prescription for China's success was spelled out in his most important writing, *The Three People's Principles*.

Disappointed by China's treatment at the Paris Peace Conference, Sun turned to the new Marxist state in Russia. Lenin and the Bolsheviks were only too happy to encourage Sun, if for no other reason than to strike a blow at their capitalist enemies. Early in the 1920s, the Soviets began to send equipment and advisors to Sun. The Soviet advisors did a particularly good job of reorganizing the Kuomintang, turning it into an effective political force, and establishing a credible army capable of launching a military offensive. Furthermore, the ranks of the nationalists were augmented in 1923 when the tiny Chinese Communist Party, founded two years earlier, allied itself with the KMT under pressure from the Soviet-dominated Communist International, or Comintern.

In 1925 Sun Yat-sen died. He was succeeded as head of the Kuomintang by Chiang Kai-shek, a young general who had received training in the Soviet Union. Chiang resumed the Northern Expedition, a military and political offensive designed to unify the nation and to bring all China under Kuomintang rule. In 1927, in the middle of this successful campaign, Chiang, who was considerably more conservative than Sun, unexpectedly turned on his communist allies and massacred them. What was left of the Chinese Communist Party retreated to a remote area of southern China, where it tried to reconstitute itself. Meanwhile, in 1928 Chiang occupied Peking and declared the KMT to be the official government of a unified and sovereign Chinese state. While the KMT was clearly the strongest Chinese force, its authority in many regions remained nominal at best. Warlords and renegades continued to enjoy considerable strength.

Chiang's success alarmed an increasingly militaristic Japan, which wanted a weak and pliable China and feared that the KMT success would undermine its position. In 1931 Japan began to tighten its grip over the important province of Manchuria. In the following year, despite Chinese protests, Japan converted Manchuria into Manchukuo, a Japanese puppet state. For the next several years, Japan systematically bullied China; then, in 1937, it launched a full-scale invasion. Chiang and the increasingly corrupt nationalists put up ineffective resistance, and Japan overran much of eastern China. In response, Chiang moved his capital inland to the distant city of Chongqing.

Throughout the 1930s, as Japan devoured China, Chiang and the KMT continued to battle the Chinese communists. The communists, having regrouped in southern Jiangxi province after Chiang initially turned on them, in 1931 proclaimed the "Chinese Soviet Republic." However, despite some initial military success, they were too weak to ward off the nationalists, who attacked relentlessly. Finally, in October 1934, a rag-tag band of communists took flight to avoid annihilation. This was the start of the legendary Long March, a journey of some 6,000 miles undertaken by perhaps 100,000 hard-core communists that lasted more than a year. During the course of the Long March, Mao Zedong, a former teacher and librarian, outmaneuvered his rivals to emerge as the leading figure of Chinese communism, a position he held until his death in 1976. When the fleeing communists finally came to rest in the caves of Yenan in northwestern China's remote Shaanxi province, only a handful of the original marchers remained.

In 1937 the nationalists and the communists formed a united front to oppose the Japanese. But this was an artificial concoction, and it soon fell apart. For the rest of World War II, the nationalists and communists spent as much time competing against each other as they did fighting the Japanese. Consequently, after the deaths of perhaps 2.2 million Chinese during World War II and the surrender of Japan in 1945, it was not surprising that civil war engulfed China. Despite significant aid from the United States, the KMT was defeated by the communists, who received considerably less aid and encouragement from the Soviet Union. On October 1, 1949, having driven Chiang and his forces from the mainland onto the offshore island of Taiwan, Mao Zedong and the communists proclaimed the People's Republic of China (PRC) with its capital at Beijing.

However, revolution in China did not end with the communist victory. Rather, during the past several decades the communists themselves have initiated a number of revolutionary programs. Some, such as the Great Leap Forward and the Cultural Revolution, have failed ignominiously; others, such as the economic reforms of Deng Xiaoping, Mao's successor, have shown great promise. In any event, all these programs represent a radical departure from Chinese tradition. Equally important, they have been carried out in a China free from foreign domination. No one today questions that China is both a unified and sovereign state.

INTERPRETIVE ESSAY
Jeffrey N. Wasserstrom

Throughout most of this century, the words "China" and "revolution" have been closely linked in the American mind. From the Wuchang Uprising of 1911 that led to Sun Yat-sen's inauguration as the first president of a Chinese Republic, to the protest movement that broke out in Beijing and other cities in 1989, the Chinese events that have made headlines in the West have often been revolutionary struggles. The relatively few Chinese names Americans have come to know during this century have typically been those of revolutionary leaders. And when American pundits have discussed China's international position in recent decades, they have often highlighted the tendency of revolutionary groups in other developing nations (ranging from Vietnam to Peru) to look to the Chinese Communist Party (CCP) for inspiration and practical assistance. Over the course of the twentieth century, in sum, we have grown accustomed to thinking of China as a country in flux, a land of revolutions.

A century and a half ago, the Western view of East Asia's largest nation was very different indeed. Foreign observers of that time typically portrayed China as a once great country that had proved unable to keep pace with the modern world, a "changeless" land whose state ideology of Confucianism inhibited all forms of social evolution. The Chinese government's efforts to circumscribe the actions of Western traders and missionaries were dismissed as a despotic regime's futile efforts to block the natural course of "progress," and Western military victories in the Opium Wars of the 1830s through the 1860s were hailed as proof of the inferiority of Confucian beliefs and practices.

One explanation for China's inability to compete with the West was that the Chinese had gone for millennia without participating in a "revolution" worthy of the name. Some Westerners insisted that China's lack of revolutionary potential was at the root of its problems. One thing that nineteenth-century foreign observers found particularly striking about the stability of China's imperial system was its perviousness to invasion as well as domestic rebellion. The Chinese historical record contained several examples of dynasties falling to armies that had come from beyond the nation's borders and been led by people who were not members of the Han ethnic group to which most people within China proper belong. It seemed, however, that even in these cases, the political status quo remained fundamentally unchanged. The case of the Qing dynasty (1644–1912) was often cited to illustrate this point.

Most China specialists now agree that nineteenth-century writers overstated the extent to which foreign dynasties adopted Chinese ways after taking power, and had a tendency to go too far in contrasting the supposed stagnation of imperial China with the alleged dynamism of the industrializing West. There is good reason to think that, despite their adoption of Confucian principles and trappings, Manchu emperors of the Qing ruled the country in a significantly different way than many of their Han predecessors. There is also evidence that patterns of social and diplomatic relations were in a state of flux throughout the final centuries of imperial rule, as merchants began to gain power in certain regions and officials in frontier areas experimented with new strategies for dealing with the rulers of neighboring states. Finally, and probably most significantly, demographic changes of enormous proportions were taking place during the century proceeding the First Opium War. Even by the most conservative estimates, the Chinese population doubled during this period, from roughly 200 million to about 400 million. This demographic explosion was both the result and the cause of a whole range of economic, technological, cultural, and political changes.

This said, it remains true that while a series of new dynasties had indeed been founded by rebel leaders during earlier periods, once in power these former insurgents had tended to make only minor adjustments to the basic bureaucratic structure of the state. Chinese philosophers had, moreover, developed a sophisticated political cosmology, centered on the concept of the Tianming (Heavenly Mandate) and a vision of dynastic cycle, that provided justification for rebellious acts (providing only that the emperor against whom one rebelled could be shown to have failed to behave benevolently) but left no room for revolutionary ones.

The concept of the Tianming, as articulated by Confucian philosophers such as Mencius, provided the clearest legitimization for righteous rebellion. The Confucian argument was that no dynasty could come to power without Heaven (Tian) bestowing a special mandate to rule (ming) upon that ruling house, but that the deity remained free to revoke its blessing at any time if the heirs of a founding emperor proved unworthy. In other words, unlike the European notion of the divine right of kings, the Tianming was not granted in perpetuity. Because Mencius claimed that Heaven "sees with the eyes and hears with the ears" of the people, any sign of popular discontent could be interpreted as an indication that the dynasty had lost or was in danger of losing its mandate. The ultimate proof lay in the rebellion's outcome: since Heaven was seen as having the power to determine the fate of human battles, whichever side won on the battlefield was considered the rightful possessor of the Tianming. The notion of dynastic cycles reinforced the motivation to rebel, by implying that no family could expect to retain its mandate forever and that the virtuous founders of new ruling houses played a crucial role in an organic process of decay and rejuvenation.

How did China go from being a land of rebellion to a land of revolutions? Why did the fall of the Qing lead to the founding of a republic rather than the establishment of yet another dynasty? How has China's vision of its own place in the world changed as Confucianism has been replaced by other state ideologies? And does the Chinese word *geming*, which is routinely translated as "revolution" but literally means "stripping of the mandate," have the same connotations as its English-language equivalent? Before attempting to answer these questions, it is worth taking some time to ask a more basic question: Does it make sense to talk about the Chinese Revolution as if it were a single coherent event, or is it more appropriate to think of modern China as having undergone a series of revolutions?

The authors of general surveys of world history and books on the revolutionary process tend to take for granted the idea that the Chinese Revolution is best treated as a single event, which began with the uprisings of 1911 and ended with the founding of the People's Republic in 1949. They typically argue, moreover, that this thirty-eight-year event should be seen as one of the relatively few "Great Revolutions" of modern times, and should be placed in the same category as the considerably shorter revolutions that began in France in 1789 and in Russia in 1917. What is thought to make these and other Great Revolutions unusual is that, far from simply affecting who was in power or even how a country was governed, they also triggered basic transformations in general patterns of social and political life.

Western scholars who specialize in the history of modern China also view the first half of the twentieth century as a time of profound changes, but tend to approach the notion of a Chinese Revolution in a somewhat different fashion. Some Chinese specialists use the term "Chinese Revolution" to refer to a long process of transformation that began in the late Qing and has continued into the communist era. However, other specialists reject the idea of viewing the Chinese Revolution as a single coherent event. Instead of speaking of an uppercase Revolution, these scholars prefer to present China's recent past as a series of interconnected but separable lowercase revolutions.

Similarly, when politicians and historians linked to the CCP and the Nationalist Party (KMT) speak of China's *geming* (which can be translated with equal validity as either its "Revolution" or its "revolutions"), they often have in mind periods that are either much shorter or considerably longer than the standard 1911–1949 time frame. In some contexts, leaders of both parties still refer to the *geming* as a single struggle, which began approximately a century ago and continues to this day. CCP and KMT versions of this Revolution differ from each other markedly in certain ways: most notably, they diverge on the question of whether communist leaders should be seen as heroes or villains. Their viewpoints often converge on key points, however, such as the notion that the Revolution's glorious legacy should be preserved for each new generation of youths, and that these youths have a sacred duty to fight for revolutionary goals that remain unfulfilled.

The CCP and KMT history textbooks written for these youths typically begin by echoing the sentiments described above, but then proceed to divide the last century and a half into several distinctive eras, each of which is described as having been shaped by the outbreak of separate revolutions or revolutionary movements. For obvious reasons, the two types of textbooks differ considerably on countless specific issues relating to interpretation and terminology. Furthermore, both CCP and KMT textbooks offer equally ambiguous answers to the question of whether China's *geming* should be treated as a single long-term quest or a series of separable struggles.

The ongoing debates relating to periodization and definition sketched out above are so important and complex that it would be foolish to attempt to resolve them in a short essay. Rather, it is better simply to draw attention to the strengths and weaknesses of various approaches to the issue, so that readers will be in a better position to make up their own minds. One way to break up Chinese revolutionary history into component parts is to differentiate between a Republican Revolution led by Sun Yat-sen, a Nationalist Revolution led by Chiang Kai-shek, and a Communist Revolution led by Mao Zedong. This self-explanatory schema puts emphasis upon three clear-cut chronological turning points: the birth of the Republic in 1912, the establishment of KMT rule in 1927, and the founding of the PRC in 1949. Implicit in this approach is a vision of the world in which the formal ideologies espoused by political parties and the activities of charismatic leaders are viewed as centrally important. Its great strength is its simplicity, and the attention it draws to the different agendas pursued by key political groups.

A second, more complex way to divide up China's recent past is to think in terms of a series of four revolutions, each of which transformed a different sphere of activity. Because no major event ever affects only one aspect of a nation's life, and because some kinds of revolutions occur rapidly while others unfold gradually over long periods of time, one needs to allow for considerable overlap when distinguishing between, say, a country's "socioeconomic" and "political" revolutions. If this is kept in mind, a potentially useful way to conceptualize China's modern transformation is to differentiate between the *political revolution* that precipitated the transition from imperial to republican institutions; the *intellectual and cultural revolution* whose high point came in the late teens and early twenties; the *diplomatic revolution* that began in the late twenties and peaked in the late 1940s; and the *socioeconomic revolution* that began early in the century but reached national proportions only in the 1950s.

The political revolution is the only one of the four that is easy to link to a specific starting date: October 10, 1911. The Wuchang Uprising, which broke out on that day, was not the first important challenge to the Qing dynasty. Throughout the nineteenth and early twentieth centuries, a wide range of revolts, ranging from large-scale peasant rebellions to attempted coups organized by secret organizations, had threatened Qing rule. None of these efforts was successful, however, until the mutiny at

Wuchang inspired military units and local authorities around the country to issue the declarations of provincial autonomy that undermined the imperial regime's authority and set the stage for the founding of the Republic.

The fact that these actions ultimately brought about the end of the imperial system does not mean that participants in the 1911 Revolution were all committed republicans. Philosophical critiques of the imperial system had appeared in various intellectual journals during the first decade of the century, to be sure, but so had vitriolic polemics deriding the Manchus as "barbarians" who had no right to control the fate of "real" (i.e., Han) Chinese, and appeals to racial pride were at least as important as appeals to republican ideals when it came to inspiring people to take action in 1911.

It is also worth noting that the most skillful political figures of the day, including Sun Yat-sen, were so adept at combining ethnic themes with political ones that it was often hard to tell where the former ended and the latter began. In their writings, the despotic nature of imperial institutions was frequently linked to the alien origins and purported inborn inferiority of the Manchu emperors. At times, the desire for a *geming* was presented as driven by a kind of filial piety toward China's last Han rulers, the last emperors of the Ming dynasty. This meant that, until the events of 1911 actually unfolded, it was not clear that if a "revolution" came it would be anything more than an effort to *ge* (strip) the Manchus of their *ming* (mandate). Even when the military mutinies swept the nation, there was no guarantee that they would end up changing anything other than the identity and ethnicity of the person who occupied the Dragon Throne.

The complex motivations of the individuals who took part in the events of 1911 made this a very real possibility. Nationalist Party historians have tried to present the Wuchang Uprising as part of a complicated master plan that was crafted by Sun Yat-sen and carried out primarily by members of his Revolutionary Alliance, the organization that later evolved into the KMT. The reality is much more complex: many participants in the 1911 mutinies had no contact whatever with the Revolutionary Alliance and knew little of Sun Yat-sen (who, incidentally, was in Denver when the Wuchang Uprising took place). Some of those involved in the revolts were indeed members of radical groups who were committed to the idea that China needed to adopt a republican form of government, but others had less explicitly political reasons for taking part in the uprisings. Some participants were motivated to act by their general distrust of the Qing "barbarians," others by anger at the way particular officials had behaved toward them in the past, and still others by an opportunistic desire to advance their careers by being on the winning side when the mandate shifted.

This diversity of grievances and the lack of a unifying ideology notwithstanding, the uprisings ended up leading to changes that were much more profound than those that typically come in the wake of coups and rebellions. The uprisings of 1911 extinguished not just a particular dynasty but a whole tradition of imperial rule. The National Assembly and the other institutions of the new Republic quickly proved ineffectual, to say the least, and as a result the country descended into a chaotic period of warlordism. The complete failure of two attempts by warlords to found new dynasties demonstrated, however, that the rules of political life had indeed undergone a profound transformation in the early 1910s.

Unlike the political revolution described above, the attempts Chinese revolutionaries have made to transform their nation's traditional belief structures and patterns of behavior are difficult to link to a particular date. The roots of this intellectual and cultural revolution can be traced back at least as far as the First Opium War (1839–1842), since the Chinese military defeats of the 1840s led many within the dominant scholar-official class to begin questioning long-standing assumptions about the inferiority of foreign cultures. The first generations of intellectuals to rethink these issues, while interested in what the West had to offer in terms of specific kinds of scientific knowledge and technological know-how, were seldom revolutionary in their approach. Their belief in the basic superiority of traditional moral codes and Confucian ideals remained unshaken, and their concern was with finding a reformist path that would allow them to hold firm to a Chinese essence (*ti*), while adapting the best that the West had to offer in terms of useful (*yong*) techniques.

The ti/yong distinction remained at the heart of intellectual debate within China for decades, until the New Culture Movement of 1915–1923 ushered in a period of genuinely revolutionary challenges to the traditional intellectual and cultural order. Most of the participants in this multifaceted event were professors and students who had either studied abroad or been exposed to foreign ideas at one of the Western-style academic institutions founded in China during the late Qing and Warlord (1912–1927) eras. They disagreed among themselves about many things, but they tended to share several basic convictions. First, they attributed much of the blame for China's current weakness to the enduring power of certain entrenched beliefs (e.g., that people should strive to recapture the glories of a past golden age rather than work to create a new kind of world) and practices (including arranged marriages and rituals associated with filial piety and ancestor worship) that they considered "Confucian" and "feudal." Second, they welcomed the best that the West had to offer in terms of moral codes and methods of critical inquiry as well as practical techniques. And finally, they felt that intellectuals needed to reach out to ordinary people and find a way to include them in the struggle for cultural renewal.

One of the key practical aspects of the New Culture Movement was the publication of a host of new periodicals filled with articles that introduced readers to the various Western ideologies (Social Darwinism, Dewey's pragmatism, anarchism, Marxism) that seemed to offer a means for explaining and resolving China's contemporary crises. Some of these new periodicals also served another purpose: written in a mode the intellectuals termed "plain speech" (*baihua*), as opposed to the less vernacular "classic style" (*wenyen*) of traditional scholarship, they were designed to inform and mobilize people outside of the academy. This literary move to break down the barriers between intellectuals and members of other classes was reinforced by public speaking campaigns intended to educate the illiterate about everything from Western ideas relating to disease to the humiliating nature of the Treaty of Versailles, under which Japan was given rights to govern parts of China that had been under German control prior to World War I.

This interest in breaking down barriers between intellectuals and the masses took an important new turn with the May 4th Movement of 1919. This event began with students taking to the streets to protest the Versailles Treaty and to call for the resignation of three "traitorous officials" of the warlord regime then in power, whom the demonstrators claimed had sold out the nation's interests in order to line their pockets with Japanese gold. The struggle soon broadened into a general fight against imperialist threats from abroad and oppression at home, and grew from a student movement into one that involved members of many social groups.

The May 4th Movement, although originally inspired by a diplomatic dispute, did not lead to a radical change in the way China related to the outside world. May 4th activists proved much more successful when it came to achieving domestic goals. Most notably, while the protests of 1919 did lead to the dismissal of the "traitorous officials," they did not prevent Japan from taking charge of the port city of Qingdao and other northern territories formerly under German control.

No diplomatic revolution could take place as long as the country lacked a strong central government committed to overturning the unequal treaties and defending China's national sovereignty. The Northern Expedition of 1925–1927, in which the KMT formed a united front with the CCP and the two parties called on the people of China to join them in a fight to the death against warlordism and imperialism, is perhaps the most logical place to start the story of China's diplomatic revolution. Major changes in China's international position did not follow directly in the wake of the KMT's victories of the late 1920s, however, for during the years immediately following his establishment of a new central government in Nanjing, Chiang Kai-shek decided that the spread of communism was more dangerous than the continuation of imperialism. This meant that throughout the Nanjing Decade (1927–1937), the Generalissimo spent a great deal of energy fighting domestic threats to his power, which came from both the CCP and from groups headed by members of the KMT who claimed that Chiang was not the most fitting successor to Sun Yat-sen. Chiang was a much more outspoken critic of the unequal treaties and Japan's increasingly aggressive brand of imperialism than any of his warlord predecessors had been, but like many of them he argued that China could not regain its place in the world until it got its own house in order.

World War II, which Chinese scholars claim (with considerable justification) began with the outbreak of Sino-Japanese hostilities in 1937, precipitated a sea change in China's diplomatic situation. China's position as one of the Allies gave Chiang Kai-shek new leverage in pushing for an end to the system of unequal relations with industrialized nations created by the treaties of the nineteenth century. In 1943 the Western powers formally renounced all claims to the concessions they had controlled for roughly a century in Shanghai and other cities on the Chinese mainland. Thanks to this decision and Japan's withdrawal from northern China in 1945, when World War II ended the Chinese state was freer of foreign influence than it had been since the outbreak of the First Opium War.

CCP historians argue, however, that even then the diplomatic revolution was not complete. These writers claim that, even though the formal structures of imperialism had disappeared, the KMT regime remained too economically and diplomatically dependent on the United States and other Western powers to be seen as a truly independent entity. The political motivations for making this claim are obvious, since CCP historians have a clear stake in making their party's rise to power appear a patriotic act. Even though this argument is often overstated and used for political purposes, it has some validity. If credit for starting the diplomatic revolution should rightly go to Chiang Kai-shek's regime, it remains true that China did not fully regain its status as an independent nation able to negotiate with other countries on its own terms until the CCP took power.

The socioeconomic revolution also needs to be seen as something that began before 1949 but did not reach fruition until the founding of the PRC. Each of the revolutions described above was both affected by and in turn triggered changes in patterns of social and economic life. To take but one example, a close look at the backgrounds of the leaders of the political revolution of the 1910s reveals that a disproportionate number belonged to newly created or newly ascendant social groups, whose members enjoyed a relatively high status within society but felt dissatisfied with the way power was allocated within the imperial system. Managers of new industrial enterprises such as Western-style steamship companies; local gentry involved in the provincial assemblies that the last Manchu rulers sanctioned, as part of a last-ditch effort to save their dynasty by introducing a broad program of reforms; officers in the permanent regional armies originally created in the nineteenth century as temporary units whose sole function was to help the central government suppress peasant rebellions; and intellectuals who had studied in Japan or the West—members of these groups had little in common except a shared sense that they deserved to rise higher than they were able to under the existing system.

The rise and disaffection of these ascendant occupational groups between the 1860s and the 1930s was an important phenomenon, since theorists of revolution often stress the leading role that "marginal elites" play in bringing about political change. Neither the development of new alignments near the top of the social ladder nor other associated socioeconomic shifts (such as the dramatic increase in the number of factory jobs available in bustling coastal cities around the turn of the century) had much effect, however, on the lives of the vast majority of Chinese, who resided in inland villages and either worked as tenant farmers or owned small plots of land. For these villagers, a socioeconomic revolution worthy of the name did not take place until the CCP launched its ambitious land reform campaigns in the late 1940s and early 1950s, during which poor peasants were called upon to publicly denounce and at times even physically assault rich peasants within their villages as well as absentee landlords. Designed to redistribute land in a way that minimized social inequality and to pave the way for ambitious forms of agricultural collectivization, these campaigns radically changed the basic structure of Chinese social and economic life.

The two schema described above both provide plausible methods for dividing up the Chinese Revolution, but there are at least three strong arguments for thinking of the *geming* as a single event. One of these has already been alluded to: participants in this struggle have often insisted that the Revolution be seen as an ongoing quest for national salvation and transformation. Chinese leaders on both sides of the Taiwan straits have continually, if at times inconsistently, argued that their legitimacy stems from their status as revolutionaries. The CCP and the KMT have very different visions of what exactly the *geming* is, and leaders of the two parties have blamed different kinds of factors (Soviet conspiracies, capitalist conspiracies, China's economic backwardness) for their inability to bring the Revolution to a close. What they share, however, is a vision of the revolutionary quest as a single enduring struggle, which will not be complete until Taiwan and the mainland are both ruled by the same government and China regains its proper place in the world as a leading cultural and political power. Party leaders are not the only ones, moreover, who think of the Revolution as an ongoing quest: some of the wall posters put up by protesters in 1989 chastised the heads of the CCP for allowing the *geming* to veer off its proper course.

A second important reason to think of the Revolution as a single event is that it forces us to focus on the continuities running through all of the various revolutions described above. For example, dividing the *geming* into republican, nationalist, and communist revolutions obscures the fact that revolutionaries of all three eras shared certain basic convictions about China's predicament and the way to solve it. All three groups of revolutionaries were convinced that China could only be saved by an approach that might best be called nationalist cosmopolitanism. That is, each sought to identify internal sources of strength and combine them with powerful new ideologies and practices associated with the West and Japan. This common thread can be seen running through the policies and proclamations of Sun Yat-sen (who combined appeals to racial pride with flourishes of republican rhetoric), Chiang Kai-shek (who flirted with ideas associated with American-style democracy, German-style fascism, and Confucianism, while simultaneously presenting himself as Sun's most devoted follower), Mao Zedong (who argued that the CCP was using Marxist principles to carry a distinctively Chinese tradition of peasant rebellion to new heights), and even Deng Xiaoping (who has justified recent experiments with market economy forces as part of an ongoing revolutionary effort to develop a form of ''socialism with Chinese characteristics'').

The third reason to think of China's *geming* as a single ongoing event is that it forces us to pay attention to those features of Chinese life that have remained relatively constant throughout the last century. Again, to take but one example, even though writings by various revolutionaries (including both noncommunist participants in the New Culture Movement and CCP leaders such as Mao Zedong) insist that one of the greatest evils of the Confucian order was its celebration of a patriarchal family system that gave men a disproportionate amount of power within the home, Chinese women continue to suffer from many of the same kinds of discrimination as their predecessors of earlier eras. Patterns of gender-based inequality exist today that are uncomfortably similar to those that New Culture Movement activists decried in their critiques of the Confucian order several decades ago. Phenomena such as these raise important questions about the appropriateness of describing China's "social" and "cultural" revolutions as completed events.

In conclusion, there are strong arguments to be made for both viewing the Chinese Revolution as a single cohesive event and for treating it as a series of overlapping but distinctively different struggles for transformation. If the definition and periodization of this (or these) *geming* remain open to a variety of different interpretations, at least one thing about this event or set of events is clear—it (or they) unquestionably did change both China and the world in important ways.

Perhaps the most striking of these changes can be linked to the strengthening of the Chinese state. Although China specialists debate whether the 1911–1949 period was one in which the state was strengthened or weakened, there is a general consensus that the Party-State of the CCP that emerged in the 1950s was a much more powerful and intrusive one than any of its immediate predecessors.

The process of strengthening the state has affected the lives of ordinary Chinese people in myriad ways, and it has also transformed the basic character of China's relations with other countries. Domestically, the changes have reshaped nearly every aspect of social, economic, cultural, and political life. For example, the Old Regime state tended to play only an indirect role in agricultural production, which was done primarily by families. Aside from paying taxes to government officials and appealing to these same bureaucrats for help when famine hit or disputes arose with other groups of farmers, these families tended to operate as largely autonomous economic units, which either worked their own land or (in the case of poorer households) negotiated directly with landlords to obtain the right to plant crops on particular fields.

The CCP Party-State has adopted a host of different policies relating to rural land ownership and agricultural production, ranging from redistributing private plots, to forcing villagers to join large-scale cooperatives, to introducing reforms that reemphasize the importance of families as economic units. All these policies, however, have at least one thing in common—each assumes that the state and its representatives should be intimately involved in deciding how the land is worked and how agricultural products are distributed. Similarly, in the case of industry, the CCP has always assumed that the Party-State should take an active role in matters relating to work, including not only the setting of quotas but also the supervision of unions.

On the positive side, the development of an intrusive, powerful, and ideologically driven state apparatus has gone hand-in-hand with a host of improvements relating to education and health care. The Party-State's commitment to social welfare programs has also helped mitigate the effects of the demographic crises that have plagued China throughout the last centuries, which can all be traced back to overpopulation.

On the negative side, many Chinese have paid a high price for the kinds of material and cultural gains described above. Not only has the regime periodically launched campaigns against intellectuals and discriminated against members of ethnic and religious minorities in a more systematic fashion, but people from all walks of life have consistently had to bow to the whims of corrupt members of the new privileged class composed of Party officials and those with powerful connections. Worst of all, perhaps, the population as a whole has suffered from a series of ideologically inspired policy blunders, such as the Great Leap Forward (in which farmers were encouraged to forget their crops and concentrate on producing iron so that China could catch up to the West) and Mao Zedong's flirtation with pro-natalist ideas (during which he claimed that the larger China's population became, the stronger the nation would be), which have exacerbated the already precarious demographic situation.

State-strengthening has had a much more positive effect, at least for China and its allies, where international relations are concerned. China entered this century a weak nation at the mercy of Western and Japanese imperialists, desperately looking to other lands for answers to its internal crises. The last several decades, by contrast, have seen China consistently try (usually with considerable success) to deal with the world's most powerful nations on its own terms. It has even served at times as a model for developing nations seeking to defend or achieve a comparable political independence.

While important transformations have occurred, it is also worth remembering that not everything about China has changed over the course of the last century. Rather, there has been a good deal of continuity even in those aspects of life that the *geming* was intended to transform. One indication of this is that many of the specific demands voiced by revolutionaries of earlier generations continue to be heard within the PRC. The China we see today is unquestionably a very different and much stronger country than it was at the beginning of the century, but it is worth closing with a reminder that when the protesters of 1989 called for an end to bureaucratic corruption and the creation of more responsive political institutions, they were asking for the very things for which some of their revolutionary predecessors of the Late Imperial, Warlord, and Nationalist eras had given their lives.

SELECTED BIBLIOGRAPHY

Bianco, Lucien. *The Origins of the Chinese Revolution 1915–1949*. Stanford: Stanford University Press, 1966. Still in many ways the best short overview of the topic.

Chow Tse-tung. *The May Fourth Movement: Intellectual Revolution in Modern China*. Cambridge, MA: Harvard University Press, 1960. A comprehensive study of a major turning point in modern Chinese history.

Eastman, Lloyd E. *The Abortive Revolution: China under Nationalist Rule, 1927–1937*. Cambridge, MA: Harvard University Press, 1974. An eclectic collection of essays by a leading scholar of KMT politics.

Fairbank, John K. *The United States and China*. Cambridge, MA: Harvard University Press, 1983. A seminal survey of China's modern history and its diplomatic relations with the United States by the century's most influential American China specialist.

Hinton, William. *Fanshen: A Documentary of Revolution in a Chinese Village*. New York: Random House, 1966. A seminal study of a village undergoing land reform.

Huang, Philip C.C. *The Peasant Economy and Social Change in North China*. Stanford: Stanford University Press, 1985. A detailed and sophisticated examination of local economic patterns.

Johnson, Chalmers. *Peasant Nationalism and Communist Power: The Emergence of Revolutionary China 1937–1945*. Stanford: Stanford University Press, 1962. A classic study that puts forth the thesis that the CCP's rise to power had less to do with its social programs and ideology than with its ability to capitalize on nationalist sentiment triggered by the Japanese invasion.

Meisner, Maurice. *Mao's China and After: A History of the People's Republic*. New York: Free Press, 1986. A thoughtful general introduction to a complex era.

Ono Kazuko. *Chinese Women in a Century of Revolution, 1850–1950*. Stanford: Stanford University Press, 1989. Edited by Joshua A. Fogel. The best single-volume history of the topic.

Pepper, Suzanne. *Civil War in China: The Political Struggle, 1945–1949*. Berkeley: University of California Press, 1978. The best single-volume overview of this complex and chaotic period.

Perry, Elizabeth J. *Rebels and Revolutionaries in North China 1845–1945*. Stanford:

Stanford University Press, 1980. This impressive work highlights the difficulties communist organizers faced when trying to force a rebellious tradition to serve a specific type of revolutionary purpose.

Schwarcz, Vera. *The Chinese Enlightenment: Intellectuals and the Legacy of the May Fourth Movement of 1919*. Berkeley: University of California Press, 1986. A superb study of the predicament of intellectuals in twentieth-century China.

Selden, Mark. *The Yenan Way in Revolutionary China*. Cambridge, MA: Harvard University Press, 1971. A seminal though controversial account of the CCP's rise to power.

Snow, Edgar. *Red Star over China*. Rev. ed. New York: Grove Press, 1968. A fascinating firsthand account of the lives and views of CCP leaders.

Spence, Jonathan. *The Gate of Heavenly Peace: The Chinese and Their Revolution, 1900–1985*. New York: Viking Press, 1981. A beautifully written survey of the Chinese Revolution, this work is centered around the life histories of several key intellectual figures.

Twitchett, Denis, and John K. Fairbank, general eds. *The Cambridge History of China*. Vols. 1–15. New York: Cambridge University Press, 1978–[1991]. Volumes 10 through 15 provide a comprehensive introduction to Western scholarship on the political, social, intellectual, and diplomatic history of late imperial and revolutionary China.

Wakeman, Frederic E., Jr. *The Fall of Imperial China*. New York: Free Press, 1975. A superb introduction to the social and political processes that led up to the 1911 Revolution.

Wasserstrom, Jeffrey N., and Elizabeth J. Perry, eds. *Popular Protest and Political Culture in Modern China*. 2nd ed. Boulder, CO: Westview Press, 1994. A collection of essays by leading specialists from several disciplines who attempt to put China's current crises into historical perspective.

Wolfe, Margery. *Revolution Postponed: Women in Contemporary China*. Stanford: Stanford University Press, 1985. An engaging study of one of the more problematic legacies of the Chinese Revolution.

Wright, Mary C., ed. *China in Revolution: The First Phase*. New Haven: Yale University Press, 1968. The most important single work on events leading up to and following the Wuchang Uprising.

8

The End of Colonialism and the Rise of the Third World, c. 1945–Present

INTRODUCTION

On the eve of World War I (1914), Western nations controlled virtually the entire globe. Beginning with the explorations of the fifteenth century and continuing through the middle of the eighteenth century, Europeans extended their domination over vast reaches. After a hiatus of about 100 years during which the Western world focused on domestic developments, the process of swallowing up the globe began again. Over the next few decades, the Western nations completed their conquest of the world.

The triumphant march of colonial conquerors did not go unopposed; however, the native peoples simply lacked the requisite technology, particularly military hardware, to resist successfully. Nevertheless, those who found themselves oppressed by colonial masters deeply resented the inferior status imposed upon them. In the years before 1914, in the Ottoman Empire, China, and India, indigenous leaders began to rebel against the racial bigotry, economic exploitation, cultural imperialism, and political subjugation that were imperialism's hallmarks.

World War I hastened this process. Many colonial soldiers fought for the mother country, and at least a few came away from this experience convinced that their sacrifice entitled their people to at least autonomy

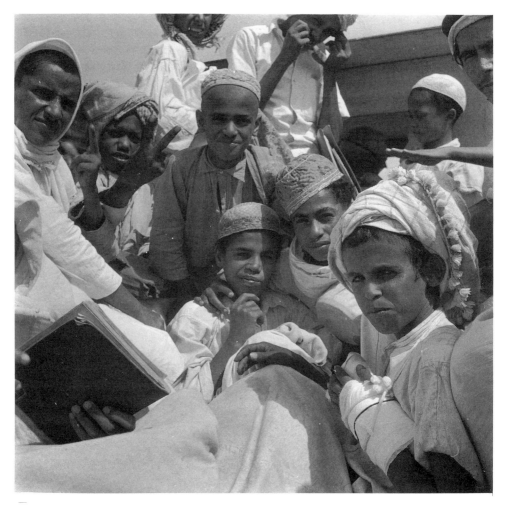

Saudi Arabian boys on their way to school. After World War II, colonial empires collapsed and more than 100 new nations emerged. (Photographic Archives, University of Louisville)

if not independence. Furthermore, although U.S. president Woodrow Wilson had not intended to stimulate anti-imperialist sentiment in Asia and Africa, his Fourteen Points (1918), which outlined an idealistic vision of the future, fired the imagination of subject peoples everywhere. More important, the 1917 Russian Revolution—a direct consequence of the war—brought to power the communists, who provided both encouragement for liberation movements among the colonial peoples (as a way of attacking their capitalist foes) and an alternative to the hated capitalism that many colonial peoples viewed as an exploitative and inhuman system imposed by their imperial masters.

Between the end of World War I and the start of World War II, Persia (which in 1935 began to call itself Iran), Turkey, and China achieved greater control of their own destiny, while India laid the groundwork for its future independence. In 1921 revolution in Persia brought to power Reza Khan, who was less inclined to do the bidding of the Western world. Mustapha Kemal, who later renamed himself Ataturk, dominated Turkey and instituted a series of reforms designed in part to free his country from subservience to the Western states. In China, the imperialists lost power as the nationalistic Kuomintang, under the leadership of first Sun Yat-sen and then Chiang Kai-shek, and a strong communist movement under Mao Zedong competed for power. Both the Kuomintang and the communists despised the Westerners who had manipulated China for much of the nineteenth century. In India, the English-educated lawyer Mohandas Gandhi led an increasingly popular struggle against the British rulers. Relying on a campaign of nonviolence and passive resistance, Gandhi undercut British authority and forced a number of concessions from the reluctant imperialists. However, Great Britain refused to capitulate on his main demand—independence for India.

World War II greatly accelerated the drive for independence among non-Western peoples. As was the case in World War I, colonial peoples supplied the war effort with necessary raw materials and finished products as well as soldiers. A strong feeling emerged among both the colonial peoples and some important segments of Western public opinion that the sacrifices of the native populations should not go unrewarded. This sentiment was further reinforced by the nature of the war, which seemed to pit the forces of good against the forces of evil. If the victory of the Allies over Nazi Germany represented the triumph of a liberal, humane, egalitarian, and democratic philosophy, how could the winners possibly continue to maintain an imperial system resting on racism, brutality, exploitation, and inequality? The professed ideals of the Western world were clearly at variance with imperialism.

Most significant, perhaps, was the destruction of the old relationship between the colonies and their imperial masters. For many in Asia, Japan's military victories reinforced the notion already born of Japan's success against Russia in the Russo-Japanese War (1904–1905) that the white man was not militarily invulnerable. Furthermore, when the Japanese—who were as imperialistic as the Europeans—supplanted white colonial rule in the colonies of Asia, indigenous leaders who had opposed colonial rule before the war formed guerrilla units to resist them. Leaders such as Ho Chi Minh in French Indochina and Achmed Sukarno in the Dutch East Indies not only established effective fighting forces, but also gained a large popular following. With the end of the war, independence movements led by figures who enjoyed the support of their people and commanded well-organized and experienced fighting units confronted the returning imperialists. Restoration of the prewar colonial status quo now became unlikely, especially as the cost to the Europeans in terms of men and precious resources desperately needed to rebuild the mother country was simply too great.

Some imperial countries, such as Great Britain and the United States, quickly grasped the lessons of World War II. Others, such as France and the Netherlands, attempted to regain control of their colonies and became embroiled in costly and exhausting warfare. The largest and most populous colony was India, where the movement for independence from Great Britain was already significant before the war. In 1947 Great Britain vacated the great Indian subcontinent; however, religious and ethnic rivalry, an all too common curse among the colonial peoples, not only led to the assassination of Gandhi in 1948 but also prevented the formation of a single state. Instead, two states were created: India, with a Hindu majority, and Pakistan, with a Moslem majority. India, under the leadership of Gandhi's disciple Jawaharlal Nehru, who served as prime minister from 1947 until his death in 1964, developed an enduring constitutional democracy, a rare occurrence in the former colonial world, where dictatorship tended to be the norm. Nehru also guided India toward a socialist economy that became the model for several newly independent countries. Except for brief periods, Pakistan has been a military dictatorship. The rivalry that divided India and Pakistan at the start has continued, resulting in several wars and a seemingly permanent state of tension between the two countries.

In 1948 Britain also granted independence to Ceylon (Sri Lanka) and to Burma, which renamed itself Myanmar in 1989. The Burmese refused to join the Commonwealth of Nations, a consultative organization of fifty former British colonies sponsored by Great Britain, preferring to follow a path of rigid isolation that has led to major human rights abuses and great poverty. Nine years later, in 1957, Britain granted independence to the peoples of the Malayan peninsula after putting down a communist insurgency.

In contrast to the bloodless emancipation of the former British colonies in Asia, the Dutch fought a debilitating colonial war from 1945 to 1949 in a futile attempt to retain the Dutch East Indies, or Indonesia. The Indonesian national liberation movement, led by Sukarno and including a large communist contingent, had resisted the Japanese during World War II and, consequently, was prepared to oppose the return of the Dutch.

France also tried to reclaim its empire in Asia. In Indochina a popular, well-organized veteran national liberation movement led by Ho Chi Minh administered a series of military setbacks to the French, culminating in the 1954 Battle of Dien Bien Phu. Depicting the struggle as a communist inspired and led rebellion rather than a national liberation movement, the French interested the United States in Indochina, with devastating results for the Americans. This was a curious turn in U.S. policy, clearly reflecting the prevailing tensions of the Cold War, as evidenced by the fact that a few years earlier (1946) the United States had willingly granted independence to the Philippines, the principal U.S. colony in Asia.

The end of colonialism in sub-Saharan, or black, Africa came rapidly and unexpectedly. Unlike Asia, where organized anticolonialism had existed for decades, black Africa had been quiescent until the end of World War II. Then, beginning in the 1950s, imperialism in sub-Saharan African collapsed in the space of about two decades, and several dozen independent, black-ruled countries emerged.

The process of African decolonization began with the British Empire. In 1957 the Gold Coast (Ghana) gained independence under its charismatic leader Kwame Nkrumah. Six years later, in 1963, Great Britain granted independence to Nigeria, its largest colony in Africa and the continent's most populous country. Britain was able to surrender its West African colonies with relative ease because so few whites lived there; however, the British were not so fortunate in East Africa, where white settlers had taken advantage of a moderate climate and good soil to settle permanently. These whites strongly resisted any suggestion of black rule. However, the unsuccessful Mau-Mau uprising in Kenya in the 1950s gave Great Britain a glimpse of how costly it would be to retain its colonies. Sobered by this experience and burdened by many problems at home, Great Britain granted independence to Tanganyika and Zanzibar in 1961 (in 1964 they merged to become Tanzania under the leadership of Julius Nyerere), to Uganda in 1962, and to Kenya under the popular Jomo Kenyatta in 1963.

In shedding its black African empire, Britain faced great difficulties in southern Africa, where a substantial number of whites had settled. Northern Rhodesia (Zambia—1964), Nyasaland (Malawi—1964), and Bechuanaland (Botswana—1966) achieved independence without undue strife, but the white settlers of Southern Rhodesia resisted national liberation until 1980, when Zimbabwe was born under the rule of black nationalist leader Robert Mugabe. The Republic of South Africa, where some whites had lived for centuries, is only now groping its way toward a compromise acceptable to black, colored, and white alike after a long period of apartheid (segregation) and rising racial tension.

In comparison to its misguided colonial policies in Asia and North Africa, France's approach to its sub-Saharan empire was positively enlightened. Not only did the French freely release their black colonies, they consciously fostered a sense of "Frenchness" among the emerging black elite and willingly gave economic assistance to the newly independent states. As a result, French influence remains strong in sub-Saharan Africa.

The authoritarian Portuguese state, whose empire dated back to the late Middle Ages, determined to hold its possessions in black Africa at all costs. Consequently, Portugal found itself mired in a seemingly endless guerrilla war with national liberation movements in both Angola and Mozambique. The war had a corrosive effect on Portuguese life and was a major contributory factor to the 1974 coup that eventually brought democracy to Portugal. In the wake of the coup, Portugal gave up the fight and liberated its African empire.

In 1960 Belgium relinquished the Belgian Congo (Zaire), its large African colony. However, because of Belgium's utter disdain for the Congolese, few if any natives had been prepared for independence. Furthermore, the colony was fractured by tribal disputes, regional differences, and rivalry among its would-be leaders. With Belgium's departure, the Congo suffered a series of armed rebellions, secessionist movements, and civil war, all aggravated by Soviet and U.S. meddling in the affairs of the hapless Congo as part of their Cold War rivalry. The end result for the mineral-rich and potentially wealthy Congo was an independent but devastated and impoverished state ruled by Mobutu

Sese Seko, an extravagant and brutal military dictator who was propped up by the United States.

The third great area where colonial empires disappeared was the Arab world, stretching from Morocco on the Atlantic to the Persian Gulf. At the end of World War II, France's empire included much of North Africa. However, as was the case in Indochina, indigenous national liberation movements that predated the war worked to drive out the French. After failing to either cajole or repress the native populations, France granted independence to Morocco and Tunisia in 1956.

For France, however, its Algerian colony held special significance. France had governed it since 1830, and with at least 1 million Frenchmen living there, Algeria was considered an integral part of metropolitan France. When France categorically refused to consider independence for Algeria, the FLN (Front de Libération Nationale) rebelled in 1954. The ensuing Algerian War lasted for more than seven years, involving 500,000 French troops and causing perhaps 1 million deaths. The war shook France to its very core, bringing that nation to the brink of civil war. In 1958 the Fourth French Republic collapsed and World War II hero Charles de Gaulle was summoned from retirement to save the nation. De Gaulle instituted the Fifth Republic, and over the objections of the French settlers and many French military men he conceded independence to Algeria in 1962.

Decolonization in the Middle East was not so rancorous for the Europeans, but it was made complicated and violent by the Israeli question. At the close of World War I, the defeated Ottoman Empire (Turkey) ceded its Middle Eastern possessions to the League of Nations, which in turn assigned them to Great Britain and France as mandates. Beginning with Egypt in 1922 and continuing into the post–World War II era, several Middle Eastern countries, including Iraq, Syria, Jordan, Lebanon, Saudi Arabia, Yemen, and Kuwait, gained their independence without much opposition from the mandate powers.

However, difficulties arose when European Jews took steps to establish a state of their own in the Middle East. Relying on the Balfour Declaration of 1917, which promised British support for a Jewish homeland in Palestine, and fleeing European anti-Semitism, which had culminated in Hitler and the Holocaust, Jewish settlers proclaimed the state of Israel in 1948. The indigenous Arab population reacted violently to the Jewish state, and war ensued on several occasions (1948–1949; 1956—the Suez War; 1967—the Six-Day War; 1973—the Yom Kippur War; 1982—the Lebanese War). Complicating matters was the interest both the United

States and the Soviet Union showed in the region. Due to the Middle East's strategic location and its massive oil reserves, both superpowers became deeply involved in its disputes. Only with the end of the Cold War and the 1993 agreements between the Israelis and the Palestinians has there surfaced even a slight possibility of peace for this region.

INTERPRETIVE ESSAY
Marijan Salopek

Since World War II, interest in the Third World has grown, largely because these nations represent nearly two-thirds of the world's population. However, the majority of Third World citizens live on the edge of subsistence. The predicament of the Third World has piqued the world's conscience. Its plight must be examined not only in the context of the damage—real or imagined—the imperial powers inflicted on these lands, but also in terms of the optimism that Third World leaders displayed on the eve of decolonization. The Third World, it should be noted, is as much a state of mind as an economic and political fact. Furthermore, the term "Third World" suggests a degree of homogeneity that does not exist, and masks the cultural, linguistic, and political diversity of the nations it characterizes.

One response to the condition of the Third World has been to denigrate imperialism in terms such as "World Revolution of Westernization," the title of historian Theodore H. von Laue's 1987 study of the Western world's impact on the globe in the twentieth century. Von Laue claims that this revolution "produced a worldwide association of peoples compressed against their will into an inescapable but highly unstable interdependence laced with explosive tensions." This interpretation reinforced the long-standing thinking of some Third World leaders and their Western allies who believed that former colonies would experience dramatic economic growth once the imperialists were displaced and an indigenous commercial and political elite assumed the reins of power.

However, these proponents of decolonization were clearly too optimistic. Their self-confidence was greater than the tools available to them to take politically and economically underdeveloped territories into the realm of the Second or First World. In short, the anticolonialists had set themselves up for a psychological fall, as their level of expectation was too high to be realized in the time frame that they had established for themselves. They arrogantly asserted that the Third World could match the industrially and economically advanced former imperial powers in a relatively short period of time, possibly a single generation. However, to be fair, their expectations had been shaped by the experience of other nations, principally the Soviet Union, which had attained Great Power status in the space of a few decades. Third World leaders expressed faith in their ability to apply the Soviet model to their circumstances. However, they totally ignored the long political and economic development of the former Russian Empire.

Imperialism reflected the institutional development of the First and Second Worlds; these nations enjoyed human and material assets, a sense of unity, nationalism, and political maturity borne of war and internal struggle. The Third World's political elite ignored these points and concentrated exclusively on the wealth that the imperial powers had extracted from the colonies; this skewed perspective blinded them to the economic and political realities of the lands they managed.

Although the decolonization era is generally thought to have begun after World War II, the movement has a long history dating back to the first contact between Europeans and the peoples of Africa, Asia, and the Americas. In a sense, the decolonization era began in the eighteenth and nineteenth centuries with the emancipation of the North and South American colonies. The second wave of imperialism in the late nineteenth century led to the creation of new empires. The peoples affected— Africans, Chinese, Japanese, and other Southeast Asians—often reacted strongly, seeking to affirm their cultural and political sovereignty. The Taiping Rebellion (1850–1864), the Boxer Revolt (1898–1901), the Chinese Revolution (1911), and the Meiji Restoration in Japan (1868–1912) were reactions to foreign intervention as much as responses to internal social and political problems. A striking feature of the decolonization movement in this period before World War II was the total lack of interaction or even contact between nationalist leaders in Asia and Africa. While aware of the events taking shape around them, the nationalists campaigned for independence in isolation.

Except for the active nationalist clubs and societies that proliferated in the former colonies, few in the industrialized world had any understanding or concern for the peoples or nations beyond Western Europe or the United States. Development of the colonies was hardly a popular topic, even at the height of the imperial era before World War I. It was even less so during the interwar years and World War II. The imperial powers, faced with domestic economic and political problems, had little surplus energy to devote to the concerns of nations on the verge of development. In fact, the terms "development" and "underdevelopment" were conspicuously absent from the vocabulary of the Europeans or Americans; both began to be used with some consistency only in the 1950s.

In the years immediately after World War II, the victorious powers understandably concentrated on rebuilding war-damaged Europe and Japan. The Europeans, the Americans, and the Japanese were the world's international players. For years they had managed the bulk of the world's trade, and it was generally assumed that the world's future prosperity depended on the revival of Europe's and Japan's economies. The needs of former and existing colonies were generally ignored.

The world's attention shifted to the nations soon to be known as the Third World as relations between the Western powers and the Soviet Union deteriorated. Thus, decolonization and the rise of the Third World must be considered in the context of the Cold War. By 1948 the world had divided into clearly identifiable political blocs, referred to by commentators of the day as the First World and the Second World. In the First World were the states of Western Europe, the United States, Canada, and the other British Dominions; in the Second World, the Soviet Union and its allies in Eastern Europe.

The term "Third World" was devised to identify the nations outside the first two blocs. Originally it had a political rather than an economic meaning, referring to the nonaligned nations of Yugoslavia, Egypt, India, Ghana, and Indonesia. Later, it was applied in an economic sense to the impoverished nations of the world. However, the Third World as a concept was open to interpretation. This is exemplified by Mao Zedong's remarks in February 1974: "In my view, the United States and the Soviet Union form the First World. Japan, Europe and Canada, the middle section, belong to the Second World. The Third World has a huge population. With the exception of Japan, Asia belongs to the Third World, and Latin America too." By Mao's definition, Africa would not even fall within the limits of the Third World, as its economic and political development was far behind that of Asia and Latin America.

The Soviet Union's moral and political support for nationalist and communist movements in Eastern Europe, Southeast Asia, and China gave the West's leaders considerable reason for concern, and they responded with a political and humanitarian campaign that highlighted the West's commitment to the underdeveloped nations of Asia and Africa. During the 1950s, the former imperial powers often presented themselves as economic saviors, and the Third World's misfortunes were ascribed to technical and structural faults in the economies of these nations. The consensus was that the poorer nations could attain prosperity with the financial assistance of the West. In essence, it was expected that the breach separating the wealthy and poor regions of the world could be narrowed easily and in a short period of time.

To some degree, the Western powers fueled the expectations of the Third World. International conventions, like the 1950 Colombo Plan, emerged from the West's suspicion and fear of communism. Confronted with the prospect of communist regimes in Asia and elsewhere, Western leaders congregated at Colombo, Ceylon (now Sri Lanka), to discuss the political and economic health of the Asian and African world. This conference marks the beginning of the West's fascination with the Third World. The expectation of the participants was that communism could be averted with a generous deployment of aid.

Undoubtedly, the imperial powers faced a dilemma about emancipating their colonies, similar to the dilemma that nineteenth-century governments faced about emancipating their slaves. Material interests aside, the humanitarian impulse cannot be ignored in any assessment of imperialism's decline. Moral arguments were advanced throughout the interwar years to justify retreat from the colonies. Furthermore, Italian and German military action in Africa and Europe highlighted the moral bankruptcy of the imperialist argument, and Europeans and Americans emerged from World War II expressing an idealistic view of a better and just world.

The Atlantic Charter, devised and interpreted by the United States, prepared the ground for the decolonization process. Led by President Franklin D. Roosevelt, the United States advanced a positive interpretation of self-determination and regarded independence as a fitting reward for colonial peoples who furthered Allied interests during World War II. As during World War I, the United States, by words and actions, whetted the colonial world's appetite for freedom.

The Soviets, avowed anticolonialists, seized the opportunity and inspired nationalists throughout the world. Thus the world's two superpowers accelerated the imperialist retreat. Each brought the issue of decolonization before the United Nations and consequently gave colonial peoples a forum to present their concerns. From this point on, Third World nationalists no longer functioned in isolation. They voiced their views on the international stage, formed political alliances, and capitalized on the conflict between the West and the Soviet Union. Special United Nations agencies were formed specifically to investigate conditions in the undeveloped world, and the reports emanating from commissions like the United Nations Economic Committee for Latin America identified global capitalism as the principal cause of poverty.

The Declaration on the Granting of Independence to Colonial Countries and Peoples, adopted by the General Assembly on December 14, 1960, is characteristic of the response to the subject. Articles 1 and 2 of the declaration provide the foundation for the anti-imperialist view. Article 1 condemns the subjugation, domination, and exploitation of peoples as a denial of fundamental human rights. Such actions not only constitute a violation of the Charter of the United Nations, but also impede the promotion of world peace and cooperation. Article 2 declares that "all peoples have the right to self-determination." Consequently, they should have political independence and be free to choose their own form of government. Likewise, they should have the right to determine their own economic system and to develop their social and cultural life as they see fit. Armed with this declaration, the anticolonialists could justly argue that imperialism was immoral, unjust, and contrary to the welfare of the world community. Since the adoption of the declaration, more than fifty new states have gained independence and subsequent inclusion in the ranks of the Third World bloc.

Left-wing, socialist, and Marxist writers boosted the cause of the Third World. These intellectuals formulated the anti-imperialist interpretation that the Third World was in a desperate state because of the policies pursued by the former colonial powers. Third World writers and thinkers like Frantz Fanon widely disseminated this point of view. Fanon, a black French West Indian psychoanalyst turned author whose most famous work was *The Wretched of the Earth*, became a major spokesman for the Marxist, anticolonialist school. According to Fanon (and others), the imperialists and colonialists had raped the Third World over an extended period of time. They had behaved like war criminals with their deportations, massacres, forced labor, and slavery. All these atrocities had been committed for the sake of profit—to enrich the capitalistic coffers of Western men and Western countries. The capitalist economic system thus bore much of the blame for the destruction of the Third World. To a large extent, Europe's wealth and power derived from the systematic exploitation of the Third World. Gold, raw materials, diamonds, cotton, wood, and humans flowed from the Third World to Europe. In fact, Europe is really the creation of the Third World, brought into existence by the wealth stolen from the underdeveloped reaches of the globe. Even though the imperialists and colonialists are now being forced out, they owe the Third World much and should be required to make restitution.

In the context of the Cold War's heightened tensions, this interpretation confirmed what many in the Third World believed—they were poor because the imperial powers were rich. The West's humanitarian campaign, described as a form of atonement for the damage done to colonial nations, was presented as one more piece of evidence in support of the Marxist interpretation of the Third World's plight.

By the mid-1960s, the Third World had become a hot academic and intellectual topic. Scholars from a variety of fields churned out works that reflected the mood of the era. In many cases, the thesis of the authors was summarized in the titles they chose: "On the Mechanism of Imperialism," *Development and Underdevelopment in Latin America, How Europe Underdeveloped Africa*. Marxist writers found in the Third World a potent vehicle enabling them to challenge the West. Colonialism, aid, development, and foreign investment became symbols of the Third World's impoverishment at the hands of the West. In the charged climate of the 1960s, jargon served as a strong weapon for anticolonial, pro–Third World advocates. "Imperialist exploitation," "neocolonialism," "core and periphery," "surplus appropriation," "polarization," "dominance-dependence relations," "dependent development," and "subservient development" were the terms of choice employed to denigrate imperialism while advancing the cause of the world's underprivileged peoples.

Historians, sociologists, geographers, and polemicists were drawn into the debate. The variety of views poses a considerable problem for the student who must struggle in many cases with the ideology and political perspective of the authors. Non-Marxist scholars and popular writers responded to the negative interpretation of imperialism. They stressed the altruism of the former colonial powers or the pragmatism of decolonization, and they emphasized that the imperial powers had consciously encouraged the transition from colonial status to independence. In making their case, they belittled the economic significance of imperial possessions. According to writers like R. Robinson and J. Gallagher, empires were acquired in a fit of absentmindedness. In *Africa and the Victorians: the Official Mind of Imperialism*, they argued that "the partition of tropical Africa might seem impressive on the wall maps of the Foreign Office. Yet it was at the time an empty and theoretical expansion."

Robinson and Gallagher pointed out that prior to 1900 Great Britain did little or nothing to exploit its African empire. The British held this empire, which had come to them almost by accident, but they virtually ignored it. Certainly commercial or imperial motives did not play an important role in Britain's penetration of Africa. It was only later, well *after* spheres of influence in Africa had been allotted, that Great Britain began to develop its holdings, and then only to make good on earlier promises of African progress and to buttress its territorial claims. The trader, the planter, and the official did not bring about or accompany the partition of tropical Africa; they only came later. Thus, the British Empire—at least in Africa—arose not from any conscious desire by capitalists in cahoots with the government to plunder the natives and exploit the land, but from minor and at the time not very pressing political considerations.

In the political and international climate in which Robinson and Gallagher developed their thesis, this interpretation stood as a clear challenge to the extreme critics of empire and colonialism. Imperialism, rather than being a deliberate act of will, happened in a haphazard, nonmalicious, nonpernicious, nonavaricious manner, with the participants failing to give serious thought to the implications of their actions. An empire acquired in such a fashion and contributing little to the national treasury could be dismantled as easily as it was put together.

However, this interpretation ignores the concern expressed in Britain, France, and the Netherlands in the 1950s and 1960s about the loss of investments and access to cheap resources. The peaceful retreat by the British from their possessions in Asia reveals the extent of the decline of British power rather than the altruism of the British government and British investors. The reality, admitted by Britons at the end of World War II, was that Britain could ill afford to defend or retain its overseas interests. In addition, it should be emphasized that while Britain might have acquired its empire in a fit of absentmindedness, these possessions were held with the assistance of the political and economic elites. Without their support, the empire would have crumbled decades before the decolonization era.

Asia's political elite, swept by the winds of nationalism and buoyed by Japan's success prior to and during World War II, had matured, and it stood ready to advance its interests before those of its colonial masters. Jawaharlal Nehru, cofounder of modern India, underscored the pride and national consciousness of Asians when he recalled Japan's initial victory over the West in the 1904–1905 Russo-Japanese War. Nehru is quoted in L. S. Stavrianos' *Global Rift: the Third World Comes of Age* that ''Japanese victories stirred up my enthusiasm. . . . Nationalist ideas filled my mind. I mused of Indian freedom . . . I dreamed of brave deeds of how, sword in hand, I would fight for India and help in freeing her.''

During the last half of the twentieth century, colonialism disappeared and each former colony groped its way toward a workable political structure. However, all too often bright promises of democratic rule faded, and dictatorships—military or civilian—became the Third World norm. With the global resurgence of the democratic spirit in the 1980s and 1990s, a number of these dictatorships gave way to tentative experiments in democracy. Nevertheless, the political future of Third World countries remains cloudy. For many of these states, the search for political stability promises to be lengthy and arduous, and there is no guarantee that it will end successfully.

In the realm of international relations, most former colonies adopted a policy known as non-alignment. First outlined by Nehru at the 1955 Bandung Conference, non-alignment called for the newly independent countries to maintain strict neutrality in the struggle between the competing superpowers. In practice, non-alignment often meant bashing the West while giving the Soviet Union the benefit of the doubt. However, with the end of the Cold War any leverage the Non-Aligned Movement might have exercised disappeared, thereby forcing many Third World countries to rethink their international position. This reevaluation continues today without any clear unifying doctrine in sight.

Because of the Third World's numerical strength at the United Nations, it tends to view the UN as a vehicle to express its concerns and to achieve its international goals. Several recent UN secretaries general, including the current one, Boutros Boutros Ghali, have come from the ranks of Third World diplomats. Nevertheless, because individual states refuse to surrender their national sovereignty to the world body, the Third World–dominated UN is often ignored and the Third World appears impotent on the global stage.

By 1980 the old imperial powers had finally relinquished their political hold over the underdeveloped world. However, the issue of economic growth remained unresolved. The gap between the developed and underdeveloped nations had grown considerably, and the optimism that greeted independence had given way to cynicism and despair. The nations that had supported decolonization, particularly the United States and the Soviet Union, balked at the cost of supporting the Third World's modernization efforts.

At one time or another, most of the Third World found itself enmeshed in Cold War rivalries. Many Third World countries were able to exploit this situation to extract aid from one superpower or the other. However, as the Cold War wound down, both superpowers tended to regard the Third World as a liability rather than an asset, and funds dried up.

As the superpowers retreated from the Third World, the smaller nations of the First World, in conjunction with the nations of the Third, addressed the issue of the north-south divide, or the geographical division between the rich and poor nations. Generally, the rich nations are situated north of the equator and the poor nations are situated south of the equator. The Vienna Declaration on Cooperation for Development, issued in 1985 at the close of the "Decolonization and After—The Future of the Third World" conference, reiterated the view that the most urgent problem of the second half of the twentieth century is the "conditions of poverty, misery, disease and degradation for two-thirds of the human race." It seemed that very little had changed since 1965 when the United Nations published a very bleak report on the condition of the underdeveloped world. Despite the concerns and lofty ideals expressed by the delegates to the Vienna conference, the Third World moved inexorably toward financial bankruptcy and possibly political irrelevancy.

Imperialism's extraordinary achievement was the creation of a world economy. It stimulated world trade and interdependence on a scale never before known, and in a sense the "world revolution of Westernization" is an appropriate descriptive phrase, stripped of its negative connotations, for the modern era. While the former imperial powers relinquished their colonial possessions, they continued to exert tremendous control over the world's flow of goods.

Initially, many Third World countries chose to ignore this reality. They rejected capitalism, the foundation of the world economy, and embraced socialism instead. However, whether it was Nehru's version of socialism, Kwame Nkrumah's "African socialism," or a variation of the Soviet or Chinese models, Third World socialism featured a high level of state planning, a large, corrupt, and stultifying bureaucracy, and grandiose plans for development that featured rapid industrialization.

In Asia, however, several former colonies opted for capitalism and have enjoyed remarkable economic growth. Noting the success of Singapore, Taiwan, Malaysia, Hong Kong, and South Korea among others, and shocked by the Soviet Union's collapse, a growing number of Third World leaders have rejected the decades-old interpretation that global capitalism is the cause of their nations' misfortunes. For example, the leaders of Mexico, Argentina, and Brazil, supported by the current generation of intellectuals, stress the liberalization of their economies as the solution to the problem of underdevelopment. Thus, in the 1990s market competition and international competitiveness have captured the imagination of the Third World's elite, who express confidence in their long-term future.

For a handful of former colonies, especially in the Middle East, lack of wealth has not been a problem. Blessed with large petroleum reserves, they were able to exploit successfully the global reliance on oil. However, questions remain about both the distribution of this fabulous wealth and its use to create a sound economic infrastructure.

In the wake of international trade, cultural imperialism intensified. Western values as expressed in art, film, television, and fashion are so pervasive that the pressing issue before the nations of the Third World continues to be the retention of their identity. In a number of countries such as Iran, the omnipresence of Western styles and forms provoked an important reaction featuring the elevation of indigenous values and the demonization of Western culture.

The achievements of the Third World are noteworthy; yet they are frequently overshadowed by seemingly insoluble problems. Certainly the mere fact of having gained independence is a signal success. So too is the production of sufficient food supplies—the so-called Green Revolution of which India is a prime example. Nevertheless, the list of problems is legion. Among the more intractable ones, one must include government instability, lack of internal cohesion, overpopulation, grinding poverty, epidemic disease such as AIDS in Africa, destruction of the environment in locales ranging from Brazil to Burma, illiteracy, and disregard of human rights.

Nevertheless, the freeing of the Third World from its colonial yoke clearly carries major importance for our world. The long-term impact of imperialism and decolonization was that it forced people to reassess their institutions and their approach to life. Because imperialism highlighted technological and organizational strengths and weaknesses, its effect must be measured in terms of its tremendous psychological impact on the way people perceive themselves and their civilization, be they in the Third World or in the First or Second.

SELECTED BIBLIOGRAPHY

Ansprenger, F. *The Dissolution of Colonial Empires.* New York: Routledge, 1989. The dismantlement of the European empires is handled in a thorough and knowledgeable manner.

Blusse, L. et al., eds. *History and Underdevelopment: Essays on Underdevelopment and European Expansion in Asia and Africa.* Leiden: Centre for the History of European Expansion, 1980. A series of critical essays on a most controversial topic.

Bruckner, Pascal. *The Tears of the White Man: Compassion as Contempt.* Translation and introduction by William R. Beer. New York: Free Press, 1986. Critique of the methods employed by the left in France to advance their interpretation of the Third World.

Cambridge History of Africa. 8 vols. Cambridge, England: Cambridge University Press, 1975–1984. Authoritative analysis of Africa. Information on all aspects of African history.

Chamberlain, M. E. *Decolonization: The Fall of the European Empires.* Oxford, England: B. Blackwell, 1985. An effective, short summary of the topic.

Clapham, Christopher. *Third World Politics: An Introduction.* London: Croom Helm, 1985. Scholarly treatment of the relevant political, social, and economic issues.

de Soto, Hernando. *The Other Path: The Invisible Revolution in the Third World.* New York: Harper and Row, 1989. A good example of the anti-Marxist interpretation of underdevelopment.

Hall, D.G.E. *A History of South-East Asia.* 4th ed. London: Macmillan Education, 1981. Standard account of events in Southeast Asia.

Hoepli, Nancy L., ed. *Aftermath of Colonialism.* New York: H. W. Wilson, 1973. Survey of the problems and politics of the Third World.

Jupp, J. *Sri Lanka: Third World Democracy.* London: Frank Cass, 1978. Overview of democracy in Sri Lanka in the years following independence.

Kreisky, Bruno, and H. Gauhar, eds. *Decolonisation and After: The Future of the Third World.* London: South Publications, 1987. Summary of the Proceedings of the Decolonisation and After Conference held in Vienna on October 7–8, 1985. Provides a summary of the experiences and aspirations of the Third World and its supporters.

Manor, James, ed. *Rethinking Third World Politics.* New York: Longmans, 1991. Survey of literature on the changing attitudes toward Third World development and aid.

Mortimer, Robert A. *The Third World Coalition in International Politics.* New York: Praeger, 1980. Covers the political evolution of the nonaligned world.

Nassiter, Bernard D. *Global Struggle for More: Third World Conflicts with the Rich Nations.* New York: Harper and Row, 1986. Excellent summary of the economic problems of the Third World.

Ottaway, David, and Marina Ottaway. *Afrocommunism.* New York: Africana Publishing, 1986. Summary examination of the Marxist regimes in Africa.

Rangel, Carlos. *Third World Ideology and Western Reality: Manufacturing Political Myth.* Foreword by Jean-François Revel. New Brunswick, NJ: Transaction Books, 1986. A stinging indictment of the Marxist interpretation of underdevelopment.

Robinson, Ronald, and John Gallagher. *Africa and the Victorians: The Official Mind of Imperialism.* 2d ed. London: Macmillan, 1981. Asserts that imperialism occurred by accident and not design.

Rodney, Walter. *How Europe Underdeveloped Africa.* London: Howard University Press, 1972. Marxist analysis of European imperialism.

Stavrianos, L. S. *Global Rift: The Third World Comes of Age.* New York: William Morrow, 1981. Outlines the development of Third World consciousness and the evolution of political and economic institutions.

Von Laue, Theodore H. *The World Revolution of Westernization: The Twentieth Century in Global Perspective.* Oxford, England: Oxford University Press, 1987.

Von Laue, an eminent historian of modernization, explores the disruptive nature of that process.

Wesseling, H. L., ed. *Expansion and Reaction: Essays on European Expansion and Reactions in Asia and Africa.* Leiden: Leiden University Press, 1978. Another very perceptive series of essays focusing on the Third World experience.

Jean Monnet (1888–1979), the "father of European unification," at work. Although still an unrealized dream, European unification has made significant headway during the latter half of the twentieth century. (Reproduced from the Collections of the Library of Congress)

9

European Unification,
c. 1947–Present

INTRODUCTION

The vision of a unified Europe is neither new nor novel. During the Middle Ages, western, or Latin, Christianity served as a conscious unifying force for much of Europe. However, the sixteenth-century Reformation, which fractured western Christianity, and the development of the nation-state during the Renaissance ushered in a new era. After the Reformation, Christianity was no longer the unifying force it had once been, and the nation-state's rigid commitment to unimpeded national sovereignty struck at the heart of European unity. For the last four centuries, European unification seemed possible only at the hands of aggressive conquerors such as Napoleon or Hitler. However, their efforts always failed, if for no other reason than that the European peoples resisted them. Nevertheless, a small handful of Europeans never abandoned the dream of a voluntarily unified Europe.

The savagery and carnage of World Wars I and II made European unity seem more attractive. These catastrophic conflicts called into question the legitimacy of the nation-state. Many reasoned that if the nation-state had brought such misery to Europe, perhaps it would be in Europe's best interest to jettison the nation-state and replace it with a unified Europe. Furthermore, the wartime destruction itself was so overwhelming that many Europeans concluded that recovery was possible only in a cooperative, noncompetitive atmosphere. This, in turn, required the subordination of the nation-state to supranational institutions. Finally, many credible leaders of wartime resistance movements demanded that a "united states of Europe" replace the nation-state system.

However, if integration was to occur after World War II, it would not be on a European-wide basis; the Cold War was rapidly dividing Europe into two camps. Eventually, the USSR unified Eastern Europe forcibly, creating for itself a large but restive empire. Politically, the individual nation-states of Eastern Europe retained a facade of independence, but real power rested with Moscow, which exercised its authority through puppet leaders and subservient communist parties. The USSR in 1949 created the Council for Mutual Economic Assistance (CMEA, or Comecon), an economic union of Eastern European countries that bolstered the Soviet economy for many years. Militarily, the Soviet Union consolidated its hold over Eastern Europe with the establishment in 1955 of the Warsaw Treaty Organization, or Warsaw Pact, which placed the armies of Eastern Europe at Soviet disposal. In international affairs, as in every other sphere, the Eastern European countries were expected to march in lockstep with the USSR. Important deviations from the Soviet norm were not tolerated. When Hungary in 1956 and Czechoslovakia in 1968 strayed too far from the Soviet course, the USSR invaded. All this, of course, was not the voluntary unification many Europeans envisioned, but rather a variation on the theme of unification by conquest. The flawed nature of this kind of European unification revealed itself in 1989 when the Soviet empire collapsed and the USSR itself moved to the brink of its ultimate dissolution.

Compared to Eastern Europe after World War II, Western Europe—although greatly influenced by the United States—was much freer to pursue its own goals. Nevertheless, driven by Cold War fears, the United States initiated several major programs that promoted Western European unification. On June 5, 1947, at a speech at Harvard University, Secretary of State George C. Marshall announced that the United States would provide massive aid for Europe's economic reconstruction. Several months later, the U.S. Congress appropriated $13 billion for the European Recovery Program, or the Marshall Plan, as it was popularly known. One of the Marshall Plan's provisions required its European recipients to cooperate with each other in planning the most effective way to employ American aid. The result was the Organization for European Economic Cooperation (OEEC), a European planning and coordinating body. The Marshall Plan was a great success in many ways, not the least being the establishment of organs of European economic cooperation.

In the military sphere, the North Atlantic Treaty Organization (NATO) matched the Marshall Plan. Once again driven by fears of Soviet expansionism, the United States joined with several Western European states to form a defensive military alliance. Beginning with the 1948 Brussels Treaty, which committed Great Britain, France, Belgium, the Netherlands, and Luxembourg to a common defense, the United States, together with Canada, the signatories to the Brussels Treaty, and Denmark, Norway, Italy, Iceland, and Portugal, established NATO in April 1949.

The Europeans took additional steps on their own initiative to reinforce the impetus toward European unification that the Marshall Plan and NATO provided. In 1948, Belgium, the Netherlands, and Luxembourg formed Benelux, a customs union or free trade zone. A year later, several European countries, including Great Britain, France, and the Benelux countries, established the Council of Europe, a parliamentary body that met at Strasbourg, France. Although the Council of Europe was a tangible sign of progress toward European unity, it nevertheless revealed many of the problems that European unionists faced. Members of the Council represented their countries' legislative bodies and were not elected by nor responsible to European voters. Moreover, while the representatives could debate and pass motions, they lacked legislative authority, since no state was willing to surrender its sovereignty to the supranational Council. Consequently, the Council proved to be little more than a high-powered debating society.

When the move toward political unity foundered on the rock of national sovereignty, those who favored further European integration looked in a different direction. Under the leadership of Jean Monnet, a dedicated French Europeanist, economic integration advanced rapidly. Sympathetic political leaders including Robert Schuman of France, Alcide de Gasperi of Italy, Konrad Adenauer of the emerging West German state, and Paul-Henri Spaak of Belgium supported Monnet's vision. In May 1950, Schuman presented a proposal calling for the integration of Western Europe's coal and steel industries. Although Monnet devised the proposal, it was named the Schuman Plan; it resulted in the European Coal and Steel Community (ECSC), which began to operate in 1952. Comprising France, West Germany, Italy, and the Benelux countries, ECSC not only assured each country access to coal and steel resources, but also coordinated the development of heavy industry for the member countries and established a viable administrative structure headed by a High Authority that wielded extensive supranational powers.

ECSC's success paved the way for another step toward European economic integration. With Monnet once again providing the vision, on March 25, 1957, the ECSC members signed the Treaty of Rome, which created the European Economic Community (EEC or Common Market) with its headquarters in Brussels. The EEC sought to eliminate all tariffs between member states, to formulate a common tariff policy applicable to nonmember states, and to facilitate the unimpeded movement of both labor and capital among the six member states. At the same time, the EEC states also created the European Atomic Community (Euratom) to conduct peaceful nuclear research. The member states also erected a supranational administrative structure comprised chiefly of technological experts committed to the idea of European unity. The EEC embraced 175 million Europeans, forming one of the largest trading blocs and one of the largest free trade zones in the world. The only sour note came when Great Britain rejected membership in the EEC.

While Western Europe made important strides toward economic integration, the drive for greater unity also encountered difficulties. The Council of Europe continued to languish, and an attempt to create a supranational European army, the European Defense Community, failed in 1954. When Charles de Gaulle became president of France in 1958, the quest for European unification became more difficult. While de Gaulle's objectives continue to generate debate among scholars, it seems that the French president supported the concept of a unified Europe as long as this Europe was led by France and worked to further French national interests above all. One thing was certain: de Gaulle resented the loose control that the United States exercised over Western Europe and wanted to oust American influence from the Continent. To this end, he removed French troops from NATO in 1966 and created a nuclear arsenal for France, the so-called *force de frappe*. While these steps certainly undercut U.S. authority, they also harmed the chances for European unification.

De Gaulle also turned his attention to the EEC, where he twice vetoed Britain's belated application for membership (1963, 1967) because he believed that Britain was acting as a Trojan horse for the United States and, perhaps more important, because he feared that Great Britain's presence in the Common Market would diminish his and France's importance. He also insisted that the EEC bend to the wishes of France, and when he could not get his way he was willing to bring EEC activity to a halt, as he did in 1965. De Gaulle resisted attempts to transform the EEC into a vehicle for the political unification of Europe and attacked the already existing supranational nature of the organization. Demanding that national interests take precedence over supranational ones, he carried the day with the Luxembourg Agreement (1966), which gave each member state of the Common Market the right to veto EEC decisions whenever it felt that its national interests were at stake.

After de Gaulle, the EEC was not quite the force for European unity that Monnet had envisioned. Rather than serving as the embryo for European political union, it more than ever became an economic coordinating and planning body where the individual European states voiced their concerns and tried—sometimes successfully and sometimes not—to balance their competing interests. Behind the Common Market's supranational facade, national sovereignty or national self-interest prevailed. This is not to say that the Common Market's member states abandoned it. In fact, the member states were well aware that the EEC was a major reason for Europe's economic prosperity, and they were not about to dismantle it. However, they would not surrender their sovereignty to it.

Despite these setbacks, the EEC experienced some significant gains between 1967 and the mid-1980s. In 1967 the EEC consolidated its numerous supranational bodies into a single organization, the European Community, or EC. In 1968 the last internal tariffs disappeared, three to six years ahead of schedule. More countries also joined. After de Gaulle resigned as French president in 1969, Great Britain joined the EC in 1973. Ireland and Denmark entered at the same time. In 1981 Greece joined the EC, and Spain and Portugal followed in 1985. Thanks to the collection of external tariffs and a 1 percent value added tax (VAT) levied in all member states, after 1975 the EC enjoyed its own source of income and the greater independence such funds provided. In 1978 the EC created the European Monetary System. Although the system did not provide for a single European currency, it was an important step in that direction. One year later, the European Parliament—consisting of the assemblies of ECSC, EEC, and Euratom, and acting as something of a successor to the moribund Council of Europe—gained the right to elect its membership directly. Henceforth, individual Europeans would vote for representatives to the Parliament rather than having the governments of the member states choose the representatives.

While the EC enjoyed great success, especially in the economic realm, many problems continued to plague the organization. In attempting to balance conflicting national interests, EC regulations grew more complex and less rational. For example, the EC's less than coherent agricultural policy led to "mountains of butter and lakes of wine" in costly storage facilities. Furthermore, with the addition of six new members in twelve years, the EC lost some of its cohesion. This was particularly true with the admission of Ireland and the three Mediterranean states, whose economies were more agrarian and less advanced than the prevailing EC norm. Margaret Thatcher, British prime minister from 1979 to 1990, proved to be as obstinate as de Gaulle had been. Moreover, despite the elimination of tariffs, other national bureaucratic and administrative practices impeded free trade. Most discouraging, perhaps, the 1973 oil embargo and the subsequent severe economic downturn revealed the fragility of European union. Faced with rising unemployment and declining production, the European countries tended to act independently of each other. This every man for himself attitude dealt a severe blow to the cause of European unification.

In the mid-1980s, the EC's member states took steps to revitalize the institution. Spurred on by the need to compete more effectively with the United States and Japan, and fearful of falling behind technologically, the EC member states recommitted themselves to Monnet's original ideas about European unification. In July 1987 they adopted the Single European Act. Hoping to create a "single Europe" by 1992, the act called for an integrated market completely free of exchange controls and barriers to the movement of capital and labor. It also provided for more coordinated industrial and agrarian policies, and it bestowed greater power on the European Parliament. Most important, perhaps, it ended the veto power that individual member states had exercised since the de Gaulle era. Henceforth, binding decisions would require only a majority vote of the EC members.

However, during the early 1990s the renewed drive toward greater unification encountered some serious problems. The Treaty on European Union, the so-called Maastricht Treaty, designed to advance the Single Act of European Union, was rejected by Danish voters in 1992. Fortunately for the cause of European union, the Danes reversed their decision the following year when all the other EC countries ratified the Maastricht Treaty. For some, however, the ratification process proved difficult. Maastricht's provisions called for "an ever-closer union among the peoples of Europe" and created a new, twelve-nation "European Union." The treaty also enhanced the powers of the European Parliament; increased cooperation among the member states on a wide range of issues including crime, the environment, and immigration; urged greater integration of foreign and security policy with an eye toward eventually creating common defense and foreign policies; and called for a single European currency by 1999.

Nevertheless, at the very time that the Maastricht Treaty was being ratified, its goal of creating a single European currency was being made more difficult to achieve. In August 1993, the European Monetary System's exchange rate mechanism (ERM), which set the value of European currencies in relation to each other, virtually collapsed under the pressure of international currency speculation. A temporary solution allowing currencies within the ERM to fluctuate against each other in bands of 15 percent rather than the previous 2.25 percent was cobbled together, but one former EC finance minister said that the crisis "meant the end of a single currency" for Europe. If in fact this is the case, then the ultimate goal of European unification must remain in doubt.

INTERPRETIVE ESSAY
Richard A. Leiby

Our century has witnessed some bold political experiments. For example, both communism and fascism sought unsuccessfully to destroy the traditional patterns of nation-state politics. The supporters of European unity also seek to change the world's assumptions about the role of the nation-state; however, unlike communism and fascism, the movement for European unity is both benign and viable. The slow but steady integration of Europe's political and economic institutions since World War II promises that the continent might become a "United States of Europe," that is, a supranational state to which the historically independent nations of Europe would surrender most if not all of their sovereignty.

Interestingly, it was the United States that initially supplied much of the impetus for post–World War II Europe's first hesitant steps toward political and economic unity. Although World War II had deeply disturbed the Europeans and led some of them to conclude that European unity was a desirable goal if not an absolute necessity for the continent's future, only the United States possessed the requisite moral and material resources to initiate the process. And the United States had good reason to start the ball rolling.

Faced with a growing communist menace, the Truman administration welcomed any arrangement that helped stabilize and strengthen its European allies. The European Recovery Program, popularly known as the Marshall Plan, gave evidence of a financial commitment, and NATO pledged the United States to defend Western Europe. Additionally, the

United States supported every European attempt at integration, including the Council of Europe, the ill-fated European Defense Community, and the European Common Market. Undoubtedly, this steadfast support, coupled with the relative security afforded by NATO's nuclear umbrella, was critical to the success of the European unity movement.

It is somewhat ironic that the first attempts at institutionalized European integration were undertaken to promote efficiency, not peace. U.S. grants and loans sent before 1947 reached Europe when its needs were most basic. Consequently, the aid was used to pay for food or energy, not infrastructure. As hardships continued into 1947, many Americans wondered if the aid had been "thrown down a rat hole." As a result, when the Marshall Plan was introduced in 1947, loans and grants were conditional upon the creation of a European organization to oversee their distribution.

Europe's response, the Organization for European Economic Cooperation (OEEC), is often touted as the initial step toward European unity; but in reality that overstates its impact. As constructed, the organization was incapable of achieving any political or economic integration. It is true that the organization rationalized aid distribution and that European trade benefited, but the free trade area it originally intended to create never emerged. Similarly, the OEEC was no embryonic European government since it was never given supranational powers. Its recommendations were subject to unanimous agreement, and if a nation abstained from voting it would be exempted from compliance. Indeed, the very fact that the United States was itself a member destroys any notion that "Europe" began with the OEEC. Although the OEEC decided which nations received grants, in the final analysis the United States retained control over the delivery of the funds.

Undaunted by the OEEC's shortcomings, Europe's attempts to forge political unity proceeded apace. Unfortunately, the unproductive Council of Europe and the defeat of the European Defense Community in 1954 left the cause of political unity in little better shape than it had been in 1945. The stalemate arose from two divergent views of integration. Some politicians who espoused unity saw integration as a means to destroy national barriers and create "Europe." Others viewed integration only as a loose confederation of independent states; in other words, as a device to bring about common economic and political revival while preserving national autonomy. For the latter group, "Europe" was more an abstraction than a definite goal, and consequently it was not about to support legislation that would limit the national right to self-determination. Clearly, many European governments were reluctant to surrender sovereignty so soon after having paid such a high price to regain it.

In those early years it would have been very easy to give up on integration. Instead of surrendering to the prevailing pessimism, some Europeans such as Jean Monnet and Robert Schuman adopted a gradualist strategy. Monnet, the son of a wine merchant, had made a name for himself as a champion of cooperation during his years as deputy secretary of the League of Nations and later as France's wartime emissary to Great Britain and the United States. He postulated that a more cautious approach, which emphasized limited integration in certain key economic sectors, would lead to further political, economic, and social integration. Working behind the scenes, Monnet devised plans to pool German and French coal and steel resources. In the belief that someone with more political clout than he should sponsor his plan, Monnet picked Robert Schuman, the French foreign minister, to present his ideas to the public. Schuman's selection proved not only practically but also symbolically effective. Born in Lorraine, a province that had changed hands between France and Germany on four different occasions between 1871 and 1945, Schuman had seen firsthand how national antagonism can lead to confrontation. On May 1, 1950, the men unveiled the Schuman Plan, a blueprint for the European Coal and Steel Community (ECSC), Europe's first true step toward unity.

The ECSC is significant for a number of reasons, but at first glance coal and steel do not seem an obvious choice for a pilot integration project. They were older industries, and because of their links to armaments production they were always considered essential to national security. But if the ultimate goal of integration was to make war not only unthinkable but materially impossible, then success would carry an enormous psychological impact. In addition, the arrangement made good economic sense. Germany's abundant coal supplies, when coupled with French iron, meant more efficient production and lower costs. Furthermore, since steel has many applications, the advantages of integration might spill over into other economic sectors. The scheme also offered a chance to manipulate the steel market, which in the early 1950s was suffering from overproduction and lack of demand. The formation of a community interest could legally rationalize distribution and oversee production before private firms could cartelize and accomplish the same thing illegally.

The Schuman Plan was an economic arrangement motivated by a desire for political cooperation. The plan entrusted decision making to a High Authority comprised of nine members (two each from France and Germany; one each from Belgium, the Netherlands, Luxembourg, and

Italy; and one at-large member) chosen for their special expertise and for their interest in the common good. The Authority's job was to make and execute "laws," including production and distribution quotas, taxes on production, and fines for noncompliance. The novelty of this institution was that its membership was to be free of national allegiances so that it might work in the name of "Europe."

Monnet and Schuman understood that a rationalization of two such labor-intensive industries as coal and steel would lead to some worker layoffs in the less productive plants and mines. To address the social costs of integration, the Schuman Plan empowered the High Authority to levy and collect a surtax on production. This money could then be used to provide assistance to dislocated workers and to retrain those who lost jobs permanently. The High Authority also committed the community to social reforms intended to bring about uniform standards and practices in the workplace.

No one doubts that the ECSC played a major role in Europe's economic revival. The elimination of coal and steel tariffs and the effective restriction of cartelization were clear successes. That the member states were sufficiently encouraged to proceed with further integration is an indication, albeit indirect, that the treaty was (if nothing else) perceived as a success. However, if one looks to production figures to corroborate this perception, distinct conclusions are elusive. Steel production did increase markedly throughout the 1950s and into the 1960s. Even though many historians have linked this dramatic increase in production to the treaty, such a conclusion is presumptuous since it is impossible to "replay" history and compare what production would have been without the ECSC. With no claim for cause and effect, it is still safe to say that the treaty made steel cheaper and more profitable to produce and that demand was stimulated. However, such accomplishments fell short for the many supporters of supranationalism who had hoped for a dramatic increase in production and trade.

The ECSC's lasting legacy was not its economic productivity but its political boldness. The treaty was a milestone in the history of international affairs, marking the first instance when national authority was willingly transferred to a supranational body. But this achievement was a far cry from unification. Integration was still confined to only one sector, and it was still uncertain whether the much hoped for spill-over effect would actually occur. Indeed, while coal and steel moved toward increased integration, economic nationalism continued unabated in other areas, including the key sectors of agriculture and transportation. Many nations clung desperately to their national product standards, labor mobility laws, and tariff schedules as ways of protecting their industry and farming. The Coal and Steel Community failed to address, let alone dismantle, such economic barriers to integration. It is best to regard the ECSC as a bold but limited political experiment. It showed that international cooperation was not only possible but also potentially lucrative. As a first step on the path to complete integration, it was an important one and provided a good foundation on which to build the process.

In 1955 delegates of the ECSC member nations gathered at Messina to begin negotiations for a larger union. Again, external events added impetus to the drive for increased integration. Egypt's seizure of the Suez Canal and the West's subsequent failure to recapture it awakened many Europeans to their dependence on Arab oil. In addition, the Soviet Union's crackdown on Hungary in 1956 further exacerbated East-West tensions and revived the old theme of Europe's impotence in world affairs. In this tense diplomatic atmosphere, the delegates of the Six (that is, the six original ECSC member nations), emboldened by ECSC success, worked to expand economic cooperation by creating a single market similar to the one already established between Belgium, Luxembourg, and the Netherlands. The Treaty of Rome was the result.

The European Economic Community (EEC or Common Market) went into operation on January 1, 1958. Its goal was to free all other commodities of customs duties and tariffs within twelve years. The agreement created a large free trade area and established a common tariff policy on goods imported from nonmember states. Its supranational institutions mirrored those of the ECSC with the important addition that decisions could be reached only by a "qualified majority," that is, both a majority of votes *and* a majority of nations had to agree, thereby protecting the interests of the smaller states against the larger nations. The treaty also established a European Social Fund, financed with production surcharges, to continue the ECSC's mandate to retrain and if necessary resettle displaced workers. A newly created European Investment Bank provided seed capital to the community's underdeveloped regions.

Unlike that of the ECSC, the Common Market's success is clearly discernable. Industrial trade barriers disappeared by 1962, and the remaining tariff barriers were all but eliminated by 1968, well ahead of schedule. Intramarket trade rose 73 percent during the treaty's first three years, and the European gross national product increased 21 percent. Standards of living within the Six reached new highs during the 1960s. But it would be erroneous to conclude that such success was easily achieved. One sector that posed particularly thorny integration problems was agriculture. For years, Europe's farmers enjoyed the benefits of national subsidies and tariff restrictions. Although government intervention helped Europe's farmers, the resulting high food prices gave farmers little or no incentive to modernize or avoid overproduction. In order to solve these problems, France (Europe's major producer of foodstuffs and perennial "victim" of protectionism) led negotiations to rationalize agricultural production. It took round-the-clock negotiations to reach a workable consensus, but on January 14, 1962, a Common Agricultural Policy (CAP) emerged. The CAP agreement guaranteed all farmers a fixed price for their produce and communitywide tariffs to bring the price of imported foodstuffs to at least the minimum commodity price.

The Common Agricultural Policy points out both the positive and negative nature of European integration. Although CAP was a clear victory for French agriculture, its significance lies in Germany's willingness to compromise, even at the expense of its own farmers—an action that boded well for supranationalism. On the other hand, the compromise was also a good example of "negative integration." The Common Agricultural Policy did not eliminate agricultural tariffs, it consolidated them. Henceforth, the tariff burdens were simply shifted to nonmember states. Consequently, Europe's farmers still had no incentive to modernize production, and food prices have remained unusually high compared to world markets.

Despite the EEC's economic success, the movement for political unity encountered further difficulty. Again, the accidents of history played a major role. When the Fourth French Republic collapsed in 1958, Charles de Gaulle, France's war hero, established the Fifth Republic with himself as president. De Gaulle had his own opinions about European unity, preferring a federal approach that would allow France to preserve its national interests. De Gaulle's intransigent nationalism had a number of unfortunate by-products. His opposition to Great Britain's application for membership clearly set back the cause of unity. In addition, his steadfast refusal to grant the Common Market's Commission the expanded powers it needed to enforce the vast array of economic and social agreements nearly destroyed supranationalism. In 1966 France partially withdrew from a number of Common Market institutions. This so-called Empty Chair Crisis led to the Luxembourg Agreement, which stipulated that an individual nation could override the Commission if that country felt its vital interests were threatened. This humiliation undermined the unity movement and demonstrated that political unity would not be achieved in the foreseeable future.

De Gaulle's retirement from politics in 1969 not only dissolved the political impasse, it also helped to bring about the most active and productive period of political negotiation. A new cadre of French politicians (notably Georges Pompidou and Valéry Giscard d'Estaing) led the way in breaking the stalemate of the 1960s. Great Britain was finally accepted for community membership; and by becoming a member, it tacitly accepted that its future lay not with its former empire but with the Continent.

Encouraged by Great Britain's commitment, the EC member nations boldly declared their intent to form a European Union. In a series of conferences beginning with the Hague meeting of 1969 and culminating at the Paris conference of 1972, the EC delegates set out to create institutions to achieve this goal. Two major efforts emerged. The boldest move was the creation of a system to keep the exchange rates of Europe's currencies relatively stable vis-à-vis each other. The scheme, called "the snake in the tunnel," stipulated that the values of European currencies vis-à-vis each other would not be allowed to fluctuate more than 2.25 percent, and that they would remain within 4.5 percent of the U.S. dollar despite the fluctuations of demand in the world currency market. Although "the snake" was essentially an attempt to end the currency devaluations of the late 1960s, many advocates of union interpreted it as the first step toward creation of a single European currency, an item without which a "Europe" could not exist. In addition, a European Parliament was fashioned from older ECSC and Common Market institutions. For the first time in many years, it looked as though the political side of the European unity movement was back on track. Few could have foreseen that events beyond Europe's control once again would derail the process, this time for fifteen years.

In 1973 war between Israel and the Arabs caused the Organization of Petroleum Exporting Countries (OPEC) to cut production, resulting in a quadrupling of the price of oil. The action sent economic shock waves throughout the world, but particularly through Western Europe, where many nations were entirely dependent on foreign sources of energy. In this hour of mutual need, the ideals of unity were suddenly and decisively shoved aside. Rather than work in concert, the EEC member governments scurried about individually in an attempt to secure special concessions from OPEC. When a second oil crisis struck in 1979, the malaise of the 1970s continued into the 1980s.

Economic statistics tell a harsh tale. Between 1980 and 1983, the combined gross national product of the EC countries grew less than 1 percent each year. Unemployment levels in 1982 were nearly double those of 1978. These statistics may be shocking, but they are not unlike similar figures recorded at that time in the United States and other industrialized countries. Furthermore, by 1983 Europe was falling far behind the United States and Japan in high-tech fields such as electronics and computers.

The oil crisis probably did more than any other single event to retard the cause of unity. It pointed out the lack of a common energy policy and tested the will to share bad as well as good times. The recession also destroyed some of the EC's economic institutions. The "snake" died as national governments withdrew their currencies from the scheme, and with it died hopes for a single currency.

Paradoxically, economic stagnation spurred political progress. Europe's ineffective response to OPEC made clear the need for a concerted foreign policy effort. The result was the European Political Cooperation agreement (EPC), which established a mechanism whereby Europe's governments could confer and reach decisions in foreign affairs. This was an important step forward, considering that foreign policy had always been the nation-state's most jealously guarded prerogative. The initiative began as regularly scheduled summit conferences, but soon took on a more formal title—the European Council. The Council, together with the new European Parliament, held out the hope that a truly supranational government was in the offing. In one of its first actions (1974), the Council reiterated that monetary union was vital to the future of European unity and, given the prevailing economic difficulties, all the more important a goal. Eventually, the European Monetary System (1979) emerged, featuring a revival of the "snake" concept called the Exchange Rate Mechanism (ERM). The reform's centerpiece was the creation of the European Currency Unit (ECU), with a value based on a set proportion of each member nation's currency.

The 1970s also saw movement toward realizing the Treaty of Rome's goals for equal employment opportunities for men and women. On February 10, 1975, the EC began what was called Positive Action, a program to eliminate gender bias in the workplace. Positive Action outlawed sex discrimination in salaries and established an equal pay for equal work policy. Gender bias in hiring, job descriptions, and job conditions was also attacked. A recommendation in the following year augmented the program, suggesting equal treatment for men and women in matters of promotion, training, and social security. Unfortunately, social legislation proved difficult to enforce. Most of the directives were optional, and compliance was at best sporadic. But as the Community pulled out of its economic malaise, it had at least the trappings of a unified social framework. In reality, much remains to be done.

Since 1985 the pendulum has again swung toward a more optimistic view of integration, evidenced by the Draft Treaty for Union and the so-called Project 1992. After identifying key problems preventing a totally free marketplace—including unnecessary border controls, excessive paperwork and huge fines for simple mistakes, divergent national product standards, differing rates of Value Added Taxation (VAT), and some remaining nationally protected markets—the EC set 1992 as its target date for the elimination of all remaining nontariff barriers to trade. The passage of the Single European Act (SEA) enhanced the process. SEA allows for majority decisions, and thereby provides for a more democratic method of decision making and precludes any single country from blocking legislation. Additionally, it gives the European Parliament de facto veto power over the Council, since its dissent would require a unanimous Council vote to override. Thus Parliament's power has actually increased.

As of 1995, the tariff goals had been largely accomplished. However, the more contentious political, social, and economic problems defy solution. The debate over the Maastricht Treaty, which would commit Europe to unity and expand the EC's supranational authority, has already resulted in the resignation of at least one major political figure, Margaret Thatcher, who stepped down as Great Britain's prime minister in 1991 rather than agree to further limitations on British sovereignty. Two years later, that very same government under John Major became the last EC member to approve the treaty. It is ironic but fitting, given the history of the European unity movement, that the British Parliament ratified the Maastricht Treaty on the same day that economic pressures on the French franc led to a collapse of the Exchange Rate Mechanism. Once again, progress and setback seemed inextricably intertwined.

The European unity movement has proceeded in fits and starts. Its history has shown that economic ventures are more easily accomplished in times of political turmoil, and political progress is more likely when economic fortunes decline. That dynamic may seem a bit convoluted, but within it lies hidden strengths. Since one sector or another is always making progress toward further integration, the Community is never totally at rest. The movement possesses an internal flexibility that enables it to take advantage of external events. Thus, the EC moves forward.

Indeed, despite various periods of inactivity, the Community's continual progress has made the question of its survival irrelevant. The Common Market is here to stay. Even the most skeptical acknowledge that withdrawal from the Community would be tantamount to committing economic suicide. Political unity, on the other hand, is still an open question. Europe's leaders have shown the will to work toward union, but as much as they want unity, their decisions are still very much dictated by national interests. Is complete integration a realistic goal? Some observers assert that total union is not and never will be the Community's goal. As evidence, they cite the Draft Treaty for Union (1985) and other documents that affirm that the purpose of political integration is not to destroy the nation-state but to enhance it. In other words, the unity movement aims to create not a monolithic superstate but a mixed government where power is shared between national and supranational authorities. Such an interpretation must disappoint those purists who still believe in complete and total union, but it strikes the neutral observer as a pragmatic attempt to bridge the hopes for continued integration with present political realities. For now, the concept of "Europe" must remain in limbo. European integration no longer aims for unity but for "an ever closer union."

Many difficult political, social, and intellectual obstacles will undoubtedly delay or derail this ever closer union. The single greatest economic stumbling block is the lack of a European currency. Until summer 1993, there was reason for optimism that the ECU might become Europe's official legal tender. It is already an established commodity on the world's financial and trade markets, and the Community sends aid to nonmember nations in ECU increments. Unfortunately, when the Exchange Rate Mechanism collapsed, it severely damaged the chances of currency unification. Can the ECU rebound to become Europe's medium of exchange? Yes, but only if the major European states find a way to stabilize the values of their indigenous currencies vis-à-vis each other. Given the present recession and Germany's apparent desire to put the reintegration of its eastern lands above the needs of the Community, the time does not seem ripe.

Social unification has also proved a difficult task. Given Europe's cultural diversity, uniform social standards are critical if a single community is to emerge. If goods, services, ideas, and even people are to traverse national borders freely, then the quality of the workplace must be ensured and employee rights must be safeguarded. The social goals promised in the Treaty of Rome, including gender-neutral pay equalization, industrial hygiene, and safety research, are still not fully realized.

Although social integration has proved difficult for even the advanced members of the EEC, it poses a greater problem for the recently admitted nations, who have resisted complying with a myriad of regulations. It is understandably difficult to bring the social standards of the twenty-first century to countries where enclaves still languish in the nineteenth. Consequently, the EEC has had to be patient with its newer partners and allow them time to bring their national social standards up to Community standards. This has slowed the tempo of integration markedly.

Although the task seems monumental, there is reason for optimism. The European Social Fund has done much to support underdeveloped areas despite the social prejudices that remain. Conquering those prejudices will remain the Community's biggest social project. The need for gender-neutral hiring practices, social insurance, and environmental laws may escape the farmers of southern Italy or the fishermen of Spain; but without such uniform social protection, a community can hardly be forged.

The movement for political unification has advanced during the last twenty years. European political parties have emerged to represent transnational interests. Their members can seek direct election to the European Parliament, a working legislature complete with lawmaking and taxation powers gleaned from the nation-states. Nevertheless, many problems still defy solution. The Community's political institutions may be well thought out and constructed, but they will never function successfully unless they command the respect of the citizens they govern. Hence, the EC's most formidable political task may have an intellectual dimension. It must create a "European" identity that can command the allegiance of its people. This will be no mean feat, since nationalism (the philosophy that the nation-state, comprised of like-minded, ethnically similar, and linguistically united peoples, is the natural form governments must take) has held sway for nearly four centuries. Ethnic loyalties will hardly disappear with the rising tide of supranationalism. If that is true, is further political integration a pipe dream?

Nationalism is a double-edged sword in that it can be used to stress both the similarities uniting peoples and the differences separating them. Twentieth-century nationalism has stressed the latter, as examples from Belfast to Bosnia will attest. But nationalism need not be negative; it can be the same unifying force that brought together the German and Italian peoples, among others, in the nineteenth century. Europe's challenge is to overcome the differences that separate its populations and to emphasize what they all hold in common. It is no accident that the model for integration has always been countries (like the United States) that have somehow earned the allegiance of their disparate ethnic and religious minorities. "Europe" can emerge only if the member nations accept each other's ethnic and linguistic individuality, and realize the strengths of a multiethnic, multicultural society. The EC must redirect Europe's nationalistic urges toward the geographical and historical uniqueness of the continent as a whole, and away from the divisive ideology of the nation-state.

If Europe succeeds, it has much to gain. The new Europe has already become one of the world's largest single trading blocs, encompassing over 320 million people. A politically united Europe, economically on par with the United States and Japan, and with a common foreign policy, would be a potent world force. Some nations, particularly in South America and the Far East, have already formed supranational trading blocs based on the European model in the hopes of increasing their economic and political status. Is it possible that we are witnessing the dawn of a new age in diplomacy, when geopolitical power blocs supplant the nation-states as the world's power brokers?

Such speculative questions are perhaps best left to the political theorists; but it is safe to conclude that the European Community has already altered traditional politics. Its very existence signals a rejection of the past, when international rivalry, competition, and war formed the status quo. It is an unparalleled attempt to forge a future for Europe based on cooperation and peace. However, as with all experiments, history's judgment will determine its ultimate success or failure.

SELECTED BIBLIOGRAPHY

Camps, Miriam. *European Unification in the Sixties: From the Veto to the Crisis.* New York: McGraw-Hill, 1966. In-depth account of a turbulent decade for European political unification.

Cecchini, Paolo. *The European Challenge 1992: The Benefits of a Single Market.* Hants, England: Wildwood House, 1988. Official EC report on the obstacles that remained for the 1992 target date, and the relative cost to the Community of nonratification.

Gillingham, John. *Coal, Steel and the Rebirth of Europe, 1945–1955.* New York: Cambridge University Press, 1991. The latest and best scholarship on the ECSC's earliest years.

Hackett, Clifford. *Cautious Revolution: The European Community Arrives.* New York: Praeger, 1990. A look at the institutions and problems of the EC.

Hill, Brian. *The Common Agricultural Policy: Past, Present and Future.* London: Methuen, 1984. Part of Methuen's EEC series, a good history of the development of agricultural policy.

Hill, Christopher, ed. *National Foreign Policies and European Political Cooperation.* London: George Allen and Unwin, 1983. Essays outlining the various national responses to a unification of foreign policy.

Lee, Roger, and P. E. Ogden, eds. *Economy and Society in the EEC.* Hantsfield, England: Saxon House, 1976. A look at the EEC's geographic, economic, and demographic trends.

Lodge, Juliet, ed. *European Union: The European Community in Search of a Future.*

London: Macmillan, 1986. A collection of essays analyzing the problems and potential of integration during the 1980s and beyond.

Ludlow, Peter. *The Making of the European Monetary System: A Case Study of the Politics of the European Community.* London: Butterworth Scientific, 1982. Explores the confluence of politics and money policy; part of Butterworth's European Studies series.

Mayne, Richard. *The Community of Europe: Past, Present and Future.* New York: W. W. Norton, 1962. An insider's account of the genesis of the Common Market.

———. *The Recovery of Europe.* New York: Doubleday Books, 1973. A more in-depth account of the early postwar years.

Minshull, G. N. *The New Europe: An Economic Geography of the EEC.* London: Hodder and Stoughton, 1980. Another look at the EEC, this time through the eyes of a geographer.

Monnet, Jean. *Memoirs.* Introduction by George Ball. Translated by Richard Mayne. New York: Doubleday, 1978. The reminiscences of the "Father of Europe."

Pryce, Roy, ed. *The Dynamics of European Union.* London: Routledge, 1989. A useful compendium of thought pieces concerning the history and development of the European Community.

Schmitt, Hans A. *The Path to European Union: From the Marshall Plan to the Common Market.* Baton Rouge: Louisiana State University Press, 1962. Dated, but perhaps still the best scholarly account of the process leading to the EEC's formation, with a particularly valuable account of the ECSC.

Tipton, Frank B., and Robert Aldrich. *An Economic and Social History of Europe from 1939 to the Present.* Baltimore: Johns Hopkins University Press, 1987. As the title indicates, this survey is strong on economic and social developments.

Tsoukalis, Loukas. *The European Community: Past, Present, and Future.* Oxford, England: Basil Blackwell, 1983. A collection of occasional papers dealing with aspects of integration in the early 1980s.

Willis, F. Roy, ed. *European Integration.* New York: Franklin Watts, 1975. Articles from historical and political science perspectives on key events in the Common Market's early history.

———. *France, Germany and the New Europe 1945–1967.* New York: Oxford University Press, 1968. A detailed account of the role these two key nations played in the Community's formation.

Mikhail S. Gorbachev, General Secretary of the Communist Party of the Soviet Union (1985–1991). The collapse of the USSR marked the end of Soviet communism and ushered in a period of instability for much of the world. (Reproduced from the Collections of the Library of Congress)

10

The Collapse of the Soviet Union, 1985–1991

INTRODUCTION

On November 10, 1982, Radio Moscow took to the airwaves with a steady stream of dirges and somber classical music, the traditional signal that an important Soviet personage had passed from the scene. And in fact, Leonid Brezhnev, general secretary of the Communist Party of the Soviet Union (CPSU) and leader of the USSR since his ouster of Nikita Khrushchev in 1964, had died. At the time of Brezhnev's death, the Soviet Union was a mighty state, universally acknowledged as one of the world's two superpowers. However, beneath this glistening facade a number of serious problems challenged the Soviet leadership.

The Soviet economic model, little changed since Joseph Stalin created it in the 1930s, was increasingly unable to meet the demands of a modern society. Untouched by market forces, which were virtually outlawed in the USSR, the Soviet Union's economy continued to produce outmoded and shoddy products more appropriate for the early stages of the Industrial Revolution than for a high-tech world. Moreover, the gigantic Soviet military establishment had first call on whatever resources the state possessed. The result was a curious anomaly in which the Soviets could project their military might across the globe and send their cosmonauts into space for long periods of time, but could neither feed their population without large and expensive grain imports nor house them properly.

In addition to the critical question of economic stagnation, other difficulties confronted the USSR. At the end of World War II, the Soviet Union had established its control over Eastern Europe. However, the Soviet satellite empire was a restive one. Poles, Czechs, Hungarians, and others chafed under Soviet domination and yearned to break free. The ethnic minorities within the Soviet Union itself, who had never fully reconciled themselves to Soviet power, were potentially even more troublesome. Although these ethnic minorities were outwardly quiescent, events soon demonstrated that the spirit of nationalism had put down deep roots among the more than 100 different ethnic groups that comprised the USSR.

At the time of Brezhnev's death, the Soviet Union also found itself seriously overextended in its pursuit of a vigorous global foreign policy. Under the leadership of Ronald Reagan, the United States, the USSR's old rival, evinced both a renewed purposefulness and a willingness to spend billions on new armaments. At the same time, the Soviet Union was increasingly bogged down in a guerrilla war in Afghanistan that not only siphoned off money and manpower but also estranged the Soviets from the Islamic world. Finally, dozens of client states in the Third World casually squandered Soviet aid and then demanded more.

Facing such an array of difficulties, it seemed unlikely that the old men who led the Soviet Union at the time of Brezhnev's death could muster the imagination and initiative to find solutions. And they couldn't. Although Yurii Andropov, Brezhnev's immediate successor, was unusually bright and sophisticated for a Soviet leader, he was already fatally ill when he came to power, and his plans for reform never got off the drawing board. Andropov's successor, Konstantin Chernenko, was a doddering old timeserver who accomplished virtually nothing from the time he was named general secretary in February 1984 until his death in March 1985.

With Chernenko's death, the CPSU finally turned to a younger person to lead the Party and the state: Mikhail Gorbachev, a fifty-four-year-old Communist Party functionary from the Stavropol region of southern Russia. The son of a collective farmer, Gorbachev had risen rapidly through the Party ranks, gaining admittance to the Politburo, or inner council of the Party, in 1979.

After being named general secretary, Gorbachev moved to establish his control over the Communist Party. Older Soviet leaders died, retired, or were removed from positions of authority. Their replacements, like

Gorbachev himself, were younger, better educated, and committed to reforming the system. Among those pushed out was Andrei Gromyko, longtime Soviet foreign minister and subsequently president of the USSR, who relinquished the latter post to Gorbachev; among those brought into the inner circle was Boris Yeltsin, an outspoken communist reformer from western Siberia.

The leadership vacuum of the previous few years had allowed the great difficulties confronting the Soviet Union to intensify. The domestic economy had slowed to almost a standstill as the rate of growth of the Soviet Union's gross national product dipped to less than 1.5 percent per year in the mid-1980s. A number of factors accounted for this precipitous decline: antiquated factories, a startling absence of high technology, costly and inefficient state and collective farms, a significant drop in oil production, which supplied the USSR with badly needed hard currency, and the diversion of badly needed resources for dubious military purposes. The *apparat*, the cumbersome, hidebound, venal, and incompetent bureaucracy that oversaw every aspect of life in the Soviet Union, greatly aggravated the situation.

Economic woes led to a decline in the already low Soviet standard of living. For a long time, a lack of good housing and an absence of decent consumer goods had plagued the average Soviet citizen. Now these conditions worsened. Furthermore, the health care system showed signs of collapse as the rate of infant mortality increased while life expectancy declined—demographic trends that were truly astonishing for an industrialized country. The amount of resources devoted to education decreased as well, and pollution in every imaginable form threatened to engulf the entire country. The Soviet population exhibited signs of serious demoralization. The divorce rate climbed, and corruption, a hallmark characteristic of both Russian and Soviet life, intensified. Alcoholism, a long-standing social problem, worsened and brought with it increased absenteeism, thereby further weakening the country's economic performance. The Soviet media's repeated references to the USSR's superpower status brought little consolation to a worn-out people.

However, even the Soviet Union's global position was in growing jeopardy. The war in Afghanistan dragged on, with mounting Soviet casualties. As always, the Eastern European peoples chafed under Soviet domination. Relations with the United States and its Western allies were less than cordial. And Third World client states drained limited Soviet resources without providing much in return.

Acutely aware of the problems confronting the USSR, and determined to sweep away the preceding decades' stagnation, Gorbachev initiated the policy of *perestroika,* or renewal/reconstruction. At the heart of perestroika was a determination to reform, but not replace, the existing Soviet system. Perestroika called for extensive decentralization of the rigidly controlled Soviet economy. Both industry and agriculture were to have greater freedom in the form of self-management, while the role of the *apparat* would be significantly reduced.

To make perestroika work, Gorbachev coupled it with the policy of *glasnost,* or openness. Glasnost allowed, even encouraged, a frank and open examination of not only the problems confronting the Soviet economy but virtually all aspects of Soviet life. Gorbachev apparently launched glasnost in order to win over public opinion and to undercut any opposition from entrenched interests threatened by perestroika.

Although never as clearly articulated as perestroika and glasnost, Gorbachev also determined to reassess the USSR's global position. He concluded that perestroika's success required better relations with the capitalist West and a reduced commitment to global activism.

Perestroika proved more difficult to implement than Gorbachev had imagined, while glasnost brought a tidal wave of criticism that challenged the Soviet state's very foundations. Sailing into uncharted waters, Gorbachev either introduced or permitted such radical (for the Soviet Union) concepts as economic decentralization, the profit motive, individual enterprise, a socialist or regulated market economy, and cost accounting. The role of the bureaucracy in general, but especially Gosplan, the omnipotent state planning agency, was curtailed. State subsidies for industries were reduced, and plans to transform the collective and state farms into private holdings were considered.

The perestroika reforms failed to achieve their objective. Deeply entrenched vested interests, including the *apparat,* factory and farm managers, much of the Party hierarchy, and some of the army opposed perestroika and successfully worked to undermine it. They were aided by the bumbling and inconsistent manner in which the naive and inexperienced Gorbachev approached his task. Industrial and agricultural production declined. Store shelves were stripped bare. Inflation skyrocketed. Economic chaos and confusion set in, and the Soviet economy began to collapse.

Glasnost also led to unanticipated and, for Gorbachev, unpleasant results. Discontent with Soviet life, repressed for decades, now burst into full view. Open criticism of leaders, policies, and institutions—at one time unthinkable in the Soviet Union—now became commonplace. Ad hoc groups that originally formed to discuss current issues began to appear more and more like rival political parties in the making. Atheism, the official policy of the USSR, was rejected, and the various religions of the Soviet people, especially Russian Orthodoxy, enjoyed renewed popularity. Even the heretofore sacrosanct KGB, or secret police, was publicly taken to task.

Most ominous for the Soviet leadership, glasnost permitted ethnic or national feelings, long condemned by the class-conscious Soviet leadership as reflective of a petit bourgeois mentality, to bubble to the surface. The Soviet Union was a multiethnic state. Of the approximately 285 million Soviet citizens, only about one-half were Russians. Nevertheless, the Russians clearly dominated the USSR, a condition that the numerous ethnic minorities greatly resented. With glasnost, these minorities now had the opportunity to vent their frustration. If the cry of "Russians Out!" was not yet heard on the streets, it was at least beginning to form in many minds.

As pressure mounted on Gorbachev, events rapidly spun out of control. Astoundingly, the Soviet empire in Eastern Europe collapsed. Taking advantage of Gorbachev's new course, the Eastern Europeans broke free of Moscow's embrace. Acts of defiance toward Moscow and the puppet Marxist rulers it had installed increased in frequency until a tidal wave of revolution rolled over the Soviet bloc in 1989. Poland withdrew from the Moscow-sponsored Warsaw Treaty Organization and the Council of Mutual Economic Assistance (COMECON, or CMEA); Czechoslovakia underwent its "velvet Revolution"; and on November 9 the Berlin Wall, symbol of the Soviet Union's domination of Eastern Europe, came crashing down. The overthrow and execution of Nicolai Ceausescu, the Stalinist dictator of Romania, on Christmas Day, punctuated the complete collapse of the Soviet Union's position.

Meanwhile, the Soviet economy came perilously close to total collapse itself. While Gorbachev's incomplete and sometimes ill-conceived reforms caused growing chaos, the entrenched elite mounted a determined opposition to his policies. Consequently, Soviet agrarian and industrial production slowed dramatically. Supplies of food, fuel, and other necessities dwindled, and a rash of crippling strikes occurred. By 1991 inflation was running at more than 250 percent annually and the Soviet Union could no longer service its multibillion-dollar foreign debt.

Emboldened by glasnost and spurred on by the Eastern European example, the economically hard-pressed ethnic minorities within the Soviet Union itself began to contemplate secession. The Baltic peoples (the Estonians, Latvians, and Lithuanians), who had been forcibly incorporated into the USSR in 1940, led the way. They were soon joined by the nations of the Caucasus (the Georgians, Armenians, and Azerbaijanis). Neither threats of repression (and in the case of Lithuania the spilling of blood) nor promises of better treatment dampened the growing sentiment for independence. The emergence of a strong nationalist movement (Rukh) in Ukraine, the Soviet Union's second largest republic, seemed to call into question the USSR's continued viability.

Overwhelmed by events, Gorbachev turned to political solutions. In particular, he determined to break the CPSU's political monopoly and move the Soviet Union closer to the Western, liberal-democratic model in the hope that this would assure perestroika's success. To that end, in March 1989 he presided over elections to the Soviet Congress of People's Deputies that were remarkably free and open by Soviet standards. Although the CPSU and its allies exercised their right to appoint 750 delegates, the Soviet people elected 1,500 delegates. Many of the elected delegates opposed the CPSU's privileged position, and some criticized Gorbachev for failing to push his reforms ardently enough. Andrei Sakharov, a leading Soviet dissident and winner of the Nobel Peace Prize, and Boris Yeltsin, maverick communist who had once supported Gorbachev but now broke with him, led the charge against the CPSU and the USSR's military-industrial complex.

Stunned by the rising tide of popular sentiment that demanded further and more rapid reform, Gorbachev offered additional political concessions. In February 1990 the Supreme Soviet, the executive body of the Soviet Congress of People's Deputies, abandoned Article 6 of the Soviet constitution, which had given the CPSU a monopoly over all political power in the USSR. Shortly thereafter, Gorbachev permitted the USSR's individual republics to hold parliamentary elections. The largest republic, the Russian Republic, elected a majority of delegates favorable to Yeltsin, who now emerged as a rival to Gorbachev for power.

While Yeltsin, who was overwhelmingly elected president of the Russian Republic in June 1991, pushed Gorbachev to quicken the pace of reform, Gorbachev's opponents within the Party and the crumbling power structure were not idle. With increased frequency and boldness, they objected to the entire program of reform and urged a return to traditional policies and methods. Buffeted from both sides, Gorbachev vacillated, first trying to placate his conservative opponents and then abruptly returning to the path of reform.

When Eduard Shevardnadze, the Soviet Union's foreign minister, resigned in December 1990, Gorbachev chose to ignore his warning of an imminent attack from the threatened hard-liners. However, several months later Gorbachev's conservative opponents attempted a coup d'état. With Gorbachev on vacation in the Crimea, a conspiratorial group of disgruntled Party chieftains, disaffected military officers, and KGB officials tried to seize power on August 19, 1991. Gorbachev was placed under arrest; but the coup failed when Yeltsin rallied his forces at the Moscow White House, the parliament building of the Russian Republic, and the Red Army refused to support the conspirators.

Although Gorbachev was freed and returned to Moscow, he was a spent force. The new man of the hour was Boris Yeltsin. The Soviet Union itself, already under attack on several fronts, was also a victim of the failed coup. Within Russia, Yeltsin proceeded rapidly to destroy the Communist Party and to lay the groundwork for Russia's secession from the USSR. As the CPSU disintegrated, other member states of the USSR moved toward independence, beginning with Ukraine, which declared its independence on August 24. Other republics followed suit, and when a Ukrainian referendum on December 1 resoundingly confirmed the decision to secede, the Soviet Union was dead. On December 25, the Soviet flag, the hammer and sickle, was lowered from atop the Kremlin, and on December 31, 1991, the USSR officially ceased to exist.

INTERPRETIVE ESSAY
Charles E. Ziegler

From its birth in the Revolution of 1917 to its demise at the end of 1991, the Soviet Union stood as the chief political, ideological, and military adversary of the Western democratic world. The Western democracies were constitutionally based systems embodying the concept of representative government, holding regular competitive elections for political office, respecting (in general) the rights and freedoms of the individual citizen, and promoting market economies with extensive private enterprise. By contrast, the Soviet Union and its East European colonies rejected the principles of "bourgeois democracy" as a sham, promoting instead the Marxist concept that the industrial working class should exercise political power without regard for the niceties of democratic procedure. The supposedly transitional phase of the "dictatorship of the proletariat" gradually solidified into a centralized, repressive dictatorship in which every facet of life—political, cultural, and economic—was regulated by the Communist Party and state bureaucracy.

Under the energetic direction of Vladimir Lenin, founder of the Communist Party of the Soviet Union (CPSU, originally called the Bolshevik

Party), all competing political forces in revolutionary Russia were either discredited as insufficiently radical, or militarily defeated in the Civil War (1918–1921). After Lenin died early in 1924, Joseph Stalin, an ethnic Georgian born Josef Djugashvili, utilized his position as general secretary of the Communist Party to gradually eliminate his rivals in the Soviet leadership, most notably Leon Trotsky, cofounder of the Soviet state.

In 1928 Stalin, his political position now secure, launched an ambitious program to transform the Soviet Union from a backward peasant economy into a highly industrialized modern system. The relaxed program of the 1920s, which permitted small private businesses and private farming in a market exchange (the New Economic Policy, or NEP), was jettisoned in favor of a series of Five Year Plans that demanded ever-increasing quotas of steel, coal, cement, and other heavy industrial goods from state enterprises. During the 1930s, all private farms were forcibly consolidated into enormous collective and state farms (*kolkhozes* and *sovkhozes*). Millions of peasants died during this period; they were shot for resisting collectivization, or simply starved to death as a result of excessive government requisitions of grain. Millions left the countryside to work in the new urban factories. Underlying these monumental transformations of Soviet society was what Robert Conquest has called the Great Terror, Stalin's paranoid, determined attempt to root out all possible forms of opposition to his absolute control. When the archives were finally opened after the collapse of the Soviet Union, estimates of those who had perished in the huge labor camp system (the Gulag Archipelago) or were shot outright ranged upward of 60 million.

Stalin established the central elements of the totalitarian Soviet state: a Communist Party headed by the general secretary acting as the definitive political authority; an intrusive government bureaucracy that controlled every facet of society and the economy; the use of force and intimidation to achieve full compliance of the population; state censorship and manipulation of information through the mass media and the educational system; and state ownership of the entire economy (industry, agriculture, and services), with minimal attention to consumer needs and fulfillment of production quotas as the primary goal.

Following the trauma of World War II, in which the Soviet Union lost some 20 million people, Stalin extended the Soviet model to the newly occupied countries of Eastern Europe, thus creating the first communist empire. Soviet control of Eastern Europe was thorough but not absolute, and weakened considerably after Stalin's death in 1953. Yugoslavia had defected from the Soviet bloc as early as 1948; Hungary and Poland challenged Soviet control in 1956. Albania threw in its lot with China after the Sino-Soviet split in 1961, and a Czechoslovak reform program that foreshadowed Gorbachev's was repressed with Soviet tanks in August 1968. Nicolai Ceausescu had promoted an independent-minded brand of Romanian national communism from his accession to power in 1965. Poland proved a constant irritant—demonstrations in 1968, 1970, and 1976 were followed by the emergence of the Solidarity movement, which challenged the Polish Party's monopoly on power from August 1980 to December 1981. Soviet attempts to organize its allies into economic (Council for Mutual Economic Assistance) and military (Warsaw Treaty Organization) alliances were only partially successful, since these pacts were not based on sovereign consent or shared interests.

The first indications of the economic problems that would eventually lead to Gorbachev's reforms surfaced during Nikita Khrushchev's tenure as general secretary from 1953 to 1964. Khrushchev's ill-fated attempts at reform alienated much of the Party and government bureaucracy, who deposed him in a bloodless Kremlin coup in October 1964. His successors—Leonid Brezhnev, who served as general secretary from 1964 to 1982, and Aleksei Kosygin, premier of the Soviet government from 1964 until his death in 1980—merely tinkered with the Stalinist structure of centralized political control and economic planning. A period of bureaucratic lethargy, what Gorbachev and the reformers would later call the "time of stagnation," supplanted Stalin's terroristic oppression and Khrushchev's amateurish experiments. Problems became more acute and obvious to younger, reform-minded Soviet leaders as the industrial economy could not keep up with the dynamic computer and information-driven economies of Europe, the United States, and East Asia.

The Soviet economy had provided the population with a modestly improving standard of living ever since Stalin's death, but it could not match rising consumer expectations. Much of Soviet investment went to feed the huge military machine, which absorbed some 20 to 25 percent of total gross domestic product. As the United States retreated from international commitments following the Vietnam debacle, the Brezhnev regime increasingly resorted to military threats, and occasionally the direct exercise of military power, to achieve its foreign policy goals. In the latter half of the 1970s, Soviet officials confidently asserted that the "correlation of forces" in world affairs had shifted in favor of socialism and against the capitalist states. By the time of Brezhnev's death in November 1982, however, the Soviet Union confronted stubborn guerrilla resistance in Afghanistan (which the Soviets had invaded in 1979), a restive population in Poland (where the Solidarity movement had openly defied the government during 1980–1981), and a conservative administration in

Washington determined to rebuild America's military strength and confront the Soviet Union around the globe. And few members of the Third World any longer admired the USSR as a model of development, preferring instead the example of newly industrializing and increasingly wealthy capitalist nations.

In sum, the early 1980s found an aging and unimaginative Soviet leadership facing intractable domestic problems and an increasingly difficult international environment. As the old guard died off or retired, a new generation of leaders, influenced more by Khrushchev's thaw than by Stalin's terror, moved into the highest echelons of power.

The dramatic changes that led to the collapse of the Soviet Union and its communist empire cannot be attributed to any one individual or factor. Certainly Mikhail Gorbachev, the relatively young Party official from Stavropol who was appointed general secretary in March 1985, deserves much of the credit for initiating the reform process. Gorbachev is not the entire story, however. Nor is it accurate to assert, as have some prominent American conservatives, that President Ronald Reagan's confrontational policies and accelerated defense spending led to the collapse of the USSR. These factors played a role, but they were overshadowed by the critical importance of internal motivations. So many domestic problems had accumulated under Brezhnev—economic stagnation, technological backwardness, corruption, environmental pollution, growing cynicism and alienation, simmering discontent among the various nationalities—that the need for reform was apparent to all but the most obdurate ideologues.

From the perspective of Gorbachev and the reformers, the economy was the greatest weakness of the system. Top-heavy central planning, with its focus on generating ever larger quotas of heavy industrial products, was clearly out of sync with the modern electronic age. Shortly after Brezhnev died, the country's top social scientists had been charged with developing a set of recommendations for economic and social reform. Gorbachev was assigned to head this task force. Many reform proposals looked back to the limited capitalism of the NEP, while others suggested adopting ideas from the Hungarian, East German, or Chinese experiments. Occasionally these internal debates spilled into the pages of mass circulation journals and newspapers. One of the most prominent voices of reform, the sociologist Tatiana Zaslavskaia, argued that rigid authoritarian methods of production established under Stalin were no longer appropriate for an educated urban work force. The recent example of Poland and instances of worker dissatisfaction throughout the USSR and Eastern Europe suggested that alienation, a Marxist concept applied until now only to capitalist systems, was a very real problem in the "workers' paradise."

When Brezhnev's simpleminded protégé Konstantin Chernenko died in March 1985, Gorbachev assumed office with literally hundreds of proposals for reform in hand. Of course, there were still conservatives in the Soviet leadership who resisted significant change, so Gorbachev had to proceed cautiously until he could develop a stronger base of support in the Kremlin. Through a series of adroit maneuvers, Gorbachev demoted or retired many of the older generation of policy makers, replacing them with younger, more reform-minded officials. By the middle of 1987 he had solidified his political position and had managed to put his ideas for change—most notably, perestroika and glasnost—at the top of the Soviet agenda. It should be emphasized, however, that neither Gorbachev nor his reformist allies had a grand strategy for change. They were experimenting, trying to reshape a moribund system and yet preserve most of the central elements of that system. It was a strategy that could not succeed.

Perestroika, broadly defined as the restructuring of the Soviet economy, was at the heart of Gorbachev's reform program, as outlined in his book of the same title. Gorbachev, who even today believes in the inherent superiority of socialism, initially sought to modernize the Soviet economy by correcting some of its more egregious failures while leaving the basic structure intact. For the first two years, Gorbachev stressed the importance of "accelerating" economic performance, improving worker discipline, and attacking alcoholism (which seriously impaired productivity). These measures had been proposed during the brief tenure of Yurii Andropov, who had been a cautious voice for reform and one of Gorbachev's patrons in the leadership. Such palliatives did not get at the root of the problem, however. By mid-1987 it was increasingly apparent that more was needed than simply adjusting the Soviet system of central planning.

The second major principle of Gorbachev's reform program, glasnost, was supposed to provide the conditions for more effective economic restructuring. Usually translated as "openness" or "publicity," glasnost was meant to expose the full extent of mismanagement, corruption, and falsification in the economic system, holding both management and workers up to the glare of public opinion. Given the long Soviet (and Russian) tradition of secrecy, most Soviet leaders, Gorbachev included, did not envision completely abolishing the government's control over information. It proved difficult to apply glasnost selectively, however. When Reactor Number 4 at the Chernobyl nuclear power station in Ukraine exploded on

April 26, 1986, the Kremlin's treatment of this disaster tested the limits of glasnost. Although the Soviet government withheld information on the true extent of the damage, domestic and international concern forced a public investigation unprecedented in Soviet history.

Chernobyl encouraged a frightened Soviet populace to demand from their government more honest reporting on a wide range of social, economic, and political issues—environmental pollution, disease, crime, official corruption, accidents, and natural disasters. As censorship weakened, the official Soviet press became increasingly critical of government actions, and subjects open for public discussion expanded to include nationality relations, military issues, foreign policy, and even the private lives of top Soviet leaders. Encouraged by Gorbachev, the media attempted to fill in the "blank spots" in Soviet history, events that had been ignored or blatantly falsified in order to portray the Soviet system in a more flattering light. Stalin's bloody dictatorship was reappraised, and such prominent "enemies of the state" as Trotsky, Nikolai Bukharin (the Party's chief theoretician in the 1920s and an outspoken advocate of the liberal policies of that period), and Alexander Solzhenitsyn, the famous dissident novelist and historian of the prison camps, were reevaluated. By the end of the 1980s, even Lenin, who had been virtually deified after his death as a prophet of Marxism and a supposedly infallible ruler, was condemned for having planted the seeds of dictatorship.

Ever since Lenin had convinced other Party leaders to ban opposing "factions" at the Tenth Party Congress in 1921, political opposition had been punished as a crime against the state. Not only were competing parties illegal; all social and cultural organizations from churches to chess clubs were tightly controlled and monitored by the Communist Party. As perestroika and glasnost evolved, political controls were relaxed and independent groups began to organize and articulate their demands. Ecology was one prominent issue that captured a great deal of attention, especially after Chernobyl, and many of the earliest "informal" groups organized to combat local environmental problems. The Soviet government's abysmal record on the environment, due to careless practices in agriculture, industry, nuclear power, and defense, contributed significantly to the crisis in Soviet health care. Environmental destruction also helped stimulate greater militancy among the Soviet Union's national minorities, who shared the belief that the Soviet government had, in classic colonial style, deliberately located heavily polluting industries in their homelands.

Of course, ecology problems were only one in a long list of resentments held by the national minorities. The elaborate federal structure of

Soviet government theoretically gave the republics, autonomous republics, autonomous regions, and national areas a certain measure of self-determination. In reality, the national aspirations of most minorities were frustrated by centralized Party control and persistent efforts at russification. Gorbachev and many of the reformers did not realize the strength of nationalism in the Soviet Union. By 1989–1990, "National Front" movements in the Baltic states, Ukraine, Belarus, and the Caucasus were demanding from Moscow sovereign control over their internal affairs; soon Lithuania would declare its outright independence from the USSR.

The Soviet government's willingness to accept social and political pluralism late in the 1980s also extended to Eastern Europe. Gorbachev encouraged Eastern European communist leaders to emulate his reforms, although the "new thinking" in foreign policy, as it was called, rejected the use of coercion as a tool to ensure compliance with Soviet practice. Moscow now abandoned its claim to be the only true defender of communist orthodoxy. As Foreign Ministry spokesman Gennadii Gerasimov explained, the Brezhnev Doctrine of limited sovereignty enunciated after the Czechoslovak invasion had been supplanted by the "Sinatra Doctrine," letting the East European states "do it their way."

As it became clear that Soviet military forces would no longer intervene to prop up unpopular communist governments, demands for change in Eastern Europe intensified. Cautious reforms were begun in Hungary and Poland, traditionally the most liberal of the communist regimes, but leaders in Czechoslovakia, Romania, Bulgaria, and East Germany resisted ceding political power. Between October and December 1989, however, a wave of revolution swept over Eastern Europe, as communist regimes fell and the Berlin Wall was torn down. The summary execution of Romania's Nicolai Ceausescu and his wife on Christmas Day marked the end of communism in Eastern Europe.

Eastern Europe's liberation provided further encouragement to the movements for greater autonomy in the fifteen union republics that comprised the Soviet Union. The Soviet constitution promised "self-determination" for Ukrainians, Armenians, Uzbeks, Lithuanians, and other major ethnic groups, but did not adequately satisfy aspirations of the various nationalities. Although some cultural autonomy was permitted, and education in native languages was available, the Communist Party exercised tight central control from Moscow over the republics' affairs. Efforts to promote a unifying Soviet identity became a thinly disguised policy of russification, antagonizing the 49 percent of the population that was not ethnic Russian. The end of the Soviet empire in Eastern Europe raised the possibility of independence for the "internal empire" as well, accelerating demands for sovereignty and in some cases complete independence.

Beyond Eastern Europe, Gorbachev's new thinking in foreign policy led to major improvements in relations with the United States, China, and Western Europe, and reversed decades of support for radical Third World causes. Successful domestic reform, Gorbachev realized, could not be achieved in an atmosphere of international hostility. Prior to 1985 no Soviet leader had ever admitted that aggressive Soviet behavior might be responsible for the poor state of East-West relations or for the Sino-Soviet split. New thinking acknowledged that confrontational Soviet foreign policies, based on Lenin's ideas of class struggle, had often proved ineffective or even counterproductive to Soviet national interests. Gorbachev and the Kremlin reformers now spoke of "universal human values" and a "common European home," promised an end to the "enemy image" that had characterized Moscow's portrayal of the West, and pledged a reduction of military forces to a level sufficient for an adequate national defense.

Despite initial skepticism in the West, new thinking produced a sea change in Soviet foreign policy. The first breakthrough—the December 1987 Intermediate Nuclear Forces (INF) Treaty signed by the United States and the USSR—eliminated an entire class of highly destabilizing nuclear weapons. In 1988 Gorbachev announced that all Soviet troops would be withdrawn from Afghanistan within a year, and at a May 1989 summit meeting in Beijing, China and the Soviet Union put an end to thirty years of bitter confrontation. A major treaty requiring the Soviet Union to undertake asymmetrical cuts in conventional forces in Europe was signed in 1990 (the CFE Treaty), and in 1991 an unprecedented agreement significantly reducing strategic arms (the START Treaty) was signed between the United States and the Soviet Union.

Although these remarkable developments in foreign policy created the relaxed international climate necessary for perestroika, many influential voices in the Soviet Union were critical of Gorbachev's "extravagant" concessions to the West and disturbed by the loss of the Soviet empire. These same conservatives were also disturbed by the increasing disorder and confusion in Soviet society, and resisted efforts to develop private enterprise and a market-oriented economy. As the 1980s drew to a close, political forces in the USSR polarized between the supporters and the critics of reform.

The radical changes in Soviet political and economic life had polarized opinions, with elites divided between such conservatives as Yegor Ligachev and supporters of more rapid reform, led by Boris Yeltsin. Gorbachev sought to occupy the middle ground, but it was a difficult balancing act. The Nineteenth Party Conference of June 1988, which illustrated the strength of conservative opposition to reform within the Communist Party, marked a watershed in political reform. Gorbachev was convinced that perestroika could not succeed barring a shift of political power from the authoritarian CPSU to elected governmental institutions. Popular pressure expressed through the electoral process, he reasoned, would compel reluctant officials to support his reform program.

The elections to a new Congress of People's Deputies, held in March 1989, were relatively free by Soviet standards. Voters could now choose among candidates and, although the outcome was biased in favor of conservative forces, roughly one-fifth of the elected deputies were ardent reformers. Unaccustomed to democracy, deputies to the Congress haggled over procedural issues and traded accusations, all of which was broadcast on national television to a fascinated Soviet audience. As might be expected, this new Congress could not immediately provide effective governance. Its emergence, however, helped legitimize the concept of representative democracy among an important segment of the population. It also marked the beginning of the end of the Communist Party's monopoly over political power.

Much of the problem in trying to effect reform stemmed from the pervasive influence of the CPSU in Soviet political life. The Party had succeeded, albeit at tremendous cost, in constructing the rudiments of a modern industrial society—an urbanized population base, factories, transportation and communications infrastructure, mass education, and science. As a consequence, Soviet society and the economy had experienced major transformations since the revolution. The moribund political system, however, had great difficulty adapting to the changing conditions of the late twentieth century. The Communist Party's obsession with secrecy clashed with the demands of the information age, its myopic focus on expanding industrial output ignored the worldwide trend toward quality and efficiency, and its centralized approach to political issues could not meet the challenge of creating community out of an increasingly diverse society. Prior to Gorbachev, the Party had resisted granting the population a larger role in governing. Lacking flexibility, the Soviet state maintained the appearance of exercising effective authority right up to the point when the system began to collapse.

As Samuel Huntington pointed out in his classic *Political Order in Changing Societies*, a political system with several powerful institutions is more likely to adapt to change than a system with only one significant institution. If one institution suffers a loss of legitimacy, the others can assume some of the weakened institution's functions. Soviet reformers, however, faced the daunting task of creating entirely new institutions— a functioning legislature, independent courts, a responsible executive, and genuine federalism—virtually overnight, to replace a rapidly disin- tegrating Communist Party. As might be expected, there was consider- able disagreement over the precise form these new governing institutions would assume.

More important, it takes time for new institutions to acquire legiti- macy. Recall that in the United States a bloody civil war was fought over federal power versus states' rights more than seventy years after the Constitution was first enacted. It would be unrealistic to assume that new institutions could be designed, staffed, and functioning smoothly within a few years, especially in the context of exponentially increasing demands from the population. Again, drawing on Huntington's study of transitional societies, political instability in the Soviet Union resulted from the rapid expansion of political participation, coupled with the in- ability of reformers to organize and institutionalize the means of recon- ciling conflicting demands. In other words, political change could not keep up with social and economic change.

The most potent source of new demands from the population was ethnic and national disaffection. Contrary to Marxian predictions, na- tionalism, not class, was the basis for revolution in the Soviet context. Few Soviet reformers, Gorbachev included, understood the strength of national feeling among the hundred-odd ethnic groups that comprised the USSR. Soviet leaders actually seemed to believe their own propa- ganda, that the tsarist "prison of nations" had been supplanted by a "family of nations" under communism. For seventy years the pressures of ideological conformity and the threat of physical force had constrained national aspirations. There were occasional glimpses of discontent bub- bling beneath the surface, as in 1978 when Georgian students took to the streets of Tbilisi to protest plans to drop their native language from the republic's constitution. But few could anticipate the tremendous surge of nationalism that accompanied the relaxation of political controls be- tween 1987 and 1991.

Revelations about official corruption and mismanagement and the ob- vious failure of Gorbachev's economic reform policies undermined the credibility of central authorities and inspired calls for greater autonomy in the provinces. Toward the end of 1990, Soviet leaders began to reev- aluate the sham federalism that had promised cultural autonomy while ensuring centralized Communist Party control over the various national republics. Plans were drawn up for a new Union Treaty to replace the one that had created the Union of Soviet Socialist Republics in 1922. Gorbachev and the reformers were finally willing to draw up a new constitution that would grant significant self-governing powers to the republics. But conservatives, who saw their influence expand in late 1990 and early 1991, argued that the establishment of genuine federalism would undermine the basis of the Soviet communist system. Ironically, the movement toward political autonomy in the republics had progressed so far that even a decentralized system patterned on the U.S. or Canadian constitution would not satisfy their demands for sovereignty or independence.

These conflicting pressures continued to mount through 1991, culminating in the coup by hard-liners opposed to the new Union Treaty on August 19–22. Reactions to the attempted takeover illustrated the highly fragmented character of public opinion toward the changes taking place in the USSR. Many courageous individuals rallied to support Russian president Boris Yeltsin at the parliament building. The demoralized Soviet army was divided—some officers ignored orders to march on Moscow and St. Petersburg, while others commanded tanks in the streets of the capital. A few regional leaders condemned the coup; most cautiously waited for the situation to clarify before committing themselves.

For the minority republics, the conservatives' bid for power, and Gorbachev's apparent inability to grasp the significance of the August events following the coup, confirmed their worst fears. In this climate full independence seemed the best guarantee against Moscow reestablishing centralized political control. Gorbachev attempted to hold the USSR together in a looser arrangement, but his authority and credibility had been so tarnished that he was doomed to fail. Starting with the three Baltic states, each of the republics declared its independence from the Soviet Union. The death blow came with Ukraine's December 1 referendum in favor of independence. Gorbachev's resignation on Christmas Day signaled the end of the Soviet experiment.

Many factors played a role in the collapse of the Soviet Union. The most important seem to have been internal, although international pressures, many linked to Moscow's inept foreign policies, also deserved some credit for the collapse. Domestic factors include the increasingly poor economic performance of the centrally planned economy, technological backwardness, a stifling and repressive political system that discouraged creativity, excessive military spending, incredible bureaucratic inefficiency, a catastrophic ecology record, and insensitivity to the national interests of the Soviet Union's diverse minorities. Confrontational foreign policies, influenced by the ideology of class struggle, alienated many Soviet allies and brought the capitalist world together in an effort to contain the perceived communist threat.

The accretion of domestic problems and international pressures coincided with a major generational change in the Soviet leadership. Gorbachev was central in planning and promoting reform, but it should be remembered that he was supported by younger officials for whom the terror of the Stalin era was only a vague memory. This generation was better educated and more critical of Soviet "achievements" than were the Brezhnevs, the Suslovs, and the Gromykos, whose careers were built over the graves of the old Bolsheviks. And lastly, we should not forget the Soviet people, who were disillusioned and impatient with a corrupt, repressive system that refused to acknowledge their humanity. The revolution that brought about the collapse of the Soviet Union may have started with the Party elite, but it ended with an extraordinary display of public affirmation that dictatorship should not be restored.

SELECTED BIBLIOGRAPHY

Banac, Ivo, ed. *Eastern Europe in Revolution*. Ithaca, NY: Cornell University Press, 1992. Historians and sociologists discuss the collapse of communism in Eastern Europe.

Brzezinski, Zbigniew. *The Grand Failure: The Birth and Death of Communism in the Twentieth Century*. New York: Collier Books, 1990. A sweeping discussion of the critical weaknesses of communism in the Soviet Union, Eastern Europe, and China.

Dawisha, Karen. *Eastern Europe, Gorbachev, and Reform: The Great Challenge*. 2nd ed. Cambridge, England: Cambridge University Press, 1990. Analyzes Soviet intentions and interests in Eastern Europe.

Feshbach, Murray, and Alfred Friendly, Jr. *Ecocide in the USSR: Health and Nature under Siege*. New York: Basic Books, 1992. A very thorough, albeit depressing, chronicle of abuse of the natural environment and the related issue of neglect in Soviet health care.

Gorbachev, Mikhail. *Perestroika: New Thinking for Our Country and the World*. New York: Harper and Row, 1987. The general secretary's explanation of his plans for reform.

Hasegawa, Tsuyoshi, and Alex Pravda, eds. *Perestroika: Soviet Domestic and Foreign Policies*. London: Sage, 1990. Assesses the links between Soviet domestic reforms and changes in foreign policy.

Hewett, Ed A. *Reforming the Soviet Economy: Equality Versus Efficiency*. Washington, DC: Brookings Institution, 1988. A superb review of the Soviet economic structure and its operation.

Hosking, Geoffrey. *The Awakening of the Soviet Union*. Cambridge, MA: Harvard University Press, 1990. An analysis of the social and cultural factors underlying the transformations of the late 1980s.

Kagarlitsky, Boris. *The Disintegration of the Monolith.* Translated by Renfrey Clarke. London: Verso, 1992. A critical look at the political forces that emerged during the reforms.

Lewin, Moshe. *The Gorbachev Phenomenon: A Historical Interpretation.* Expanded ed. Berkeley: University of California Press, 1991. Lewin, a leading economic historian, places Gorbachev's reforms in the context of the major socioeconomic transformations that took place in the USSR.

Mason, David S. *Revolution in East-Central Europe: The Rise and Fall of Communism and the Cold War.* Boulder, CO: Westview Press, 1992. This useful work discusses the relationship between the Soviet reform process and the East European revolutions.

McAuley, Mary. *Soviet Politics 1917–1991.* Oxford, England: Oxford University Press, 1992. This slim volume cogently analyzes the political factors that formed and transformed the Soviet state.

McGwire, Michael. *Perestroika and Soviet National Security.* Washington, DC: Brookings Institution, 1991. Relates the shift in Soviet concepts of security from confrontation to cooperation.

Remnick, David. *Lenin's Tomb: The Last Days of the Soviet Empire.* New York: Random House, 1993. Remnick, formerly Moscow correspondent for the *Washington Post,* delivers a penetrating portrait of Soviet life during the reform period.

Sakwa, Richard. *Gorbachev and His Reforms: 1985–1990.* New York: Prentice-Hall, 1991. Examines the interactions of the principal individuals, institutions, and ideas that dominated the reform period.

Smith, Hedrick. *The New Russians.* New York: Random House, 1991. A perceptive survey of the impact of Gorbachev's economic, social, and political reforms on the Soviet people by one of the West's leading journalists.

White, Stephen. *After Gorbachev.* Cambridge, England: Cambridge University Press, 1993. A sophisticated analysis of the reform process under Gorbachev by a leading British scholar.

Woodby, Sylvia. *Gorbachev and the Decline of Ideology in Soviet Foreign Policy.* Boulder, CO: Westview Press, 1991. A concise discussion of Gorbachev's foreign policy reforms.

Yeltsin, Boris. *Against the Grain: An Autobiography.* Translated by Michael Glenny. New York: Summit Books, 1990. Russia's controversial president chronicles his career.

Ziegler, Charles E. *Foreign Policy and East Asia: Learning and Adaptation in the Gorbachev Era.* Cambridge, England: Cambridge University Press, 1993. The Soviet reassessment of foreign policy toward East Asia is analyzed as part of a learning process within the broader context of Gorbachev's reforms.

Appendix A

Glossary

Armistice. An armistice is a cessation of hostilities preliminary to the signing of a peace treaty. At the end of World War I, an armistice stopping the war was put into effect on November 11, 1918.

Atlantic Charter. This statement, approved by Franklin D. Roosevelt and Winston Churchill at a conference in 1941, outlined the principles that should guide the Allies in World War II. It endorsed self-determination and access for all to raw materials, and suggested a postwar organization to guarantee peace. The United States and Great Britain also abjured territorial gain as a result of the war.

Bandung Conference. Held in Ceylon in 1955, the Bandung Conference brought together representatives from a number of Asian and African countries. The conference laid the groundwork for Third World cooperation at the United Nations and stimulated the formation and growth of the Non-Aligned Movement.

Beer Hall Putsch. In November 1923, Adolf Hitler joined with the former World War I general Erich Ludendorff in an attempt to overthrow the German (Weimar) Republic. Based in Munich, the coup attempt or putsch failed. It was called the Beer Hall Putsch because the conspiracy was hatched in the back rooms of Munich's taverns.

Berlin Wall. Constructed in August 1961 to halt the exodus of people from East Germany, the Berlin Wall separated East Berlin from West Berlin.

The wall came to represent the post–World War II division of Europe in general and Germany specifically. A continual source of irritation between East and West, the Berlin Wall was destroyed in November 1989, thereby signaling the end of the communist regime in East Germany and clearing the way for German reunification.

Boxer Revolt. The Boxers were a secret society in China that launched a terrorist campaign against foreigners in 1900 with the tacit support of the government. A multinational military force relieved the besieged diplomatic community in Peking, and diplomatic pressure finally resulted in the suppression of the Boxers.

Catholic Popolari. The Catholic Popolari was an Italian political party founded in 1919. Sometimes called the Christian Democrat Party, the Catholic Popolari enjoyed widespread support among Roman Catholics opposed to the anticlericalists who had governed Italy since its founding in 1860. Beyond support for Roman Catholicism, the Catholic Popolari had no coherent or unifying philosophy.

Comintern. Officially known as the Third International or Communist International, the Comintern was formed in Moscow in 1919. Firmly under the control of the Bolsheviks, the Comintern attacked less radical socialists, promoted world revolution, and served the interests of the Soviet state. Joseph Stalin abolished the Comintern in 1943 as a concession to his wartime allies, the United States and Great Britain.

Commonwealth. Formerly known as the British Commonwealth of Nations, the Commonwealth of Nations or Commonwealth is an organization consisting of the United Kingdom and many of its former colonies that have gained independence. It is a consultative body pulling together a diverse group of nations from all corners of the globe.

Confucianism. Confucianism is a philosophy based on the writings of Kongfuzi (Confucius), who lived in the fifth and sixth centuries B.C. Confucianism placed great emphasis on righteousness and restraint in order for people to achieve harmony with nature. For centuries, Confucianism provided the philosophy by which the Chinese lived.

Cultural Revolution. The Cultural Revolution was a radical movement in Mao Zedong's China between 1966 and 1976. It was disruptive in the extreme, causing serious political, economic, and social instability in its drive to create a state of "permanent revolution."

Darwin, Charles (1809–1882). Charles Darwin was a British naturalist who developed the theory of evolution by natural selection and survival of the fittest. Under Social Darwinism some of his followers applied his ideas to individual humans, nations, and/or races.

Doughboy. Doughboy was a nickname given to American infantrymen during World War I.

Dow Jones Industrial Average. The Dow Jones Industrial Average is an index of the New York stock market performance based on the value of the stock of thirty leading industrial corporations. The "average" is calculated by means of a mathematical formula that is periodically adjusted in such a way as to make comparisons of past and present performance meaningful.

Dzerzhinsky, Felix (1877–1926). Born into a Polish noble family, Felix Dzerzhinsky became a revolutionary in tsarist Russia. He is best known for establishing the first Bolshevik secret police, the Cheka.

Entente. A French term meaning a friendly understanding or agreement, entente also came to designate the cordial relationship among Great Britain, France, and Russia on the eve of World War I. At the outbreak of the war, this relationship solidified into a formal alliance.

"Flanders' Fields." "Flanders' Fields" refers to that area of northern France and western Belgium bordering the North Sea. During World War I, several ferocious battles were fought there, resulting in a staggering number of casualties.

Freud, Sigmund (1856–1939). A Viennese physician turned psychologist, Sigmund Freud is universally regarded as the father of psychoanalysis. In 1900 he published *On the Interpretation of Dreams,* and ultimately suggested that human behavior is rooted in the irrational rather than the rational.

Great Leap Forward. Between 1958 and 1961, Mao Zedong attempted to stimulate China's economy. The Great Leap Forward featured a sustained propaganda barrage, collectivization of the peasants, and decentralization of industry. The Great Leap Forward was a disaster, as economic production declined and famine stalked the land.

Marianne. Marianne is the personification of the French Republic in much the same manner that Uncle Sam is the personification of the United States. Frequently Marianne is portrayed in flowing robes with a liberty cap and a tricolor cockade.

Marx, Karl (1818–1883). A German publicist, historian, philosopher, and sociologist, Karl Marx is generally regarded as the father of modern socialism. The most cogent synopsis of his ideas is found in his *Communist Manifesto* (1848).

Mau-Mau. From 1952 until 1956, the Mau-Mau, a secret society of Kenyan natives committed to driving the British imperialists from their homeland, waged a campaign of terror against British settlers. Although the Mau-Mau were defeated, the cost was so high that Great Britain decided to grant independence to its East African colonies rather than fight to retain them.

Meiji Restoration. Lasting from 1868 until 1912, the Meiji Restoration or era was a period of intense reform in Japan. In order to preserve its sovereignty from Western encroachment, Japanese reformers during this era adopted Western technology and ideas to modernize the Japanese state and make it capable of resisting the West.

Mensheviks. The Mensheviks were the non-Leninist faction of the Russian Social Democratic Party. Although sometimes cooperating with Lenin's Bolsheviks, the Mensheviks were less rigid and conspiratorial. In 1922 the Bolsheviks suppressed the Mensheviks.

New Deal. The New Deal refers to the series of socioeconomic reforms inaugurated by U.S. President Franklin D. Roosevelt at the height of the Depression. Among the more permanent reforms were Social Security, federal insurance for bank depositors, and laws limiting the work week, child labor, and discrimination against labor unions.

NKVD. NKVD is the Russian abbreviation for the People's Commissariat of Internal Affairs, the Soviet security force or secret police. A successor to the Cheka, the NKVD later changed its name to become the KGB.

Old Bolsheviks. The term Old Bolsheviks applies to those who belonged to Lenin's Bolshevik faction of the Russian Social Democratic Party prior to the 1917 Russian Revolution that brought the Bolsheviks to power. Joseph Stalin, who always suspected the Old Bolsheviks, eliminated most of them during the purges of the 1930s.

OPEC. This acronym stands for the Organization of Petroleum Exporting Countries, a cartel created by oil-rich nations to regain control over their resources from the various oil companies that had received favorable concessions. In the 1970s, OPEC worked to raise prices and nationalize foreign-owned production facilities.

Paris Peace Conference. The Paris Peace Conference is the official name given to the peace negotiations that concluded World War I. Held in Paris from January to June 1919, the conference's main participants were Woodrow Wilson of the United States, David Lloyd George of Great Britain, Georges Clemenceau of France, and Vittorio Orlando of Italy. In all, thirty-two nations were represented, with thousands of participants and over sixty commissions dealing with specific problems.

Plebiscite. A plebiscite is a direct vote of the population on a specific issue put to them by the government, or on the government itself, or on the leader of the government.

Pogrom. From the Russian, a pogrom is an organized and usually officially condoned attack on a minority group. Pogroms have most frequently been directed against Jews, especially the Jews of eastern Europe.

Rapprochement. From the French, rapprochement is a term used frequently by diplomats to describe a warming of relations between two countries.

Red Army. Founded by V. I. Lenin in 1918 and built into an effective fighting force by Leon Trotsky, the Red Army defended the Soviet state from its external enemies. After World War II, its name was changed to the Soviet Army.

Reichstag. Reichstag is the name formerly given to the German legislative assembly or parliament.

Reparations. Reparations are payments made by the loser or losers of a war to the victor or victors to "repair" damages done by the former to the latter during the course of the war. At the Paris Peace Conference ending World War I, this definition was stretched to make Germany liable for virtually the entire cost of the war, thereby creating fiscal chaos in Europe until the 1924 Dawes Plan restructured Germany's payment schedule.

Sino-Soviet Split. The Sino-Soviet split was the breakdown in relations that occurred between the Soviet Union and the People's Republic of China during the 1950s and 1960s. By 1969 war appeared imminent, but cooler heads prevailed. Nevertheless, Sino-Soviet relations remained frigid for many years.

The Six. The Six is a synonym for the original six members of the European Coal and Steel Community—Belgium, France, Italy, Luxembourg, the Netherlands, and West Germany.

Social Darwinism. Derived from Charles Darwin's pioneering nineteenth-century work on evolution, Social Darwinism concluded that the struggle for existence and survival of the fittest applied to man as well as plants and lesser animals. This concept served to justify a number of injustices, including racism, belligerent nationalism, genocide, and monopoly capitalism.

Social Revolutionary Party. Commonly referred to as the SRs, the Social Revolutionary Party was a radical political movement active in Russia in the late nineteenth and early twentieth centuries. The SRs supported collective ownership of the land and enjoyed great support among the Russian peasantry. The SRs were suppressed by the Bolsheviks after the Russian Revolution.

Spanish Civil War. Precipitated by fundamental disagreements over the nature of the Spanish state, the Spanish Civil War, which began in 1936 and ended in 1939, pitted a loose coalition of republicans, socialists, communists, anarchists, and syndicalists against the forces of tradition—clericals, aristocrats, monarchists, big businessmen, army officers, and Falangists or Spanish fascists. Aided by Benito Mussolini and Adolf Hitler, the traditionalists or nationalists under the leadership of General Francisco Franco defeated the loyalists or republicans, who were aided by Joseph Stalin.

Status quo ante bellum. From the Latin, status quo ante bellum means the existing condition or state of affairs before the outbreak of a war.

Syndicalism. Syndicalism was a radical, working-class movement that was particularly strong in Italy and France in the late nineteenth and early twentieth centuries. It called for direct action such as the general strike in order to deliver the means of production into the hands of the working class.

Third Reich. This term was applied by Adolf Hitler to the German state after he came to power. Hitler saw the Third Reich as the legitimate successor to the First Reich, or Holy Roman Empire, and the Second Reich, or Otto von Bismarck's German Empire. Intended to last for a thousand years, the Third Reich disappeared along with Hitler in 1945.

Appendix B

Timeline

1900	World population is estimated at 1.6 billion
	Sigmund Freud publishes *On the Interpretation of Dreams*
1902	Alliance between Japan and Great Britain
	Boer War ends
1903	Wright brothers make first powered flight
1904–1905	Russo-Japanese War
1904	Anglo-French Entente
1905	Revolution in Russia
	First Moroccan Crisis
	Albert Einstein publishes "On the Electrodynamics of Moving Bodies"
	All-India Muslim League founded
1907	Formation of the Triple Entente (Great Britain, France, Russia)
1908	Bosnian Crisis
1909	Selma O. L. Lagerlof of Sweden is first woman to win Nobel Prize for Literature
1910	Revolution in Mexico

	Establishment of Union of South Africa
	Japan annexes Korea
1911	Chinese Revolution
	Second Moroccan Crisis
1912–1913	Balkan Wars
1914–1918	World War I
1914	Ulster Crisis
	Assassination of Archduke Franz Ferdinand
	First Battle of the Marne
	Battles of Tannenberg and the Masurian Lakes
	Panama Canal completed
1915	Italy enters World War I
1916	Battle of Jutland
	Battle of Verdun
	Battle of the Somme
1917	Russian revolutions; Bolsheviks come to power
	United States enters World War I
	Dada movement influences cultural and intellectual world
1918	Treaty of Brest-Litovsk
	Collapse of Austro-Hungarian, German, and Ottoman empires
1919	Paris Peace Conference; Treaty of Versailles
	Civil war in Russia
	Establishment of Weimar Republic in Germany
	Revolution in Egypt
	May 4th Movement in China
1920	League of Nations founded
1921	New Economic Policy (NEP) introduced in Russia
	Chinese Communist Party founded
1922	Benito Mussolini seizes power in Italy
	USSR established
	Mandate System in the Middle East
1923	Ruhr occupied
	Hyperinflation in Germany
	Turkish Republic founded

1924	First Labour government in Great Britain
	Vladimir Lenin dies
1928	Joseph Stalin leads Soviet Union; First Five-Year Plan introduced
1929	U.S. stock market collapses; beginning of the Great Depression
1930	World population is estimated at 2 billion
	Getulio Vargas comes to power in Brazil
1931	Manchurian Crisis; Japan threatens China
	Credit-Anstalt collapses
	Great Britain abandons the gold standard
1932	Franklin D. Roosevelt elected president of the United States
1933	Adolf Hitler comes to power in Germany
1934	Lazaro Cardenas comes to power in Mexico
1935	Mussolini invades Ethiopia (Abyssinia)
1936	Hitler remilitarizes the Rhineland
	Spanish Civil War begins
	J. M. Keynes publishes *General Theory of Employment, Interest, and Money*
	Purge trails begin in USSR
1937	Japan seizes Nanking from China
1938	Germany annexes Austria (Anschluss)
	Munich Conference
1939–1945	World War II
1939	Nazi-Soviet Non-Aggression Pact
	Germany invades Poland
	USSR invades Poland
	"Winter War" between USSR and Finland begins
1940	Germany conquers France
	Winston Churchill becomes prime minister in Great Britain
	USSR absorbs Estonia, Latvia, and Lithuania
	Atlantic Charter
	Battle of Britain
1941	Germany invades the Soviet Union

Japan attacks the United States

Mohammed Reza Pahlavi comes to power in Iran

1942   Battle of Stalingrad begins

1943   Battle of Kursk

Italy surrenders

1944   Allies invade Nazi-occupied France

1945   Yalta Conference

Roosevelt dies

Mussolini executed

Hitler commits suicide

Germany surrenders

Potsdam Conference

Labour wins election in Great Britain; Churchill
replaced by Clement Attlee

United States drops atomic bombs on Hiroshima and
Nagasaki; Japan surrenders

United Nations established

USSR begins to establish empire in Eastern Europe

Cold War begins

1946   Juan Peron comes to power in Argentina

1947   Truman Doctrine

Marshall Plan

India and Pakistan achieve independence; Jawaharlal
Nehru comes to power in India

1948   Communist coup in Czechoslovakia

Berlin Blockade begins

Israel established; First Arab-Israeli War

Stalin feuds with Yugoslavian communist leader
Marshal Tito (Josip Broz)

Organization of American States established

1949   North Atlantic Treaty Organization (NATO)
established

The Dutch are forced to leave Indonesia

Federal Republic of Germany (West Germany) founded

German Democratic Republic (East Germany) founded

	Council for Mutual Economic Aid (Comecon or CMEA) established
	Chinese communists win civil war
1950	North Korea invades South Korea
1951	European Coal and Steel Community (ECSC) established
	Oil nationalization crisis in Iran
1952	Gamal Abdel Nasser comes to power in Egypt
1953	Stalin dies
	James Watson and Francis Crick discover DNA double-helix structure
1954	The French are forced to leave Indochina
	Beginning of revolt against French rule in Algeria
1955	Bandung Conference
	Warsaw Treaty Organization (WTO) established
1956	Nikita Khrushchev denounces Stalin at Communist Party of the Soviet Union's Twentieth Party Congress
	Suez Crisis
	Hungarian Revolution suppressed by USSR
1957	Treaty of Rome establishes the European Economic Community (EEC)
	USSR launches Sputnik (first orbiting satellite)
	Colonialism in black Africa begins to disappear
1958	Start of the Great Leap Forward in China
	Charles de Gaulle named president of France; establishment of the Fifth French Republic
1959	Cuban Revolution; Fidel Castro comes to power
1960	World population is estimated at 3 billion
1961	Increased U.S. involvement in Vietnam War
	Berlin Wall constructed
1962	Independence for Algeria
	Cuban Missile Crisis
	Sino-Soviet split
1963	John F. Kennedy assassinated

	Organization of African Unity founded
	Vatican II begins work
1964	Nehru dies
	Krushchev ousted; Leonid Brezhnev comes to power
	Military seizes power in Brazil
	China detonates a nuclear device
1966	Beginning of Cultural Revolution in China
1967	Arab-Israeli Six-Day War
	Civil war (Biafran War) in Nigeria
1968	USSR invades Czechoslovakia
	Martin Luther King, Jr., assassinated
	Unrest in major Western countries including the United States and France
1969	United States lands man on the moon
1970	Beginning of detente
1971	People's Republic of China replaces the Republic of China in the United Nations
1972	SALT I agreement
1973	Third Arab-Israeli War (Yom Kippur War)
	Start of Arab oil embargo
	Salvador Allende overthrown in Chile
1974	Beginning of world economic recession
	Richard Nixon resigns
	Marxist revolution in Ethiopia
	India detonates a nuclear device
1975	End of Vietnam War
	Last European empire in Africa (Portugal) ends
	Helsinki Conference on European Security and Cooperation
1976	Mao Zedong dies
1979	Camp David Peace Accords between Israel and Egypt
	Margaret Thatcher becomes prime minister in Great Britain
	USSR invades Afghanistan
	Sandinista revolution in Nicaragua

	Revolution in Iran brings fundamentalist Islamic regime to power
	Saddam Hussein comes to power in Iraq
1980	Solidarity movement in Poland
	Ronald Reagan elected U.S. president
	Deng Xiaoping comes to power in China
	Iran-Iraq War begins
1982	Brezhnev dies
	Israel invades Lebanon
1983	Argentina returns to civilian rule
1984	Indira Gandhi assassinated
1985	Mikhail Gorbachev named to head Soviet Union
	Brazil returns to civilian rule
1986	Chernobyl nuclear power station accident
1987	Intermediate Nuclear Forces Treaty (INF) signed
	Montreal Protocol limits substances that deplete the ozone layer
	Start of Palestinian uprising (Intifada)
1989	China crushes movement for democracy
	Ayatollah Khomeini dies
	Revolutions in Eastern Europe
	Berlin Wall falls
1990	World population is estimated at 5 billion
	Germany reunified
1991	Persian Gulf War results in defeat of Iraq
	USSR collapses
	Rajiv Gandhi assassinated
1992	European Community achieves full economic integration
1993	Apartheid in South Africa ends
	Israeli-Palestinian peace accords
	North American Free Trade Agreement (NAFTA)

Appendix C

Population of Selected Countries (in Millions)

	1900	*1920*	*1940*	*1960*	*1980*	*1990*
United States	76	106	131.7	179	226	248
United Kingdom	38	45.5	47.1	51.7	55.9	56.9
France	38.5	40	41.9	45.7	53.7	56.2
Germany	56.3	60	69.3	72.8	78.3	79.6
Russia/USSR	104	147	192.6	214.4	262	288
China	370	400	457.8	670	1027	1135
Japan	45	77	78.2	93.6	116.7	123.4
India (including Pakistan and Bangladesh)	294	315	365	532	837.1	1093
Egypt	10	12.6	16.1	26.1	41.9	54.1
Brazil	20	24.5	41.3	68	123	150.3
Mexico	13.6	16	19.4	34.6	71.9	88.6
Italy	33.6	36	45.3	50.7	57.1	57.3
Ottoman Empire/ Turkey	26.8	14	17.8	27.8	45.3	55.6
Persia/Iran	9	10	16	20.6	38	55.5

	1900	1920	1940	1960	1980	1990
Dutch East Indies/ Indonesia	36	49.5	55.7	92.6	151.8	180.5
Nigeria	—	15.1	20.6	34	77.1	113

Appendix D

States Achieving
Independence since 1945

Present Name of Country	Colonial Name (if Different)	Colonial Authority	Year of Independence
Algeria		France	1962
Angola		Portugal	1975
Antigua and Barbuda	Antigua	United Kingdom	1981
Bahamas		United Kingdom	1973
Bahrain		United Kingdom	1971
Bangladesh	East Pakistan	Pakistan	1971
Barbados		United Kingdom	1966
Belize	British Honduras	United Kingdom	1981
Benin	Dahomey	France	1960
Bhutan		United Kingdom	1949
Botswana	Bechuanaland	United Kingdom	1966
Brunei		United Kingdom	1984
Burkina Faso	Upper Volta	France	1960
Burundi		Belgium	1962
Cambodia	French Indochina	France	1953
Cameroon		France & U.K.	1960
Cape Verde		Portugal	1975
Central African Republic	Ubangi-Shari	France	1960
Chad		France	1960
Comoros		France	1975
Congo		France	1960
Côte d'Ivoire	Ivory Coast	France	1960
Cyprus		United Kingdom	1960

Present Name of Country	Colonial Name (if Different)	Colonial Authority	Year of Independence
Djibouti	Afars & Issas	France	1977
Dominica		United Kingdom	1978
Equatorial Guinea	Fernando Pu & Rio Muni	Spain	1968
Eritrea		Ethiopia	1993
Fiji		United Kingdom	1970
Gabon		France	1960
Gambia		United Kingdom	1965
Ghana	Gold Coast	United Kingdom	1957
Grenada		United Kingdom	1974
Guinea	French Guinea	France	1958
Guinea-Bissau	Portuguese Guinea	Portugal	1974
Guyana	British Guiana	United Kingdom	1966
India		United Kingdom	1947
Indonesia	Dutch East Indies	Netherlands	1949
Israel	Palestine	United Kingdom	1948
Jamaica		United Kingdom	1962
Jordan	Transjordan	United Kingdom	1946
Kenya		United Kingdom	1963
Kiribati	Gilbert Islands	United Kingdom	1979
Kuwait		United Kingdom	1961
Laos	French Indochina	France	1949
Lesotho	Basutoland	United Kingdom	1966
Libya		United Kingdom	1951
Madagascar		France	1960
Malawi	Nyasaland	United Kingdom	1964
Malaysia	Malaya	United Kingdom	1957
Maldives		United Kingdom	1965
Mali	Sudanese Republic	France	1960
Malta		United Kingdom	1964
Marshall Islands		United States	1991
Mauritania		France	1960
Mauritius		United Kingdom	1968
Micronesia	Caroline Islands	United States	1991
Morocco		France	1956
Mozambique		Portugal	1975
Namibia	South West Africa	South Africa	1990
Nauru		Australia	1968
Niger		France	1960
Nigeria		United Kingdom	1960
Pakistan	India	United Kingdom	1947
Papua New Guinea	New Guinea	Australia	1975
Philippines		United States	1946
Qatar		United Kingdom	1971
Rwanda		Belgium	1962

Present Name of Country	Colonial Name (if Different)	Colonial Authority	Year of Independence
Saint Kitts and Nevis		United Kingdom	1983
Saint Lucia		United Kingdom	1979
Saint Vincent and The Grenadines		United Kingdom	1979
São Tomé and Principe		Portugal	1975
Senegal		France	1960
Seychelles		United Kingdom	1976
Sierra Leone		United Kingdom	1961
Singapore		United Kingdom	1965
Solomon Islands		United Kingdom	1978
Somalia		Italy & U.K.	1960
South Yemen	Aden	United Kingdom	1967
Sri Lanka	Ceylon	United Kingdom	1948
Suriname	Dutch Guiana	Netherlands	1975
Swaziland		United Kingdom	1968
Syria		France	1946
Tanzania	Tanganyika and Zanzibar	United Kingdom	1961
Togo	Togoland	France	1960
Tonga		United Kingdom	1970
Trinidad and Tobago		United Kingdom	1962
Tunisia		France	1956
Tuvalu	Ellice Islands	United Kingdom	1978
Uganda		United Kingdom	1962
United Arab Emirates	Trucial States	United Kingdom	1971
Vanuatu	New Hebrides	France & U.K.	1980
Vietnam	French Indochina	France	1954
Zaire	Belgian Congo	Belgium	1960
Zambia	N. Rhodesia	United Kingdom	1964
Zimbabwe	S. Rhodesia	United Kingdom	1980

Index

About the Editors and Contributors

BRUCE F. ADAMS is professor of history at the University of Louisville. He received his Ph.D. from the University of Maryland and is the translator and editor of V. V. Shulgin's *Days of the Russian Revolution: Memoirs from the Right, 1905–1917* (1990) and the author of articles on late imperial Russia.

GEORGE P. BLUM is professor of history and chairman of the department at the University of the Pacific. He received his Ph.D. from the University of Minnesota and has contributed articles to *Great Lives from History: Twentieth Century* (1990), *Research Guide to European Historical Biography* (1992–1993), and *Statesmen Who Changed the World* (1993).

FRANS COETZEE of George Washington University received his Ph.D. from the University of Chicago. He is the author of *For Party or Country: Nationalism and the Dilemmas of Popular Conservatism in Edwardian England* (1990) and, with Marilyn Shevin-Coetzee, editor of *World War I and European Society: A Sourcebook* (forthcoming) and *Authority, Identity, and the Social History of the Great War* (forthcoming).

MARILYN SHEVIN-COETZEE of George Washington University received her Ph.D. from the University of Chicago. She is the author of

The German Army League: Popular Nationalism in Wilhelmine Germany (1990) and with Frans Coetzee editor of *World War I and European Society: A Sourcebook* (forthcoming) and *Authority, Identity and the Social History of the Great War* (forthcoming).

JOHN E. FINDLING is professor of history at Indiana University Southeast. He received his Ph.D. from the University of Texas and is the author of *Dictionary of American Diplomatic History* (1980; 1989), *Close Neighbors, Distant Friends: United States-Central American Relations* (1987), and *Chicago's Great World's Fairs* (1995). He is the editor of *Historical Dictionary of World's Fairs and Expositions, 1851–1988* (1990) and, with Frank W. Thackeray, *Statesmen Who Changed the World* (1993).

RICHARD A. LEIBY is chairman of the history department at Rosemont College. He received his Ph.D. from the University of Delaware and is the author of articles on twentieth-century Europe. He is currently writing a narrative history of the immediate post–World War II era.

MARIJAN SALOPEK teaches in the department of history at the University of British Columbia in Vancouver. He received his Ph.D. from Cambridge University and has contributed to *Statesmen Who Changed the World*. He is currently working on a study of the French ministry of colonies from 1894 to 1914.

LOWELL J. SATRE is professor of history at Youngstown State University. He received his Ph.D. from the University of South Carolina and is the author of several articles on late Victorian and Edwardian Britain. He is currently writing a biography of Thomas Burt, a nineteenth-century English coal miner and politician.

FRANK W. THACKERAY is professor of history at Indiana University Southeast. He received his Ph.D. from Temple University. He is the author of *Antecedents of Revolution: Alexander I and the Polish Congress Kingdom* (1980) as well as articles on Russian-Polish relations in the nineteenth century and Polish-American relations in the twentieth century. With John E. Findling, he is editor of *Statesmen Who Changed the World* (1993). He is a former Fulbright scholar in Poland.

LARRY THORNTON is associate professor of history at Hanover College. He received his Ph.D. from the University of Illinois and is the author of articles on human rights and numerous book reviews. He is currently researching a comparative study of Indiana and British students' opinions about war in the 1920s and 1930s.

JEFFREY N. WASSERSTROM is associate professor of history at Indiana University. He received his Ph.D. from the University of California at Berkeley. He is the author of *Student Protests in Twentieth Century China* (1991) and the co-editor of *Popular Protest and Political Culture in Modern China* (1992; 1994). He is currently working on a book about competing versions of Shanghai history.

THOMAS PHILIP WOLF is professor of political science and dean of the division of social sciences at Indiana University Southeast. He received his Ph.D. from Stanford University and has contributed to *Great Lives in History* and *Statesmen Who Changed the World*. He is editor of the "British Politics Group Newsletter."

CHARLES E. ZIEGLER is professor of political science at the University of Louisville. He received his Ph.D. from the University of Illinois and is the author of *Foreign Policy and East Asia: Learning and Adaptation in the Gorbachev Era* (1993) and *Environmental Policy in the USSR* (1987), as well as numerous articles on the Soviet Union. He is director of the Louisville Committee of the Council on Foreign Relations.